Out of the Cold

Out of the Cold

The Cold War and Its Legacy

EDITED BY

MICHAEL R. FITZGERALD

WITH ALLEN PACKWOOD

BLOOMSBURY

NEW YORK • LONDON • NEW DELHI • SYDNEY

Bloomsbury Academic

An imprint of Bloomsbury Publishing Inc

1385 Broadway	50 Bedford Square
New York	London
NY 10018	WC1B 3DP
USA	UK

www.bloomsbury.com

Bloomsbury is a registered trade mark of Bloomsbury Publishing Plc

First published 2013

Churchill
Archives
Centre

© Churchill Archives Centre, Cambridge, 2013

Library of Congress Cataloging-in-Publication Data

Out of the cold : the cold war and its legacy / edited by Michael R. Fitzgerald with Allen Packwood.

pages cm

Includes bibliographical references and index.

ISBN 978-1-62356-891-7 (pbk.)– ISBN 978-1-62356-330-1 (hardcover) 1. Cold War. 2. Cold War–Influence. 3. World politics--1945-1989. I. Fitzgerald, Michael R., 1947- editor of compilation. II. Packwood, Allen, editor of compilation.

D843.O87 2013

909.82'5–dc23

2013017195

ISBN: HB: 978-1-6235-6143-7
PB: 978-1-6235-6891-7
ePub: 978-1-6235-6998-3
ePDF: 978-1-6235-6330-1

Typeset by Fakenham Prepress Solutions, Fakenham, Norfolk NR21 8NN
Printed and bound in the United States of America

CONTENTS

LIST OF PHOTOGRAPHS

FOREWORD

Professor Sir David Wallace
Master of Churchill College
University of Cambridge

This book is the published version of the conference "The Cold War and its Legacy," which was held at Churchill College, Cambridge, on November 18 and 19, 2009. In the course of two full days we were treated to a stellar cast of panelists and speakers from around the world. Old adversaries were brought together, academic experts mingled with politicians, diplomats, military leaders, and scientists, and students of the era had the chance to ask questions of those who had played a role in shaping the great events of our recent past.

The conference was held under the auspices of our Churchill Archives Centre, home to the personal papers of Prime Ministers Winston Churchill, Margaret Thatcher, and John Major, as well as a host of their contemporaries. What could be more fitting? It was Churchill who popularized the phrase "Iron Curtain" in his celebrated speech at Westminster College, Fulton, Missouri on March 5, 1946 at the very beginning of the Cold War, and it was Margaret Thatcher who led Britain's response to its end, culminating in the fall of the Berlin Wall in November 1989, some 20 years before this gathering. The Archives Centre contains some of the most important British sources for the period, but the intention of this conference was always to widen the perspective and to look at the Cold War through the eyes of many different nationalities.

Margaret Thatcher, Nancy Reagan, and Mikhail Gorbachev all supplied letters, read out at the opening of the conference, and it is perhaps worth quoting from these here:

From Margaret Thatcher came:

> In the years that have passed there has been a tendency to diminish the importance of the Cold War. We have since discovered the true economic,

political and military fragility of the Soviet Union. But the dangers to mankind during the Cold War years were horrendous and urgent.

From Nancy Reagan:

My husband predicted that the (Berlin) wall would fall and that communism would 'end up on the ash heap of history' and for his beliefs he was called a dreamer and an ideologue.

From Mikhail Gorbachev:

Outcomes are not predetermined, they depend on both events and purposeful actions. To meet new challenges, we need to change our mentality just as we did to end the Cold War. We need to take down the wall that separates us from our future.

Of course, these are just the strong opening statements in what became a far-ranging, thematic, nuanced, and increasingly complex analysis of the conflict that dominated the late twentieth century, and which might have ended human history.

As I revisit the events of 2009 I have to record my thanks to the organizing team at the Churchill Archives Centre and their international partners at the University of Tennessee, including Senator Baker himself, Chancellor Jimmy G. Cheek, and the staff at the excellent Howard H. Baker Center for Public Policy. The occasion could not have happened without the support of its sponsors; B&W Y12, Oak Ridge National Laboratory, The Haslam Family Foundation, The Rushbrook Charitable Trust, SSC Service Solutions, EnergX, GS&N (Oak Ridge), The Coffer Group, Marshall of Cambridge, Price Waterhouse Coopers, Resolution Property, RAND Europe, Stolichnaya Russian Vodka, Mr. Michael Lewis, Mr. David C. and Mrs. Antigoni Newton, Dr. Irwin M. and Mrs. Cita Stelzer, Dr. Anthony H. and Mrs. Anna Wild, Oak Ridge Associated Universities, Dr. June Hopkins, Mr. Arthur and Mrs. Susan Seymour, and Mr. Sam Mrs. Ann Furrow. This publication owes its existence to the further generosity of Anthony Wild, Leslie Buckland, and Werner Gerstenberg.

Finally, I would like to thank Dr. Michael Fitzgerald, Professor of Political Science at the University of Tennessee, for his dedication in pulling the text together and preparing it for publication.

Professor Sir David Wallace
11 February 2013

PREFACE

Allen Packwood
Director of the Churchill Archives Centre
Churchill College
University of Cambridge

The future is bright, it is the past that is unpredictable.
SOVIET SAYING, RECITED BY SUSAN EISENHOWER

The aim of this conference was to bring together former Cold War warriors and academics from both sides of the old "Iron Curtain," and from as many nations and relevant areas of expertise as possible, to shed light on the origins, struggles, conclusion, and legacy of the Cold War: a conflict that dominated the second half of the twentieth century, and had a global impact that continues to reverberate to this day, in continuing East/West tension, in weapons of mass destruction, and in the ongoing instability of many regions.

The timing was no accident. The conference date was chosen to coincide with the fiftieth anniversary of Churchill College, itself a Cold War foundation, and with the twentieth anniversary of the fall of the Berlin Wall. It was also timed to accommodate a visit by a large number of Archives Centre friends from the Howard Baker Center and the University of Tennessee. While Senator Baker's health sadly prevented his attendance, he was ably represented by his friend, Senator John Warner, and by Chancellor Jimmy Cheek of the University of Tennessee. Indeed, the conference was the second in a series of remarkable joint ventures by the Baker Center and the Churchill Archives Centre, Henry Kissinger having delivered the keynote speech at the first conference, hosted in Knoxville in 2006; so we knew that we had a lot to live up to.

The international tone, the caliber, and the range of the debate were all set in the very first session. Senator Warner spoke movingly of the role of Ronald Reagan and how he had initially doubted the wisdom of the President's 1987 Brandenburg Gate speech, in which the American leader called on Gorbachev to "tear down this wall, concluding, "*I* have never been more wrong." Grigory Karasin, the Deputy Russian Minister of Foreign Affairs, described the start of the Cold War as a bilateral process, with the United States and Great Britain bearing a lot of responsibility because of their "ideologically charged foreign policy." He argued that all attempts to say who won and who lost were doomed to failure, and that the end came primarily because Russia chose to withdraw and to renounce the ideology that had pushed the Soviet Union into conflict. Susan Eisenhower injected a more personal dimension, reminiscing about her meetings with Churchill and Khrushchev in 1959 when President Eisenhower ordered the deployment of his grandchildren, but she also commented on the role of the Eisenhower presidency in shaping US Cold War policy, on her own frequent visits to the Soviet Union between 1987 and 1991, and her belief that the Cold War ended because the Russian people came out of their own internal exile.

This publication, expertly edited by Michael Fitzgerald, captures what followed. Letters were read into the conference record from the late Winston S. Churchill, from Nancy Reagan, from the late former Prime Minister Margaret Thatcher, and former President Gorbachev. There was expert witness testimony from participants in key events. Hugh Lunghi, an interpreter attached to the British Chiefs of Staff Mission in Moscow during World War II, spoke of his encounters with Stalin. To him the Russian leader appeared small, courteous, and good mannered, "very careful not to exceed any boundaries of protocol" with a strong Caucasian accent and a marked aversion to looking anyone in the eye while speaking to them. The Marshal came across as very controlled, needing few notes, and with an occasional dry laugh. Hugh also talked about the conditions in which the British Mission had to work, and in particular the suspicion and hostility of their Russian hosts and supposed allies.

As the sessions unfolded, the Russian perspective proved particularly interesting. Professor Vladimir Pechatnov reminded his audience that the Red Army had suffered 55 times more than American forces during World War II, and inflicted 93 percent of German combat losses between 1941 and 1944. While Professor Alexander Likhotal, former spokesperson and advisor to President Gorbachev, referred to the scale of Soviet losses in Afghanistan in the 1980s and its impact on decision-making in Moscow.

But I have hardly scratched the surface. There were panels on the different phases of the Cold War, on the role of technology and intelligence, and on specific theaters, such as the Far East. Gary Powers Jr. opened the second day with a moving presentation about how his father became a pawn in the Cold War when his U-2 spy plane was shot down. Discussion flowed and debate raged, both in and out of the formal sessions, and over the dinners. There were powerful contributions from Britain and the United States, but also vital and different perspectives from China, Germany, India, Japan, and Romania. The Churchill Archives Centre owes an enormous debt to the speakers and sponsors who gave so willingly of their time and resources to make this all happen.

Allen Packwood
11 February 2013

ACKNOWLEDGMENTS

The confrontation between the Soviet Union and its former World War II allies, known as the Cold War, established a bipolar world that defined international relations from 1945 through the close of the twentieth century. This vast ideological, economic, and political competition between the two great power blocs, led by the United States and the Soviet Union, was global in its scope and impact. Its legacy endures to shape the multipolar world of the twenty-first century.

The 2009 International Conference on the Cold War and its legacy brought together a renowned and remarkably eclectic assembly of diplomats, public officials, journalists, and scholars. In an intensive and extensive two-day dialogue, energized by lively audience participation, those who had waged, covered, and studied both sides of the Cold War reflected on what it all meant. Conference participants focused largely on the opening and closing stages of the Cold War, as well as its long-term consequences.

These essays are based on the memories and perspectives of individuals who witnessed and participated in the major events of the Cold War. Their first-person perspectives are intimate, compelling, and immediate. A more analytic, but no less compelling, perspective on the great Cold War is offered by a distinguished group of media experts, analysts, and scholars. The contributions of members of the conference audience are reflected in each essay through the integration of information that emerged during the lively question and answer sessions associated with each panel.

It was my privilege to serve on the program planning committee and participate in two major international conferences jointly sponsored by the Churchill Archives and the Howard H. Baker Jr. Center for Public Policy: "The United States and Great Britain: The Legacy of Churchill's Atlantic Alliance," March 29–30, 2006, and "The Cold War and Its Legacy," November 18–19, 2009. I am deeply grateful to my friends and colleagues, Allen Packwood, Director of the Churchill Archives Centre, and Alan Lowe, former Director of the Howard H. Baker Jr. Center for Public Policy, for this remarkable and fulfilling experience.

The completion of a project of this scope incurs significant debt, especially to the distinguished men and women who produced the essays in this volume. Working with and for them has been a great honor. I am deeply indebted to Allen Packwood, Director of the Churchill Archives, for his inspiration, confidence, and unflagging support for this work. His funding for the project is deeply appreciated. Allen is the exemplary leader of an extraordinary institution. Julie Sanderson, Archives Administrator at the Churchill Archives Centre, provided invaluable assistance in coordinating communication among the authors.

This volume could never have been written without the inspiration and outstanding editorial assistance of my brilliant wife Dr. Amy Snyder Fitzgerald, and the excellent research work of my doctoral students, Natalie Manayeva and Alexandra Brewer. I am grateful for the encouragement provided by the former Director of the Howard H. Baker Jr. Center for Public Policy, Professor Carl Pierce. A special debt is owed to Dr. Nissa Dahlin-Brown, Associate Director of the Baker Center. In addition to her organizing staff support for the US contribution to the Cold War Conference, Nissa arranged for the audio transcriptions that constituted the early foundation of the work.

It is important to acknowledge the contribution of Marie-Clair Antoine, former Senior Acquisitions Editor for Politics and International Relations at Continuum International Publishing Group/Bloomsbury, whose early encouragement support made publication possible. I deeply appreciate Ally Jane Grossan (Assistant Editor) and Kaitlin Fontana (Editorial Assistant) at Bloomsbury Academic for their exemplary professional guidance in bringing the manuscript to press.

In the end the greatest debt is owed to my family, Amy, Heather, and Michael. Their love and support makes all things possible.

Michael R. Fitzgerald
Creswell Court
1 March 2013

ACRONYMS AND ABBREVIATIONS

ABM	Anti-Ballistic Missile
CFE	Conventional Forces in Europe Treaty
CIA	Central Intelligence Agency
CIS	Commonwealth of Independent States
CPSU	Communist Party of the Soviet Union
CSCE	Conference on Security and Cooperation in Europe
EDC	European Defense Community
EEC	European Economic Community
EU	European Union
FRG	Federal Republic of (West) Germany
G-20	Group of 20 finance ministers and Central Bank governors from major world economies
GDR	(East) German Democratic Republic
GRU	Glavnoye Razvedyvatelnoye Upravlenie (Soviet military intelligence)
ICBM	Intercontinental Ballistic Missile
INF	Intermediate Range Nuclear Forces
KGB	Komitet Gosudarstvennoy Bezopasnosti (Committee for State Security)
MAD	Mutually Assured Destruction
MI5	Military Intelligence 5 (UK Security Service—internal)
MI6	Military Intelligence 6 (UK Secret Intelligence Service—foreign)

MIRV   Multiple Independently Targetable Reentry Vehicle

MRBM   Medium-Range Ballistic Missiles

NATO   North Atlantic Treaty Organization

NSA   National Security [SIGINT] Agency (US)

NSC   National Security Council (US)

OSCE   Organization for Security and Cooperation in Europe

PRC   People's Republic of China (communist mainland)

ROC   Republic of China (non-communist Taiwan)

SALT   Strategic Arms Limitation Talks

SDI   Strategic Defense Initiative (Star Wars)

SIGINT   Signals Intelligence

SLBM   Submarine-Launched Ballistic Missile

SSBN   Ship Submersible Ballistic Nuclear (Submarine)

START   Strategic Arms Reduction Treaty

UK   United Kingdom

UN   United Nations

US   United States

USSR   Union of Soviet Socialist Republics (Soviet Union)

CHRONOLOGY

1945
February   Yalta Conference
July   US detonates first atomic bomb; Potsdam Conference

1946
February   Kennan's Long Telegram
March   Churchill's Iron Curtain Speech

1947
March   US announces Truman Doctrine

1948
April   US Congress approves Marshall Plan
June   Soviets blockade Berlin—US-UK respond with Berlin Airlift

1949
April   NATO established
August   USSR detonates its first atomic bomb
October   (Communist) People's Republic of China (PRC) established

1950
January   NATO established
April   US NSC issues NSC-68 on "containment"
June   Korean War begins

1951
September   US-Japan Security Treaty signed

1952
November   US detonates the first hydrogen bomb

1953
March   Stalin dies—succeeded by Khrushchev
June   Soviets suppress uprising in (East) German Democratic Republic (GDR)
July   Korean War ends with armistice
August   USSR detonates its first hydrogen bomb

1954

January   US announces "massive nuclear retaliation" strategy based on NSC 162/2

1955

May   (West) Federal Republic Germany (FRG) enters NATO; Warsaw Pact established

July   First post-war summit between UK-US- France-USSR in Geneva

1956

February   20th Party Congress in USSR

July   Suez Crisis begins

November   Soviets suppress Hungarian Revolution; Suez Crisis ends

1957

October   USSR launches first man-made satellite Sputnik

1958

November   Khrushchev threatens unilateral treaty with GDR

1959

September   Khrushchev-Eisenhower hold summit in United States

1960

May   Soviet downing of U.S. spy plan leads to collapse of Paris Summit

1961

April   US-sponsored Bay of Pigs operation fails in Cuba

June   Kennedy-Khrushchev summit in Vienna

October   GDR closes border—construction of Berlin Wall begins

1962

October   Cuban Missile Crisis

1963

June   Kennedy visits West Berlin

August   UK-US-USSR sign Partial Nuclear Test Ban Treaty

1964

October   Khrushchev "retires"—succeeded by Brezhnev

1965

March   United States sends combat troops to South Vietnam

1966
August   The Cultural Revolution begins in PRC

1967
June   Arab-Israeli Six-Day War

1968
April   Prague Spring in Czechoslavakia
July   UK-US-USSR sign the Nuclear Non-Proliferation Treaty
August   Soviet-led Warsaw Pact forces invade Czechoslovakia
November   Brezhnev Doctrine announced

1969
March   Soviet and PRC forces clash at Ussuri River

1970
August   Moscow Treaty signed by FRG and USSR

1971
September   UK-France-US-USSR sign Quadripartite Agreement on Berlin
November   PRC admitted to UN

1972
February   Nixon visits PRC
May   Nixon-Brezhnev sign SALT I and ABM Treaties in Moscow
December   FRG and GDR sign Basic Treaty establishing formal relations

1973
January   US-North Vietnam sign peace agreement ending Vietnam War
October   Arab-Israeli Yom Kippur War

1975
August   Helsinki Final Act signed

1976
September   Mao Zedong dies

1977
August   PRC ends the Cultural Revolution

1978
October   Polish Archbishop Karol Wojtyla elected Pope
December   United States and PRC establish formal diplomatic relations

1979
May   Thatcher becomes British Prime Minister
June   US-USSR sign SALT II Treaty; Pope John Paul II visits Poland

November	Iranian Hostage Crisis begins
December	Soviet invasion of Afghanistan

1980

January	Carter Doctrine as US reaction to Soviet invasion of Afghanistan
July	United States boycotts Moscow Olympics
August	Strike at Gdansk shipyard in Poland

1981

January	Reagan becomes US President; Iran Hostage Crisis ends
October	Reagan announces expansion of U.S. strategic nuclear forces

1982

October	Helmut Kohl becomes FRG Chancellor
November	Brezhnev dies—succeeded by Andropov

1983

March	Reagan announces Strategic Defense Initiative
October	NATO deploys intermediate nuclear forces

1984

February	Andropov dies—succeeded by Chernenko
July	USSR boycott of Los Angeles Olympics

1985

March	Chernenko dies—succeeded by Gorbachev
November	Reagan-Gorbachev at Geneva Summit

1986

February	Gorbachev announces glastnost and perestroika at Party Congress
October	Gorbachev-Reagan summit at Reykjavik

1987

June	At Berlin Wall Reagan calls upon Gorbachev to "Tear down this wall!"
December	Reagan-Gorbachev sign INF Treaty at Washington Summit

1988

December	At UN Gorbachev announces unilateral reductions in Soviet conventional forces

1989

February	Soviets complete withdrawal from Afghanistan
June	Pro-democracy demonstrations in Tiananmen Square violently suppressed by military in PRC

July	Warsaw Pact affirms member's right to self-determination
September	Hungary opens border with Austria to GDR citizens with visas
October	Gorbachev criticizes GDR for failure to reform at fiftiethh anniversary celebration
	Mass demonstration against communist regime in Leipzig and East Berlin
	Moderate Krenz replaces hardliner Honecker as GDR leader
	Warsaw Pact denounces Brezhnev Doctrine
November	Spontaneous checkpoint opening at Berlin Wall—dismantling of Wall begins
December	Gorbachev-Bush declare Cold War is over at Malta Summit

1990

February	In Moscow FRG Chancellor Kohl pledges economic aid for USSR—Gorbachev accepts German unification "in principle"
June	Gorbachev-Bush sign trade and exchange agreements at Washington Summit
July	NATO declares Warsaw Pact is no longer a threat to Western Europe
September	German Unification Treaty signed in Moscow
November	NATO-Warsaw Pact sign Conventional Forces in Europe Treaty

1991

March	Warsaw Pact is disbanded
July	Bush and Gorbachev sign START agreement
August	Coup against Gorbachev fails
November	Communist Party abolished in Russia
December	Gorbachev resigns as Soviet President—USSR formally dissolved

CONTRIBUTORS

Christopher Andrew, Professor of Modern and Contemporary History, University of Cambridge

Victor Ashe, former American Ambassador to Poland

Gordon Barrass, former British diplomat and Chief of the Assessments Staff at the Cabinet Office

Sir John Boyd, former Master of Churchill College, University of Cambridge, and former diplomat and UK Ambassador to Japan

Sir Anthony Brenton, former diplomat and British Ambassador to the Russian Federation

Susan Eisenhower, President of Eisenhower Group Inc., Chairman of the Eisenhower Institute's Leadership and Public Policy Programs, granddaughter of President Eisenhower

Graham Farmelo, Senior Research Fellow at the Science Museum in London, and Adjunct Professor of Physics at Northeastern University, biographer of Paul Dirac

Michael R. Fitzgerald, Professor of Political Science, University of Tennessee-Knoxville

Stefan Halper, Director of American Studies, Department of Politics and International Studies, University of Cambridge

Jonathan Haslam, Professor of the History of International Relations, University of Cambridge

Peter Jay, writer, broadcaster, and former British Ambassador to the United States

Grigoriy Karasin, Deputy Foreign Minister of the Russian Federation and former Russian Ambassador to the United Kingdom

Anthony Kelly, Emeritus Professor and Life Fellow of Churchill College, University of Cambridge

Bridget Kendall, Diplomatic Correspondent for the British Broadcasting Corporation

Konstantin Khudoley, Professor and Dean of the School of International Relations, St. Petersburg State University

Mark Kramer, Professor and Director of Cold War Studies, Harvard University

Rear Admiral Roger Lane-Nott, former Flag Officer Submarines and NATO Commander Submarines Eastern Atlantic

Alexander Likhotal, President and CEO of Green Cross International, former Deputy Spokesman and Advisor to the President of the USSR

Hugh Lunghi, former chief interpreter for the British Chiefs of Staff during World War II and former head of Central European Service broadcasting for the BBC World Service

Sir Roderic Lyne, former diplomat and British Ambassador to Russia

Sir Christopher Mallaby, former British Ambassador to Germany and France

Thom Mason, Director of Oak Ridge National Laboratories

Franklin C. Miller, former Pentagon and NSC staff official, Principal at the Scowcroft Group, and independent defense consultant

Air Marshal Chris Nickols, former British Chief of Defence Intelligence

Allen Packwood, Fellow of Churchill College and Director, Churchill Archives Centre, Churchill College, University of Cambridge

Vladimir Pechatnov, Chair of European and American Studies, Moscow State Institute of International Relations

Hella Pick, consultant and project coordinator for Lord Weidenfeld's Institute for Strategic Dialogue

Andrei Pippidi, Professor and Director of the Romanian Institute for Recent History and Professor, University of Bucharest

Lord Powell of Bayswater, former Private Secretary to Prime Minister and advisor on foreign affairs

Kishan Rana, former Indian diplomat and ambassador

David Reynolds, Professor of International History and Fellow of Christ's College, University of Cambridge

Hermann Freiherr von Richthofen, former German Ambassador to the UK and Representative to NATO

Ying Rong, Vice President and Director of the South Asian Studies Center, China Institute of International Studies, Beijing

Yoshihide Soeya, Professor of Political Science and Director of the Institute of East Asian Studies, Keio University

John Swenson-Wright, Fuji Bank Senior University Lecturer in Modern Japanese Studies and Fellow of Darwin College, University of Cambridge

James A. Thomson, President emeritus and former CEO, RAND Corporation

Professor Sir David Wallace, Master of Churchill College, University of Cambridge

John Warner, former Secretary of the US Navy, and US Senator from Virginia

Lord Watson of Richmond, Chairman of CTN Communications and former broadcast journalist

David Woolner, Associate Professor of History, Marist College Senior Fellow and Resident Historian, Franklin and Eleanor Roosevelt Institute

Lord Wright of Richmond, former diplomat, ambassador, and Permanent Under Secretary of State and Head of British Diplomatic Service

Waqar Zaidi, Historian of Science and Technology at the Centre for the History of Science, Technology and Medicine, Imperial College, London

CHAPTER ONE

Setting the context

A plethora of complex issues surrounded the origins of the Cold War. Grigoriy Karasin and Susan Eisenhower address these issues and explain how post-World War II attitudes shaped global politics and international relations well into the 1950s. Deputy Foreign Minister Karasin's standpoint is that of a career Soviet and Russian diplomat and politician. Eisenhower offers a unique perspective on the people and events of the Cold War, as she witnessed many of them as the granddaughter of President Dwight Eisenhower, and later in her life as an expert visitor to the Soviet Union and Russia. Thus, from strikingly different points of view, Karasin and Eisenhower examine the deleterious effect of political ideology as a feature of the Cold War and its aftermath. Despite their differences, both express deep concern for the unresolved problem of integrating the Russian Federation into the social, economic, and security framework of Europe.

The ideological confrontation between East and West had a life of its own

Grigoriy Karasin

We live now in a world radically different from the Cold War era. Still, the period of bipolar confrontation continues to affect the ideology and practical policies of many countries in such a way that we continue to feel the Cold War's repercussions. What is needed at present is a clear and fair assessment of the Cold War and its legacy on contemporary international affairs.

It is obvious that there are no simple, unambiguous answers to the question as to who was responsible for starting the Cold War, or the nature of its conduct and outcome. Detailed historical research does not

corroborate the popular belief that the Cold War was unleashed as a
Western response to the Soviet Union's refusal to cooperate with its World
War II allies due to the return to prewar communist expansion. Historical
records show that slipping into the Cold War was at least a bilateral
process. The United States and Great Britain for their part must bear a
great deal of responsibility for initiating their roles. It was, in fact, a revival
of policies toward Soviet Russia that existed in the period between the
two World Wars. It was adjusted to accommodate the greatly enhanced
capabilities of the Soviet Union.

In 1946, Winston Churchill's "Iron Curtain" speech in Fulton, Missouri
and George Kennan's famous long telegram[1] did not set any course of
predetermined events. Rather, they contributed to an ideological choice
that had yet to be sold to Western public opinion. The inevitable conclusion
is that our wartime Western Allies simply returned to the same old track
of ideologically charged foreign policy that was an underlying cause of
World War II. The ideological extremes of European thinking during the
interwar period explains why ruling elites in leading Western democracies
were so enthusiastic in supporting Hitler's Germany as a stronghold against
Bolshevism. Neither Nazism nor anti-Semitism could dissuade them from
supporting Hitler as doing so seemingly led to success. As soon as the
Allies' common goal of defeating fascism was achieved, Western countries
returned to many of their prewar attitudes toward the Soviet Union.

The Soviet Union, in performing its monumental role in defeating Nazi
Germany, had overstretched its capacities by the end of the war. Moscow
was simply unable to initiate any confrontation with its former anti-Hitler
coalition allies. It is natural to suppose that the USSR, in having paid
such a dreadful price to achieve victory, was willing to play by the rules
and to compromise with its former allies. Henry Kissinger has admitted
that the United States through its own actions, gave the Soviet Union
the impression that it was trying to put the USSR in a permanent no win
situation. Kissinger observed that Washington failed to fully realize that
the security needs of a continental power were significantly different from
those of the powers surrounded, like the United States, by oceans.[2] At the
end of World War II George Kennan, who later authored the containment
concept, advocated a compromise agreement between the United States, the
UK, and the USSR based on a final delimitation of spheres of influence in
Europe.[3] Therefore, it is difficult to understand what in 1945–6, apart from
ideological preferences, and perhaps the ephemeral hope of preserving the
US nuclear monopoly, prevented the implementation of the principles that
provided the basis for détente in the 1970s. The postwar militarization of
Western economies and foreign policies were factors in starting the Cold
War. The Anglo-American concept of containment envisaged not only
blocking Moscow's expansion, but also the demolition of the Soviet system
itself as the final objective of the Cold War. It therefore is simplistic to say

that the Cold War was started by the Soviet Union, or that the actions of the Soviet Union were the real reason for such a tough line by the West.

The ideological confrontation between East and West assumed a life of its own during the Cold War; a life having nothing to do with common sense, which continues to shape our political relationships. A recent American report, prepared at the request of the Pentagon, demonstrates that US administrations intentionally and persistently overestimated the aggressiveness of the Soviet Union. It shows, for example, that the USSR never in fact based its military strategies on the concept of the preemptive strike.[4]

The Yalta and Potsdam Conferences did not determine postwar developments in the Central and East European countries. It was the sudden shift of American and British policy-makers toward a posture of noncooperation and confrontation that played the key role in shaping their future. The Western powers cast aside previous understandings about the Soviet sphere of influence. Instead, they sought to control postwar events and government in this Central and Eastern Europe. This Cold War policy left no incentive for Stalin to pursue a more creative and moderate policy in that region, and is confirmed by the events that took place at end of the 1946 through the beginning of 1948. It is a subject that should be seriously explored by scholars. The United States and Britain need to open their archives, which would shed light on the initial period of the Cold War.

The beginning of the Cold War had a negative impact on the internal development of the Soviet Union, as it prevented whatever reforms might have been contemplated. The renewal of the USSR that might have been generated by the tragic experience of the war was thwarted and delayed for many years after. Social, economic, and political reform was necessary in the USSR immediately following World War II due to the widespread destruction and suffering caused by the war. If the West had taken a more constructive line of engagement with the Soviet Union in 1946, things might have turned out differently in the Soviet Union. This probably would have given Stalin no choice but to proceed with social and political reform. It would have removed his excuse for refusing reform and developing a system centered on his own person—his cult of personality.[5]

Engagement is a brilliant human invention. When you engage issues you achieve much more than confronting each other. That is why the Soviet Party Congress in 1956 is so important. At that meeting "peaceful coexistence" was first proposed to the senior levels of the Soviet government as an alternative to the vicious confrontation with the West. Before that, peaceful coexistence was contrary to the line of the ruling party in the Soviet Union. This made possible the subsequent Soviet proposal on collective security in Europe. This draft treaty was aimed at preventing the establishment of the European defense community and the remilitarization of West Germany. The Cold War, however, was already in force and had gained its own momentum. This analysis of events persuades us that the Cold War, with its drastic shift from the Allied policy of cooperation to ideological confrontation, rather than being historically predetermined, represents an aberration in international relations.

The Cold War provides common lessons for all of us. These lessons include: the inevitable harm that results from national infallibility complexes, the futility of efforts to impose social and political systems against a people's own will, the danger of militarizing international relations, and the fallaciousness of using military force to solve problems instead of settling them through political and diplomatic means. We should realize that attempts to answer the questions of who "won" and who "lost" the Cold War are doomed to failure. For many unbiased analysts, it is clear that Russia simply withdrew from the Cold War by renouncing the ideology that pushed the Soviet Union into it. This was the choice made by the Russian political elite, the Russian people, and by the other republics of the former USSR. Russia managed to avail itself of its potential in order to produce this extremely difficult change in the intellectual and spiritual sphere. At the same time, the realpolitik of the West was engulfed by a euphoria that had little to do with meaningful, long-term analysis. During the two decades since the fall of the Berlin Wall, our partners, primarily the United States, have pursued the "nothing has changed" course driven by the spirit of triumphalism and a desire to move into the geopolitical space that was left by the Soviet Union. The recent interview with former US Secretary of State James Baker in *Der Spiegel*, together with many other materials on the subject, cast a new light on the double game played by Western leaders in persuading Gorbachev not to oppose reunification of Germany.[6] Furthermore, many of us were shocked when Lech Walesa recently said in Berlin "We were lucky that the Soviet Union at that time had such a weak leader."[7] These triumphalist attitudes are unhelpful.

The problem of European integration could easily have been solved much earlier than it was. It could have occurred, without dissolving the North Atlantic Treaty Organization (NATO), by making the Organization for Security and Cooperation in Europe (OSCE) a full-fledged regional organization in accordance with Chapter 8 of the UN Charter. This would have enabled Europe to deal with the whole range of Euro-Atlantic issues. It could have produced a collective security system in the region that was open, understandable, and guaranteed unity. Our Western partners, unfortunately, took a different path and expanded NATO. It seems appropriate again to cite George Kennan, who viewed NATO enlargement as "The greatest mistake of the West in the last 50 years."[8]

The world is undergoing one of the turning points of history. The current financial and economic crisis demonstrates the failure of attempts to return to a so-called pure liberal capitalism. At the same time the elusive hope of creating a unipolar world adds a special acuteness to this situation. There is an ongoing radical and irreversible transformation of the world's landscape. We are witnessing the emergence of a new polycentric world in all levels of politics, economics, and finance.

The West originally drew basically incorrect conclusions about social and economic development at the conclusion of the Cold War. Many, for example, considered the socially oriented economies of Western Europe a vestige of the Cold War and not its positive byproduct. There were attempts to destroy this economic model, such as through the unsuccessful *Lisbon Agenda* of the European Union (EU) promulgated in 2000.[9] These unsuccessful efforts produced the current global financial and economic crisis.

The scale of global challenges makes it necessary to adopt an integrated agenda in international relations today. During the general debate in the UN General Assembly in September 2009, this was the opinion of practically everyone, including President Obama. There is a growing understanding that today the main priority of world politics is the harmonization of international relations based on the rapprochement and understanding of different economies and cultures. The activities of the G-20 aimed at overcoming the global crisis most vividly demonstrate that the international community is increasingly aware that there are no alternatives to coordinated actions. This is illustrated by modernization and economic development, which is the goal of Russian foreign policy.

So, not for the first time, there opens a window of opportunity for developing relations of open partnership in the Euro-Atlantic region. The partnership could be based on collaboration between Russia, the EU, and the United States. President Medvedev repeatedly has expressed his belief that such collaboration should become a backbone of political unity in the Euro-Atlantic area. We hope that the process of resetting the Russian-American relationship and a renewal of cooperation between Russia and NATO will contribute to a new beginning for Euro-Atlantic politics.

Certainly, the momentum of the past is still strong. This is evidenced by the desire of certain nations to act based on zero sum thinking, which assumes that the security and economic interests of some states are insured at the expense of others. There are those who would like to draw a new ideological dividing line in Europe. For example, during a recent hearing of the US Helsinki Commission, US Senator Sam Brownback insisted that the Obama administration should expedite the entry of Ukraine and Georgia to NATO so as to protect them from Russian military aggression. Such messianic enthusiasm is a shortcut to repeating the mistakes made in European affairs in the 1990s, and earlier in the mid-1940s. This is misguided because the bonds between Russia and the countries of the former USSR, like those with Central and Eastern Europe, are so strong and long-lasting that any attempt to make these countries choose between joining a strong NATO or weak Russia can cause a profound destabilizing effect.

The crisis in the Caucasus in 2008, provoked by the irresponsible policy of the Saakasvhili regime in Georgia, demonstrates that the use of force in today's world is usually counterproductive. In this instance Georgia lost its territorial integrity through the fault of its leaders. Nevertheless, today there is an increasing awareness of the new realities in global affairs. Network diplomacy is the logical alternative to outmoded, hierarchical security structures. We welcome the proposal for building a global security network recently offered by the former US National Security Advisor Zbigniew Brzezinski.[10] In this context, the construction of an indivisible security network from Vancouver to Vladivostok is an increasingly urgent task. It can only occur when Cold War era, bloc-based confrontational approaches to security are abandoned.

I hope that no nation will resort to militarizing their economies as a means to recover from the current global economic crisis, as was the case

PHOTO 1.1 *Susan Eisenhower at "Cold War and its Legacy" Conference at Churchill College in November 2009 (Courtesy of Churchill Archives Centre)*

after the Great Depression. It is beyond doubt that security can be insured only with the involvement of all states, as well as the relevant organizations in the Euro-Atlantic area. This is exactly the approach that our European Security Treaty initiative is based on. We are proposing to translate political commitments into legal ones. The core commitment is that no one may insure their security at the expense of the security of others. Security should be fair for all. This cornerstone principle was endorsed within the NATO-Russia Council, but it is not being implemented and practiced.

American President Eisenhower used to say that peace and justice are two sides of the same coin. Peace and justice require the construction of structures for their realization. To facilitate this construction we must, in a variety of venues, brainstorm the path forward and discuss even the most complicated issues with a view to mutually acceptable solutions. We are convinced that agreeing to a comprehensive Euro-Atlantic treaty would be a most decisive step to break with the erroneous ideologies and practices of the Cold War era.

Reflections of a child of the Cold War

Susan Eisenhower

Now is the time to look at the Cold War and its current implications because we are still living with many of the effects of that period. How could it be otherwise? Young people today are not focused on the Cold War. Most of those attending college have little knowledge about the long confrontation between the West and East and how it continues to shape the world in which they live. For example, I gave a lecture not long ago to a group of young women and tried to explain my career in dealing with the nuclear legacy of the Cold War in the former Soviet Union. In the course of my work I had travelled extensively, visiting nuclear weapons facilities in the Russian federation, uranium enrichment facilities in Kazakhstan, and research reactors all over the former Soviet Union. In my presentation I told students that during the Cold War the United States and the USSR had the capacity to blow themselves up as many times over. During the question and answer session a young girl of the back of the room raised her hand and she said, "I have just one question for you Ms. Eisenhower, why wasn't once enough?" Well, that is an excellent question. Not only do people fail to recognize the challenges we face today in dealing with the nuclear legacy of the Cold War, there is little conception of the size of the weapons programs that bred the problem.

Today if you were to ask any average college physics class how many nuclear weapons the US and the USSR held in their arsenal, probably no one would be able to answer the question with any degree of accuracy. For example, a friend of mine who is a professor at a major university in the United States recently asked this question in his class with the result that not one college student had an answer. Eventually a student at the back of the room raised his hand and wondered whether it was ten! This demonstrates the enormous job before us. We must produce an accurate history of the Cold War era and shine light on its relevance to our present and future. This task reminds me a little bit of a great Soviet joke with the punch line "the future is bright it is the past that is unpredictable."

The Cold War and Its Legacy Conference held at Cambridge University in 2009 marked the fiftieth anniversary of the founding of Churchill College as well as the fiftieth anniversary of the summit meeting between President Eisenhower and Soviet Premier Khrushchev. During the Soviet Premier's visit to the United States he visited my grandparents' farm in Gettysburg, Pennsylvania. We commemorated this historic meeting in September 2009 with a conference sponsored by the Eisenhower Institute at Gettysburg College. At this event I shared memories of the 1959 meeting with my old friend Sergi Khrushchev, son of the Soviet leader. In this essay, as I did with Sergi, I will discuss personal memories from the Cold War, which I witnessed as the young granddaughter of President Eisenhower. Then I offer a perspective on the end of the Cold War based on my professional experience in the Soviet Union.

I was exceedingly fortunate to be related to one of the people who was directly involved in the Cold War, President Dwight Eisenhower. Because of this, for example, as a child in 1959 I met both Winston Churchill and Nikita Khrushchev. Especially memorable was that two-week visit to the United States of the Soviet Premier. During this famous trip Eisenhower and Khrushchev were deeply involved in discussions about the future of Berlin and other difficult issues, but could not achieve any significant progress toward agreement. When nothing else seemed to work, Eisenhower decided to try another tactic and "deploy" the grandchildren at Gettysburg Farm. This was my personal introduction to the Cold War.

When Khrushchev arrived at the Gettysburg Farm my siblings and I were dressed up and ready for his visit. It was soon revealed that Nikita Khrushchev was not sure he wanted to board the helicopter for the trip to the farm. It was only after my grandfather reminded the Soviet leader that the Russian-American Igor Sikorski had designed the aircraft, and that the President would accompany him, that Khrushchev relented. Upon meeting us kids, Khrushchev mentioned that he wanted very much for my grandfather to bring his grandchildren to Moscow in 1960 for a reciprocal visit.

At the end of his visit Khrushchev dipped into his pocket and pulled out little red star pins and placed them on our lapels. As soon as the helicopter had taken off my mother demanded that we remove and give her those pins. I do not know what happened to the pins, but I suspect she threw them away. At the recent commemoration, Sergei Khrushchev and I laughed about the incident.

I did not get to make the trip to Moscow that Khrushchev hoped would occur. It was immediately clear to me that the grandchildren were not going to accompany the President of the United States to Moscow—our parents had the idea that we should stay home and work on our studies. It was U-2 Incident, of course, that actually derailed the presidential trip. Few people know that Khrushchev, through back channels, later approached the Eisenhower administration and tried to reinstate that visit.[11]

It took me twenty-five years to get to the Soviet Union. My first reaction was that I could not believe my eyes. I was struck by the crumbling infra-structure. I was struck by the fact that my private conversations with Soviet citizens were open and rambunctious—even before the full public effects of perestroika were evident. From 1987 to 1991 I made roughly thirty trips to the Soviet Union. During those critical years I personally observed unfolding events and listened to policy-makers discussing the situation in the Soviet Union.[12] I am struck in retrospect by the extent to which I had absorbed my grandfather's worldview and how it affected my perspective. I remember from dinner table conversations how granddad rigorously demanded that if you were going to posit an idea, which, of course, we all did and we were given free reign to do so, that you would not be permitted to go through your argument without analyzing how it looked to the other guy. This perhaps produced for me a slightly unconventional view of the Cold War and how it ended. In analyzing the people and events in the Soviet Union from 1987 to 1991, I strove to understand how it looked to the Russian side. I find it distressing, therefore, to attend so many conferences at which American speakers are unable to discuss what was happening on the Soviet side. Their stock response is to say, "Well, you know, we are not Soviet experts."

The worldview that I somehow absorbed from my grandfather was broad and reflected the analytic ability to see things from a variety of perspectives, including those with whom he disagreed. Eisenhower was unique among presidents in the fact that he had lived abroad for lengthy periods of time before he became President of the United States. He lived in Europe following both world wars, in Central America in the1920s, and in Asia and the Philippines in the 1930s. This produced a truly broad worldview.

When Eisenhower took office in January 1953 the situation in internal affairs was undergoing profound change, which produced a range of challenges for the new administration. There were growing tensions over the future of Europe. The United States and the USSR were rapidly arming with nuclear weapons. China had fallen to the communists and America was engaged in the Korean War. The Truman administration had vastly increased defense spending relative to the rest of the national budget.

Within two months of the Eisenhower inauguration, in March 1953, Stalin died. In August of that year the Soviet Union broke the American monopoly on the hydrogen bomb. The hydrogen bomb and the development of intercontinental ballistic missiles were game changers. At the same time the collapse of colonialism around the world gave rise to new weak states, with a high potential for failure.

In contending that the Eisenhower administration was the first to bring about a coherent American Cold War policy, I must acknowledge its roots in the great debate over US strategy that occurred during the Truman administration between a group centered on Dean Acheson and Paul Nitze and a group led by George Kennan and Chip Bohlen. This vigorous debate revolved largely around the nature of the struggle between the United States and the USSR and the essential nature of the Soviet regime. In 1950, the Policy Planning Staff of the National Security Council (NSC), led by Paul Nitze, produced NSC-68, the top secret report that had far-reaching implications during the Cold War. The authors of NSC-68 argued that the USSR was inescapably militant because it possessed a worldwide revolutionary view, was the inheritor of Russian imperialism, and because it was a totalitarian dictatorship. It noted that, for the moment the US atomic retaliatory capability was probably adequate to deter the Kremlin from a deliberate, direct military attack against the United States or other free people. If, however, the Kremlin leadership calculated that it possessed sufficient atomic capacity to make a surprise attack on us that would nullify US atomic superiority, a military situation effectively in its favor would occur. In such a case, the USSR might be tempted to undertake a nuclear first-strike. George Kennan and Chip Bohlen argued strenuously against this perspective on Soviet intentions before NSC-68 was issued. And they continued to argue their views to the end of the Truman administration.[13]

President Eisenhower was well versed in organization and in policy-making. He saw the Truman administration as erratic in its decision-making and incoherent in its policy implementation. The first thing Eisenhower did to end the ongoing debate within the government over Cold War strategy, in addition to reorganizing the NSC, was to forge a coherent strategy through a long-term planning exercise known as Project Solarium.[14] The Solarium Project was organized into three competitive teams and each was tasked with the analysis of a different fundamental strategic approach to US-Soviet relations. The results of their analyses were presented in July 1953 at a special meeting of the NSC at the White House—with the President and the administration's senior security leadership in attendance. The product of Solarium was the promulgation of NSC-162/2, which detailed the critical assumptions about Soviet objectives and American capabilities that would guide US strategy throughout the Cold War. It reflected Eisenhower's fundamental rejection of the thinking behind NSC-68. The President was convinced that the free world needed to maintain a security situation that deterred the Russians, but which did not exceed what was necessary for achieving this purpose. Eisenhower believed it was critical that the free world mitigate the risk of war through cooperative action until the eventual and inevitable decline of the Soviet Union.[15]

President Eisenhower never swerved from his conviction that the Free World was stronger than the Soviet bloc and the USSR would eventually implode. After leaving office Eisenhower on many occasions advised leaders in Washington to distinguish between those who rule and those who are ruled. Failure to make this distinction could be a grave mistake. In Eisenhower's judgment the Soviet leaders were pragmatic, determined to stay in power. The Soviet regime that he knew from World War II would never risk the security of their country or the continuance of their regime by bringing about a nuclear holocaust. He especially believed in a realistic estimate of enemy strength as well as our own. He worried that military spending alone would be equated with security. Eisenhower believed that in addition to military strength the country's fiscal health was also a key component of national security. Of the many things accomplished by the Eisenhower administration, I am proud of the fact that they balanced the national budget three times in eight years. That is remarkable given the revolution in military technology and strategic thinking during the period.

Eisenhower knew the Cold War would be a long struggle. For the Free World to prevail over the thirty years or more necessary to prevail in that struggle, the United States needed strong defense, strong alliances, and a program to engage the Soviet Union. This commitment to engagement explains why the first agreement that was signed between the United States and the Soviet Union after World War II provided for exchanges in cultural, technical, and educational fields. This agreement is illustrative of Eisenhower's conviction that cultural exchanges and people-to-people diplomacy were also critical aspects of "waging peace" with the Soviet Union.

It is a very important to remember that cultural exchanges between the United States and the USSR were an important part of a multilayered strategy during the Cold War. The United States aimed to maintain a strong military to assure its capability for deterring an attack. But we were also laying the groundwork for a set of exchanges that would enhance mutual understanding. I know that sounds soft by today's standards. We now tend to discount the soft approach. But when you think of how little we knew about one another as people, the cultural exchanges proved essential to our long-term strategy. My grandfather used to speak of the dangers of "paranoid uncertainty" and how important it was to dispel it, lest we make a deadly miscalculation.

President Eisenhower's vision of how to conduct the Cold War included the conviction that it was important to engage the Soviets in negotiations, especially talks about arms control. Indeed, one of my grandfather's greatest achievements was his Atoms for Peace Program. It took great political courage for the President to offer this program to the world just months following the Soviet's first successful test of a hydrogen bomb. Eisenhower had many reasons for undertaking this initiative, but one of his chief objectives was to bring the Soviet Union back to the bargaining table around nuclear issues. In response, the Soviet Union matched the President's initiative by declassifying a whole area of nuclear science— nuclear fusion.

The tension between different strategies for dealing with the Soviet Union during the Cold War has never really dissipated in the United States. The different approaches to national security championed by Kennan-Bohlen and Acheson-Nitze in the Truman administration, which Eisenhower sought to reconcile through the Solarium process, have resurfaced in some form today. The United States continues to debate the nature of the threats to its security, and the extent to which the deployment of hard or soft power is appropriate for meeting them. It continues to struggle with the appropriate approach to regimes and organizations that threaten international stability and security.

Drawing the right lessons from the experience of the Cold War is an important guide for the development of security strategy. I am therefore surprised that so much of the literature about the end of the Cold War overemphasizes the role of the Strategic Defense Initiative (SDI) in producing the collapse of the Soviet Union. I traveled extensively to the Soviet Union during this period. I saw with my own eyes a nation of people come out of their internal exile to, as one Russian has described it, "Squeeze out the slaves in ourselves drop by drop." I personally witnessed the transformation and knew well many of those, such as Andrei Sakharov, who were so important in producing the transformation. I had many opportunities to meet and talk to people within the Communist Party of the Soviet Union and know that in large measure it was they who "put themselves out of business"—just as George Orwell predicted when he wrote that it would be the attitude of the ruling elite itself that would be decisive when the end of a regime would come.

The end of the Cold War is a very complicated issue. It was produced by many intertwining events that took place—some of them human, some tactical, and some strategic. At the end of the day, all of them were important. In 1965, my grandfather said that when the day comes that the Soviet Union is well educated and its people are able to travel as the West, there would be either a radical reform of communist regimes or a violent overthrow of those very regimes.

An important lesson from the Cold War experience is that unbridled ideology can be a very detrimental factor in political affairs. Today, the world seems so far removed from the consequences of its actions. This makes ideology a convenient way to mobilize people. As a pragmatist, I worry that when ideology is asserted—as if there are no consequences—it can be particularly dangerous.

With respect to post-Soviet Russia, I regret to say that our work is not done. It is noteworthy that Germany, which brought about the greatest destruction of any country in the twentieth century, entered the twenty-first century integrated economically and militarily into the West. Yet Russia, which kicked the communists out of power themselves and absorbed great economic dislocation in this transition, remains to this day estranged from the West. This is only one indication that we have a tremendous amount of work to do.

Notes

1 See "X" [George F. Kennan], "The Sources of Soviet Conduct," *Foreign Affairs* 25, no. 4 (July 1947): 566–82.

2 Vladimir Pechatnov, "Fulton Revisited," *Russia in Global Affairs*, no. 2 (April/June 2006), http://eng.globalaffairs.ru/number/n_6572

3 Wilson D. Miscamble, *George F. Kennan and the Making of American Foreign Policy, 1947–1950* (Princeton: Princeton University Press, 1992), 179–82.

4 John G. Hines, Ellis M. Mishulovich, and John Shull, *Soviet Intentions 1965–1985: An Analytical Comparison of US-Soviet Assessments During the Cold War*, Volume I (BMD Federal: McLean, VA, September 1995).

5 Vladimir Pechatnov, "The Soviet Union and the World, 1944–1953," in *The Cambridge History of the Cold War, Volume 1: Origins*, (eds), M. Leffler and O. A. Westad (New York: Cambridge University Press, 2010a).

6 "James Baker on the Fall of the Wall," *Der Spiegel Online*, 9/23/2009, http://www.spiegel.de/international/world/0,1518,druck-650801,00.html

7 "It's Good that Gorbachev Was a Weak Politician," *Der Spiegel Online*, 11/6/2009, http://www.spiegel.de/international/europe/0,1518,659752,00.html

8 George F. Kennan, "A Fateful Error," *New York Times*, February 5, 1997, A23.

9 The economic strategy plan for the the European Union between 2000 and 2010.

10 Zbigniew Brzezinski, "An Agenda for NATO: Building a Global Security Web," *Foreign Affairs* 88, no. 5 (October/September 2009): 2–20.

11 See John S. D. Eisenhower, *Strictly Personal: A Memoir* (New York: Doubleday, 1974).

12 Susan Eisenhower, *Breaking Free: A Memoir of Love and Revolution* (New York: Farrar, Straus and Giroux, 1995).

13 See Melvyn Leffler, "The Emergence of an American Grand Strategy,

1945–1952," in M. Lefler and O. A. Westad, *The Cambridge History of the Cold War, Volume 1: Origins* (New York: Cambridge University Press, 2010a) and John Lewis Gaddis, *Strategies of Containment: A Critical Appraisal of American National Security Policy During the Cold War*, revised and expanded edition (New York: Oxford University Press, 2005a), chapters 2–6.

14   Robert R. Bowie and Richard H. Immerman, *Waging Peace: How Eisenhower Shaped an Enduring Cold War Strategy* (New York: Oxford University Press, 2000), chapter 8.

15   Bowie and Immerman, *Waging Peace*, 49.

CHAPTER TWO

Origins and preliminaries

Memories of the origins and early stages of the Cold War have faded with the passing of the generation that endured World War II. Hugh Lunghi, one of the few surviving interpreters for the Tehran, Yalta, and Potsdam Conferences refreshes our collective memory. Lunghi met Stalin, Churchill, Eden, and Molotov, and was present at many of their most intimate and important meetings. He offers a first-hand view of the leaders who were influential in shaping the postwar world. Lunghi's description of wartime service Moscow, including Soviet espionage efforts to penetrate the British Military Mission there, provides unique insight into the atmosphere in the USSR as a prelude to the Cold War era.

Building from Lunghi's personal recollections, American, British, and Russian historians examine the origins and early events of the Cold War. This includes a discussion of the importance of the deeply divisive and intractable problems associated with the political and territorial status of postwar Germany as well as of Central and Eastern Europe, most especially Poland. Attention is paid to the distinctive Russian, American, and British mindsets at the end of World War II, which set the stage for the Cold War and to an important degree shaped its conduct through to its conclusion.

Vladimir Pechatnov explains the beginning of the Cold War from the Soviet perspective. He describes the breakdown of the wartime alliance among the Big Three, emphasizing the importance of differences over spheres of influence in postwar Europe and the long history of mutual mistrust. David Woolner provides the American view of the beginning of the global rivalry that emerged after World War II. Woolner places the Cold War in its context by describing the most significant people, decisions, and events of World War II, highlighting the particular importance of Franklin D. Roosevelt.[1] David Reynolds provides the British perspective and explains the significance of Anglo-American relations, and the European origins of the Cold War.[2]

PHOTO 2.1 *Big Three at the Teheran Conference in November–December 1943 (Courtesy of Churchill Archives Centre)*

Reminiscences of the wartime Big Three

Hugh Lunghi

My first sight of Stalin at the Big Three Conferences has to be set in the context of what I had seen and read about him in the press and on the radio. The mass media in Britain following Hitler's invasion of Russia painted a generously favorable picture of Stalin and the Red Army. They were portrayed as heroes, led by a hero with a kindly, but strong face. Far from being the heroic, upright, soldierlike figure I had been led by press reports to expect, I saw a little old uncle who was modest in demeanor—yet there was an air of menace about the man. Perhaps it was his eyes. He avoided looking directly at you.

Stalin was smaller than I had imagined him to be from the ubiquitous, flattering posters and portraits gracing all public and private offices and homes. He was certainly smaller than Churchill. Stalin's built-up heels made Churchill appear even taller. Stalin seemed more relaxed with his shorter lieutenants, for example, with his foreign minister, Vyacheslav Molotov and his Russian Revolution comrade-in- arms and cavalry general, Kliment Voroshilov. Although diminutive in stature, these were powerful men.

On formal occasions and in business meetings Stalin spoke quietly, moved smoothly, and was cat-like. Spiteful and bullying to his own company, Stalin was careful to be courteous and good mannered with foreigners. He was visibly anxious not to exceed any boundaries of protocol, avoiding bad language. Living in Russia one soon learned under deep secrecy that he was cruel and murderous among his own.

Stalin appeared restrained, far from crude, even displaying what used to be called in Britain "Victorian manners." During conference discussions he was most impressive, refraining from speaking too much as Churchill and Roosevelt tended to do. Stalin rarely used notes or briefing papers, or referred to documents, during meetings. Occasionally, he would have a notebook on the table. Otherwise he would avoid notes.

Stalin's attitude toward the Soviet Foreign Minister Molotov was that of a headmaster to a leading pupil. He was much more formal with his interpreter, Vladimir Nikolayevich Pavlov, listening carefully to his translation from the English and sometimes correcting Pavlov's Russian. When he wanted to increase the pace of a conference session, Stalin would interrupt his interpreter asking, "Is that all?" Although ostensibly addressing his interpreter, it was obvious Stalin intended his opposite numbers to get to the point.

When necessary, Stalin readily displayed his self-control. At social occasions he would join in somewhat restrained laughter. During the Yalta Conference he was most relaxed. By then he was, after all, playing the host. Everything had gone well for him by the time of Yalta. Most of East and Central Europe had already been occupied by the Red Army with its troops and security services.

As much as it was all important for Churchill and Roosevelt to keep each other in the war, both knew it was vital to keep Stalin too. Rather more than to each other, they made up to Stalin throughout the conferences. Although he was not exactly deferential, Churchill, like Roosevelt, seemed inclined to show he agreed with Stalin. He clearly had no illusions about the communist system. He was a lifelong, inveterate anti-communist.

To Soviet citizens and foreigners who lived and worked in Moscow, or indeed anywhere in the Soviet Union, it was obvious that the tension between the Allies about the Second Front was a point of origin of the Cold War. It was at their first meeting in August 1942 that Stalin berated Churchill over the failure, as he saw it, of Britain, to open a Second Front against the German forces invading Russia. Following a bad-tempered, first-round plenary session of talks with military advisors present, Stalin invited Churchill into his personal quarters for a round of private talks. "The talk with the snacks," as Stalin called it, went on right through the night. During this second session they fell into a discussion of history and military strategy. It touched upon Churchill's illustrious military ancestor, John Churchill, the Duke of Marlborough whose biography Churchill had written. It had been published just before the outbreak of World War II. Clearly Stalin had been well briefed about the work. Sharing meals and drinks Churchill and Stalin built some rapport. In this way Churchill was able to separate his judgment of the system from the man who ruled it.

I worked in the British Military Mission in Moscow during the war in addition to serving as an interpreter at the Big Three Conferences. My expectations of what it would be like to work in Moscow with the Russians were shaped by the British and American press. Based on the media coverage of Russia at war I arrived in the Soviet Union full of good will. After only a few months I found it very difficult to accomplish the task of helping the Soviet Union in its war effort. The Russian people received us warmly. They recognized us as allies and were friendly. Eventually, of course, they realized that although we were allies it was dangerous to befriend us. Russians who associated with foreigners were confined to forced labor camps, the Gulag. Only two years after the end of the war a decree was issued forbidding Soviet citizens to pass "any" information to foreigners. Without special written permission it became impossible for foreigners to travel beyond a distance of ten, later twenty kilometers from the center of Moscow—a measure later reciprocated in respective foreign countries during the Cold War.

Even more serious for us was that we were being hampered in every possible way in our work. We were in Moscow to assist the Russians in their war effort. But it seemed as if we were regarded as the enemy. It was vital, for example, for the Russians no less than for us, to protect the Arctic convoys bringing supplies to Russia from German U-boats. The convoys were especially vulnerable on the approach to Murmansk and to the port of Archangel, where the White Sea narrows. We requested facilities to station a squadron of Hampden Bombers for anti-submarine operations. At first the Soviet naval authorities, in fact Stalin, as we later learned, agreed, but after the equipment was delivered to the base in Russia, visas for our pilots were denied. The squadron was never used for its immediate purpose. The senior Soviet naval officials were not told why the visas had been refused and were afraid of taking the initiative themselves. Personnel at Royal Navy hospitals in Archangel and Murmansk were also refused visas for many months.

Then there was the silly affair of the carrier pigeons. These birds were carried on the Catalina Flying Boats patrolling the main sea routes taking people from Britain to the Soviet Union. The pigeons were on the aircraft in the event of radio failure. As absurd as it now sounds, the Russians refused to allow us to exercise the pigeons on their soil. Eventually, of course, when it finally went to the top senior man in Murmansk, the Soviet general said, "This is nonsense. Let the pigeons in."

All foreign establishments in the USSR were allocated staff provided by a Russian government agency. It was no close secret that these people were compelled to work for the secret police. We assumed our offices were bugged. I shared a room and an office in the Military Mission with a colleague. To counteract the microphones we used various well-known methods, such as tapping desks vigorously with pencils. Within a few months of the end of the war, I discovered thirty-three microphones in the Military Mission building. An American signals officer inspected the offices with a detection device. He found the microphones hidden in plaster behind skirting boards in various rooms of the building. That was the kind of atmosphere within which we lived and worked in Moscow during the war.

A Soviet perspective on Cold War origins

Vladimir Pechatnov

There are various interpretations of the origins of the Cold War depending on how you see the main driving forces behind it. Was it realpolitik, great power rivalry, or ideology? Or, was it perhaps a clash of cultures, which had been going on for on for centuries? My view is that the Cold War was about all of the above; it was a messy mixture of ideology, realpolitik, geopolitics, and culture. Realpolitik and geopolitics were very important in the wake of World War II, which left only two great powers, and many power vacuums between them in the strategically important areas of Central and Eastern Europe, the Far East, Northern Asia, and the Near and Middle East. As soon as the common enemy was defeated and the Axis Powers disappeared, the competition for influence over those areas began in earnest, destroying the Big Three Alliance from within.

The United States and its allies tried to prevent the emergence of a hegemonic Eurasian power in World War I and World War II. For American and British planners, the Soviet Union with its ideology and huge military capability became the next logical candidate after Nazi Germany for the role of Eurasian hegemon.

For the Soviet Union, the American-led Western bloc was aimed at depriving it of its well-deserved fruits of great victory, and ultimately at its destruction. The Soviet geopolitical aims in the wake of World War II, as we are now able to document from the recent archival findings, included building a buffer zone of pro-Soviet states on the western borders as they were in 1941.[3] Also, the Soviets sought to keep Germany and Japan enfeebled and wanted to regain the Czarist possessions in the Far East lost in the Russo-Japanese War early in the twentieth century. They wanted as well to acquire a controlling influence over the Black Sea Straits, as well as trustee status over the former Italian colony Tripolitania on the Mediterranean. Stalin also planned to create an enclave in northern Iran to cover the vulnerable Soviet southern flank where most of the Soviet oil deposits were located. Soviet efforts in 1945–6 to implement this program met with stubborn Western resistance and that led to serious tension among the former allies. But without the ideological factor, the geopolitical rivalry would have assumed more traditional and more restrained forms.

The Cold War was not just about geopolitics; it was also a struggle between two worlds "for the soul of mankind." Ideology made the Cold War more intense, global, and dangerous. More global because both sides believed in the universal nature of their principles and wanted to spread them to the whole world. More intense because each side believed it had a monopoly interest and was determined to win. And more dangerous because ideological hostility led to exaggerated suspicions and fears, which in turn pushed both sides to overkill in providing for their security.[4]

Culture was also a complicating factor. In civilizational terms Russia has always been a lonely country, torn between the East and the West and never truly belonging to either. Ever since the thirteenth century, Russia's relationship with the West had been particularly difficult. For Russia, the more prosperous, modern, and technologically advanced West was a cultural and security challenge, a source of many invasions through indefensible western borders. For the West, the heart of the Russian problem, especially from the nineteenth century onward, was a combination of huge natural and manpower resources, with an alien authoritarian regime capable of using those resources freely against Western interests. Even Marx and Engels, the founders of Marxism, subscribed to this basic view of Russia's role in European politics. When the Bolsheviks came to power the gap between Russian and Western values widened. This increased Russia's isolation, and made the traditional task of defending its vulnerable Eurasian landmass against real and potential enemies even more difficult. The Soviet system aggravated the brutality of Russian culture in which human life had always "not been worth a kopek" to quote a Russian proverb. At the same time democracy advanced in the West, enhancing human rights and individual dignity. Bolshevism was a daring attempt to catch up with and overtake the capitalist West in technological development by means of central planning, a nationalized economy, and the one-party state.

The Cold War originated in a messy mixture of ideology, geopolitics, and culture that mutually reinforced each other. For all of these reasons the Cold War was, in my view, largely inescapable, although it could have taken different forms. It would have been slightly better had both sides, but especially the more preponderate West, been more flexible and ready to negotiate. Alternatively, it could have been much worse had it not been for the restraining impact of nuclear weapons and cooler heads prevailing in Soviet and Western councils during various Cold War crises. It could have turned into a large-scale hot war between the contending blocs.

It is useful to consider what the world looked like from Moscow between 1945 and 1947. To Stalin and his circle, the Soviet postwar geopolitical agenda seemed a moderate and legitimate compilation of Soviet security requirements, given the tragic lessons of World War II and the experience of the preceding interwar period. The geopolitical legitimacy at the core of Stalin's desideratum was recognized in the West during the war as necessary to provide for in-depth defense of the Soviet Union. What was strategically justifiable in Stalin's eyes was also morally right to Stalin and his circle. They saw their claims as a fair share of the spoils of the war, won by a great sacrifice and contribution to the defeat of the common enemy. And it was a decisive contribution. By general accounts, the Red Army suffered fifty-five times more casualties than did American forces, and inflicted ninety-three percent of German combat losses between the German invasion of Russia and the Allied invasion of France on D-Day. Counting operations in all the war theaters, the Soviet share of the total Allied effort according to Soviet estimates was about seventy-five percent. So it was morally right in Stalin's view for the Soviet Union to have this share of the spoils of war. This sense of entitlement was enhanced by a deeply felt desire in the Kremlin for recognition of the Soviet Union as a new great power. This was a very important psychological factor behind Stalin's postwar agenda.

The Soviet Union thus became a key member of the victorious Grand Alliance. Germany and Japan, its two mortal enemies, lay prostrate, and Soviet military predominance over the Eurasian landmass seemed assured. This provided a unique window of opportunity. Now was the time to restore Russia's historical rights, which had been lost in the previous ill-fated wars of the nineteenth and twentieth centuries. It was time to convert gigantic losses and tremendous victories into lasting security for the Soviet Union and its ruling circle. Looking ahead, Stalin realized that it would be hard to attain his agenda. Well versed in Russian history and mythology, he expected the ever-tricky West to follow its usual pattern of behavior: use Russians as cannon fodder, lure them to fight with promises of major strategic gains, and leave them emptyhanded in the end. In Stalin's words cited by Molotov at the war's end, "Czarist Russia was used to win wars, but was unable to enjoy the fruits of her victories. Russians are remarkable warriors but they do not know how to make peace. They are deceived and underpaid."[5]

Having been deceived by Hitler in 1941, Stalin was determined not to be deceived again. As the war moved toward its end, Stalin and Molotov were braced for tough bargaining with their allies. They were ready to pursue their primary agenda with their allies' consent if possible, and without their consent if necessary. In the end, it proved to be impossible to reconcile Stalin's security agenda with maintaining the cooperative wartime alliance.

So the Kremlin had to sacrifice the latter to secure the former. There was no doubt in Stalin's view as to who was responsible for the Cold War. In one of his documents there was a note on the margins: "We're not waging Cold War," he wrote to himself, "it is the United States and its allies who are doing this."[6] To put it bluntly, in Stalin's own style, the Anglo-Americans reneged on their wartime promises. They tried to deprive the Soviet Union of its well-deserved fruits of victory, most especially Soviet control over Eastern Europe and part of Germany. The Allies were wrong in refusing to pay the Soviets their due. The United States and Britain, in Stalin's view, wanted to revise the results of World War II, which had been won largely by Russian blood. As Molotov put it himself in his oral reminiscences, "We had to consolidate what we had conquered. Hungary, Czechoslovakia, and other countries were in a messy condition. So we had to introduce socialism to squeeze out the bourgeois order. Hence, the Cold War."[7]

Stalin and Molotov were not entirely wrong about Anglo-American Cold War aims. One of which, according to declassified American documents, was the retraction of Soviet influence; that is getting the Soviets out of Germany and Eastern Europe. Following the same causal connection further, it can be argued that the Soviet presence in the heart of Europe at the end of the war was possible because of the Anglo-American reluctance to fight the main Wehrmacht forces head on until the summer of 1944. In other words, to save Anglo-American lives, the Western Allies first let the Russians into Europe and then tried to push them back, but again, without having a big war that would cost Western lives. Thus, the origin of the Cold War may be traced back to the belated Second Front. I would not go as far as to say that this was the reason for the Cold War, but it was a very important factor in setting Stalin's view, because it fed his suspicions about the Allies' ultimate aims and intentions during the war.

In considering the breakdown of the Grand Alliance, attention must be paid to British-Russian relations, especially regarding the status of Central and Eastern Europe. It is true that mutual suspicion between the Soviet Union and the British, which would eventually contribute to the Cold War, predated their alliance against Hitler. The British concern over the Treaty of Non-Aggression between Germany and the Soviet Union in 1939 and its secret protocol is often cited as an example.[8] But, this can be overestimated as a source of Soviet-British contention, as circumstances may not be so simple. The situation created by the Molotov-Ribbentrop Pact was complex, especially with regard to its consequences. Stalin's move into the Baltic states and eastern Poland was not entirely unwelcomed by the British. Churchill seemed almost to welcome it. At the time he said that he would rather have Russians coming there as liberators, not as occupiers, because that was still better than Germany moving in there. So, the Molotov-Ribbentrop Pact was not entirely harmful to British-Soviet relations or negative in its impact on the British mindset.

Poland was one of the major controversial points between the Allies, on a par with Germany as a factor in the origin of the Cold War. Poland was the place where both sides had almost diametrically opposed positions. Stalin himself put it very well at Yalta, when Churchill spoke about a British moral obligation to Poland. When Churchill said, "That is how we started the war and we are committed to a democratic, free and strong Poland," Stalin responded that for the Soviet Union it was a matter of ultimate security. Poland had been a corridor of aggression more than once in our history and Stalin was bound to stop this. Stalin proceeded to observe that the Soviets were interested in a strong Poland, but it should be friendly; it should be essentially a pro-Soviet Poland. To have a free and pro-Soviet Poland was impossible, because a free Poland would not be pro-Soviet.

Aside from Poland, which was a special case, I do not believe that Stalin had a clearly developed plan to "Sovietize" all of the Eastern European countries. The main thing for Stalin was to assure that these countries were pro-Soviet. The degree to which they would have to control those countries was still unclear, as late as 1946. In some places like Hungary and Czechoslovakia, the non-communist elements were still in power. So, imposing control throughout Eastern Europe was an improvisation in part. Therefore, I do not think Stalin had a plan of brutal Sovietization. Given the opportunities that arose, however, he went in that direction easily. As the Cold War opened, it became a struggle about who would control the governments in Europe. At that point the United States and Soviet spheres of influence began to stiffen, especially the Soviet one. For Stalin it was unthinkable to have any subversive anti-Soviet elements in the governments of Eastern Europe. So, once the Cold War was in full swing, Stalin undertook Soviet-style mass repression to insure his control of the region.[9]

Perhaps the Cold War's origins preceded the tension over the Second Front. It is possible that it began with Hitler's attack on Britain and France, which George Kennan, the architect of the American containment strategy called a "colossal betrayal of western civilization."[10] If so, had Hitler been contained in the 1930s, there would have been neither World War II nor a Cold War.

An American perspective on Cold War origins

David Woolner

To understand the American perspective on the origins of the Cold War, it is necessary to understand the hopes, expectations, and strategy of the one man who stood at the center of US politics from 1933 to 1945: Franklin D. Roosevelt. Indeed, given Roosevelt's central position in the direction of US policy vis-à-vis the Soviets, one of the great unanswered questions concerning the origin of the Cold War is what would have happened if FDR had not died on 12 April 1945? This, of course, is a question that can never be answered, but posing it often leads to a second set of equally vexing questions: might Roosevelt have prevented the onset of the Cold War? Or was his behavior at the end of the war a major contributing factor to the onset of that half-century struggle?[11]

Of course, there is no question that FDR played a part in this story. But all too often, FDR's role in the history of the Cold War is taken to begin at the Yalta Conference in 1945. Yalta, however, as David Reynolds has frequently pointed out, was just one of many wartime conferences. It was never expected to be the last conference of the European war, nor was it "intended to be the last word on the future of Europe."[12] In fact, it is far more accurate to see Yalta as but a brief moment on a longer road; an important moment to be sure—perhaps the first time we see the Allied powers begin to make the transition to a new postwar phase in their relationship—but Yalta was not, nor was it ever meant to be, the conclusive gathering it was later portrayed to be. Indeed, when looking at Yalta, it is striking to see how much was left undone during the conference, especially with respect to postwar Germany.

So, to understand the origins of the Cold War from the American perspective, we need to gain a greater understanding of the trajectory of US-Soviet relations both before and after Yalta. Above all, we need to understand the evolution of Roosevelt's thinking, not only about the Soviets, but also about America's place in the world as he struggled to meet the twin crises of depression and war in the difficult period between 1933 and 1945.

To begin with, we must remember that from the American perspective, World War II was intimately linked to the worldwide economic crisis that Americans refer to as the Great Depression. Today's generation tends to treat these two crises as two separate historical events, but for the generation that lived through the depression and war, nothing could be further from the truth. Perhaps no other official within the Roosevelt administration felt this more keenly than FDR's Secretary of State, Cordell Hull. Born in back-woods Tennessee, Hull would serve in both the House and the Senate and was a significant force within the Democratic Party by the time Roosevelt was ready to run for national office. Hull was an unabashed champion of freer trade and by the early 1930s he became convinced that it was the deprivation caused by the Great Depression that led to the rise of Nazism in Germany and other forms of fascism in Europe and in Asia. Hull often said, "If goods don't cross borders, armies will" and in an effort to stem the growing likelihood of war launched his Reciprocal Trade Agreements program in the mid-1930s in the hope that greater international cooperation and prosperity might prevent the outbreak of another major conflagration.[13] Needless to say, Hull's efforts were not successful, but by September of 1939 both Roosevelt and Hull shared the view that World War II had largely economic causes.

This determination would have important consequences for the future, for it meant that for both Roosevelt and Hull, World War II was not just about achieving an Allied victory, it was also about opening the world's markets, providing greater access to raw materials, and establishing a new world financial and economic order. Indeed, for many officials within Hull's State Department, this was nearly as important as defeating the Germans and the Japanese.[14] Almost from the moment the German Wehrmacht crossed into Poland, therefore, American planners began thinking about how the United States might fashion a new postwar economic order.

A second major factor that we must take into consideration if we are to fully understand America's perspective on the Cold War involves FDR's geopolitical thinking—what the diplomatic historian Alan Henrikson has called FDR's "mental maps."[15] For Roosevelt, the outbreak of the war in Europe marked a significant escalation in the "epidemic" of international lawlessness that began in Manchuria in 1931 and would expand to Abyssinia, Spain, and China before the decade was through. Hampered by a wary public and the non-interventionists (isolationists) in Congress who pushed through a series of neutrality laws in the mid-1930s, there was little the President could do to stop the tide of war, and even after war broke out in Europe, it would take roughly a year and a half before he could offer Britain—and later the Soviets—America's full support in the form of Lend-Lease.[16]

But Roosevelt's inability to act decisively does not mean that he was unaware of the danger facing the United States in the 1931–1941 period. On the contrary, FDR was keenly aware of the geopolitical challenges the nation faced and in an effort to strengthen America's global position undertook such moves as the recognition of the Soviet Union in 1933 (which he hoped might give pause to an expansionist Japan) and the launch of a major naval buildup in 1934. FDR also worked hard to convince the American public that the United States could not afford to ignore the global security crisis posed by the aggressive policies of the Germans and the Japanese and, as we shall see, by the time the United States had entered the war in December of 1941 had already laid the framework for future American involvement in world affairs.

A third factor in the development of the Cold War involves FDR's military/political strategy. Roosevelt never doubted that the greatest threat to America's—and indeed the world's—security came from Nazi Germany. As such, FDR fully concurred with his military advisors' "Germany first" strategy and in the wake of Pearl Harbor came to the conclusion that it was absolutely vital to get the United States involved in the European/ Atlantic Theater in 1942. He pushed for a joint operation in this theater in his early conversations with the British. This ultimately led to the decision to launch Operation Torch, which brought Allied forces into North Africa in November 1942. As Michael Howard has pointed out, the duration of the campaign in North Africa and other complicating factors led to the British-American Mediterranean strategy in 1943.[17] But the expansion of Anglo-American operations in the Mediterranean delayed the opening of the Second Front that Stalin so desperately wanted until June 1944. This was quite late in the conflict and, in view of Soviet advances, predetermined in many respects the fate of Eastern and Central Europe.

Taken together, these three factors—the desire to create a new postwar economic order, the realization that the United States must play a major role in world affairs that would be supported by the American public, and the military strategy that FDR launched in the war itself—all played a significant part in the development of the Cold War and American perspectives about that conflict.

If we look at American policy vis-à-vis Germany, for example, which most historians would agree stands at the center of the East-West dispute at the heart of the Cold War; we can see that the direction of US postwar policy toward Germany was largely determined during the war itself. This is best exemplified by the brief but serious dispute within the Roosevelt administration over the so-called Morgenthau Plan. The latter involved a proposal issued by FDR's Secretary of the Treasury, Henry Morgenthau, at the Second Quebec Conference in September 1944 which was based on the idea that the Allies should deindustrialize Germany after the war.[18] Hull was immediately and vehemently against any notion of German deindustrialization. Long before the war was over, and in keeping with his economic agenda, Hull knew that a viable German economy was going to be vital for Europe, as well as for the rest of the world's economy. Although Hull played a very minor role in the FDR's wartime conferences and often seemed to be ignored by the President in the exercise of wartime strategy, he nonetheless prevailed in this bitter dispute with Morgenthau. Thus, even before we get to Yalta and the last months of the war, it became clear that American policy toward postwar Germany would ultimately be based on the idea that Germany must be economically rehabilitated once the conflict was over. This was significant, for the American decision to rehabilitate her former enemy would run directly counter to the Soviet desire to keep Germany weak, all of which would become a major element in the onset of the Cold War.

If we delve deeper into Roosevelt's determination to see the United States play a major role in world affairs, we can see that this also played an important part in setting the stage for onset of the Cold War. Here, it is important to examine the dual function or roles that the President played as a world leader during the war years. The first role was to inspire the world to become a better place—a goal that was very much in keeping with FDR's effort to convince the American people they must take on a greater degree of responsibility for world affairs. As noted, FDR launched this effort even before the American entry into the war. Roosevelt first articulated this vision in January 1941, arguing in perhaps his most famous address of the war that the American people's sacrifices in support of the British war effort were part of a larger effort to create a world based—not on the tyranny of the Nazis—but on four fundamental freedoms: freedom of speech and expression, freedom of worship, freedom from want, and freedom from fear. Roosevelt's reference to the four freedoms resonated with people the world over. In simple yet elegant terms, the President seemed to capture the essence of what separated the Western democracies from the demonic policies of the Axis powers, not only in political terms—through freedom of speech and religion—but also in economic terms, through freedom from want. FDR had already initiated a major effort to rid the United States of freedom from want through his launch of the New Deal, which restructured and reformed the American economy. As such, his arguments about the need to rid the world of poverty carried special significance. And, in the dark days of 1941, when the German war machine seemed unstoppable, his call for freedom from fear carried equal weight. Taken together, FDR's call for the Four Freedoms—"everywhere in the world"—created a great deal of expectation in every corner of the planet about a better future as a consequence of the war. At home, meanwhile, the economic and rhetorical dimensions of FDR's performance as a wartime leader combined to produce an equally strong desire on the part of officials within the State Department, the US Treasury, and within other agencies of his administration to remake the world in an American image. Critics sometimes see this determination as a malevolent effort to force an American economic and security agenda on the rest of the world, but for the generation that fought the war, it was more often seen as a benevolent idea.

To bring all of these ideas together, and to ensure that the American people would be directly tied to an American-led effort to ensure peace and prosperity after the war, FDR needed to create the structural institutions that would prevent any possible return to the prewar isolationism that had so limited his government's freedom of action in the 1930s. This effort first took shape in the promulgation of the Atlantic Charter in August of

1941, and would be further expanded through the establishment of such institutions as the International Monetary Fund, the International Bank for Reconstruction and Development (later the World Bank), and of course the UN. Roosevelt used his rhetorical skills to marshal public support for these institutions, but their creation brings us to the second major aspect of his role as wartime leader: as the pragmatic head of the American government; as the individual, who, in short, needed to protect and promote America's vital interests.

It is this aspect of FDR's leadership that we see most clearly in his dealings with his wartime allies, especially the Soviet Union. However, in bargaining with the Soviets over such critical issues as the fate of Poland or the status of postwar Germany, and in the horse trading and give-and-take of great power geopolitics, Roosevelt's dual functions placed him in a great dilemma. For these were hard-headed negotiations that went on underneath FDR's rhetorical call for a world without spheres of influence, or balance of power of politics. If FDR were here today, he would probably smile and say that he could have worked out the contradictions in his policies once the war was over. Roosevelt had great confidence in himself—perhaps a bit too much at times. Ultimately, FDR thought that the American alliance with the Soviet Union could be transformed into postwar cooperation, which was his primary goal at the end of the war. If you read the speeches that Roosevelt makes in the latter part of his life, particularly at the very end of his life, it is quite clear that he recognizes that the kind of unparalleled violence that came with World War II could not be repeated. The world simply could not go through this again.[19]

In the speech that Franklin Roosevelt was working on the day he died, for example—a speech that was never delivered due to his untimely death—the President wrote:

> Today we have learned in the agony of war that great power involves great responsibility...
>
> We, as Americans, do not choose to deny our responsibility.
>
> Nor do we intend to abandon our determination that, within the lives of our children and our children's children, there will not be a third world war.
>
> We seek peace—enduring peace. More than an end to war, we want an end to the beginnings of all wars—yes, an end to this brutal, inhuman, and thoroughly impractical method of settling the differences between governments ...
>
> Today we are faced with the preeminent fact that, if civilization is to survive, we must cultivate the science of human relationships—the ability of all peoples, of all kinds, to live together and work together, in the same world, at peace.[20]

These were not hollow words. FDR firmly believed that above all else, he must do everything in his power to prevent a third world war. This was Roosevelt's view even before the atomic bomb. Hence, he saw cooperation with the Soviet Union as absolutely vital to the building of a more peaceful world in the future. And that is why, for example, FDR regarded the Soviet agreement at Yalta to more or less embrace the American recommendations on voting procedures at the UN as a major step forward. This, despite the fact that Roosevelt knew full well what was going on in Central Europe; he knew that Russian actions in Poland and Eastern Europe were very problematical. He knew the Red Army's presence in the heart of Europe would need to be addressed, as is apparent when one examines the flurry of telegrams among Stalin, Churchill, and Roosevelt in the last few months of FDR's life. But FDR also understood that Soviet power was here to stay, it was not going to disappear after the war, and for him the critical issue was to maintain the cooperation that had been established among the Big Three in the struggle against Hitler. This would require compromises on such difficult issues as the geopolitical makeup of Eastern Europe; compromises that would later be viewed, not as a necessity of war, but rather as the appeasement of a great power, much like the appeasement of Hitler in the late 1930s.

So Roosevelt played a role in the story of the beginning of the Cold War. Unfortunately, he was not around to try and influence these events. It is nevertheless important to recognize these deeper roots of the origins of the Cold War, and also to recognize Roosevelt's enduring commitment to a policy of engagement with the Soviets. As we have seen, Roosevelt was engaged with the Russians almost from the start of his administration. He extended diplomatic recognition to the Soviet Union in 1933 because he recognized Russia as a potential ally against the Japanese in Asia, much like President Nixon recognized China vis-à-vis the Soviet Union years later. This initial attempt at a US-Soviet alliance did not go as far as the Soviets or the Americans wanted, but the point here is that he established a policy of engagement that was followed from the very beginning. FDR never lost sight of the geopolitical reality of the power of Russia. He was not happy about the Molotov-Ribbentrop Pact and was distressed by Russia's Winter War against Finland in 1939–40. But Roosevelt was always mindful that the West would need the Soviet Union in the fight against Hitler and would need Russian cooperation in the postwar world if there were to be any hope of maintaining the principles he first enunciated in the Atlantic Charter. Hence, the critical issue so far as he was concerned was to bring the Soviet Union into the UN, especially into the Security Council where the Big Three along with France and China could work out their differences without recourse to war.

Following Franklin Roosevelt's death, US relations with the Soviet Union deteriorated at an ever-increasing pace. FDR believed he could continue to accommodate Stalin and maintain cooperation. Truman resolved instead to stand up to the Soviets in a confrontational fashion, and he never really put accommodation to the test. Therefore, at his first meeting with Molotov shortly after Roosevelt's death in April 1945, Truman applied blunt diplomacy, only to discover that it did not get him where he wanted to go. Following the Allied victory in Europe, and in an effort to reverse the decline in US-Soviet relations, Truman sent FDR's trusted confidant, Harry Hopkins, to Russia to speak with Stalin to reestablish more cordial relations with the Soviet regime, but this failed to alter things significantly. With little experience in foreign affairs, Truman tended to regard the Soviets

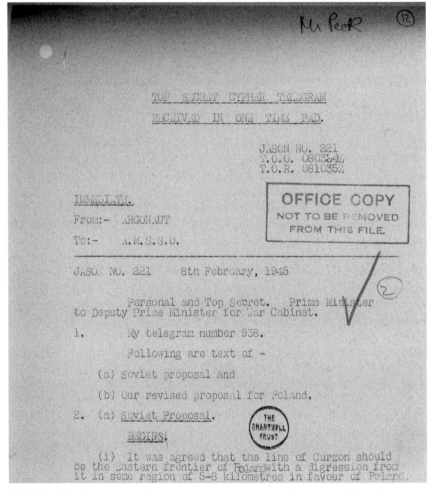

PHOTO 2.2 *Top secret telegram on negotiations with Soviets on Poland in February 1945 (Courtesy of Churchill Archives)*

with deep suspicion; and he was far less sympathetic about the Soviet need for security. At base, Truman never fully understood or accepted the Russian demand for a sphere of influence in Eastern Europe and he tended to interpret that demand, not as a logical extension of Russia's critical need to protect itself from the possibility of further German aggression, but, rather, in much the same way that Stalin would later interpret the Anglo-American decision to rehabilitate Western Germany, as a threat to the reestablishment of liberal, capitalist democracy in those parts of Europe liberated by the Allies—in other words, as a threat to vital American and Western European interests. Ironically, it was FDR's tendency to describe World War II as a gargantuan struggle between democracy and totalitarianism that helped frame Truman's world view—a worldview that would lead to the ever-increasing determination to stand up to the Soviet menace, as best exemplified by the Truman Doctrine.

Franklin Roosevelt's approach to spheres of influence—in spite of his rhetoric to the contrary—was based on a more open concept. He hoped that in the long run the United States could ameliorate Soviet behavior in Poland and elsewhere, and that there would be economic and cultural ties between the East and West that would help secure this process. Unfortunately FDR was not there to direct the West toward that goal and thanks to his untimely death, we will never know if the man Winton Churchill called "the greatest man I have ever known" might have been able to avert the half-century struggle known as the Cold War.

A British perspective on Cold War origins

David Reynolds

What follows is not a formal academic essay but a series of informal reflections on the issues addressed in this chapter. To begin any discussion about how the beginning of the Cold War appeared from the British perspective, one must make the obvious point that Britain was the weakest of the three major powers coming out of the war. Alexander Cadogan, the Permanent Undersecretary of the Foreign Office at the end of the war, wrote in his diary that the Big Three were really the "Big Two and a Half." There was a distinct sense of Britain's limitations in many ways. Obviously, there were the financial limits. By the end of the war Britain had lost approximately eighteen percent of its economic assets. All that is very familiar now, because it fits into our perspective of the story of the British role in the world as one of being in inexorable decline from then on. But, from the perspective of the time and certainly for British policy-makers at the time, there was still a sense that Britain did matter in a major way in world affairs. It is worth remembering that when American political scientist William Fox coined the term *superpower* in 1944, he described three superpowers: the United States, the Soviet Union, and Great Britain.[21]

Fox recognized Britain as a superpower because at the end of the war, it remained a vast empire. The Empire had worked well in World War II in mobilizing huge amounts of resources and manpower. We often forget the role of Canadian, Australian, New Zealand, and Indian troops in almost every theater of the war. At the end of the war and well into the late 1940s, Britain had more than a million men and woman under arms in the armed forces of the Empire. This was a time when France was ruined, weak, and politically divided. There were no other powers in Western Europe in 1945.

There are two important points to be considered from this perspective. First, among British policy-makers there was still a sense that, "Yes, we are weakened, but we are still a major force in world affairs and we have a part to play in it." That was their perspective of the events of the 1940s. Second, it is important to consider, despite her weakness, how Britain related to the other two major powers.

How did the British view the Americans? British policy-makers, like all policy-makers, were influenced by the experiences of their own past, what they had been through. At war's end, for most British policy-makers, there was a keen desire to avoid the withdrawal of the United States from Europe in the way that had happened after World War I. British policy-makers well remembered the whole fiasco of the League of Nations, designed principally by an American president who then was unable to get it through Congress. Franklin Roosevelt at wartime conferences told Churchill and Stalin very clearly, "Do not expect that I can keep American troops in Europe for more than a couple of years after the end of the war." That is worth remembering given that we now assume the American presence in Europe was axiomatic for the whole of the Cold War. So from the British point of view, a fundamental axiom of policy was to try to draw the United States into European commitments. Because that was the only way Britain could hope to deal with the huge problems of postwar Europe.

The British had a certain conceit here that had developed over the course of the war. They considered the Americans as being somewhat junior in the business of being a world power. Britain, on the other hand, considered it had a great deal of experience and *savoir-faire* as a power, and could somehow persuade the Americans to remain in Europe after the war; that, at least, was the British mentality. John Maynard Keynes was a member of the British delegation negotiating a large loan from the United States to Britain after the war. During one of the meetings in Washington there was a little note left afterward by some British diplomat that goes something like this:

In Washington Lord Halifax
Once whispered to Lord Keynes
'It's true *they* have the money bags
But *we* have all the brains.'

The idea was that somehow the combination of British brains and American brawn and finances would prevail, if the Americans could be kept in postwar Europe.

The Americans, of course, had their own agenda, but this was certainly the basic point of British policy. And it is worth remembering that when we talk about Churchill's Iron Curtain Speech, it raised issues beyond what Churchill said about Soviet control of Central and Eastern Europe. True, he warned of an iron curtain descending upon Europe, but Churchill also spoke about the importance of negotiation with the Soviet Union. He was not talking about another war; he was advocating negotiation from a position of strength. Strength would be provided, in Churchill's view, by a close Anglo-American relationship, by a special relationship. So that is the basic point of British policy after the war—to try and draw the Americans in and keep them in.

How did the British view the Soviets? They saw the Russians with a certain degree of suspicion throughout the period. British distrust of Stalin and the Soviet Union can be traced back at least as early as the Molotov-Ribbentrop Pact in August 1939. That agreement was a complete bombshell as far as the British were concerned. It still affected the British mindset toward the Russians when going into the alliance after the German invasion of Russia in June 1941. British policy-makers never imagined that communist Soviet Union and Nazi Germany, which had declared themselves as absolute ideological enemies in the 1930s, would suddenly cozy up to each other. Once it happened, however, it was not forgotten. It was always in the back of British minds that if Stalin had gone that way once, he might do so again. And so the Soviet-German pact created an element of doubt that was always present in the alliance.

From the other point of view, after the British and the French negotiated the Munich Agreement with Germany in September 1938 to settle the Czech crisis, Stalin concluded that there was no reason to expect much from the British and the French in the way of serious help against the growing German threat. So, he made the best deal he could with Hitler in 1939. Stalin never believed that the British were serious allies. He always felt the British played things their own way when it suited them. Indeed, Stalin's main fear as late as June 1941 was that are the British were trying to push him into a war with Germany. He held this view, rather than looking at the evidence before his eyes about the German buildup, right up to the Nazi invasion. Stalin was deeply suspicious of the Hess peace mission in May 1941.[22] He saw it as evidence that Britain and Germany were collaborating against the Soviet Union. It worried him so much that three years later, during Churchill's Moscow visit in 1944, Stalin pressed the Prime Minister as to what Hess was up to. Churchill vehemently denied any collusion with the Germans. Clearly, there was an element of mutual mistrust on both sides that is overlaid during the war by cooperation. Throughout the war years there was this element of doubt on both sides, which contributed to the mindsets of both sides at the beginning of the Cold War.

The extent of the Russian contribution to victory over Nazi Germany was not fully clear to the British or the Americans at the end of the war, despite the wave of enthusiasm in the middle of the war for the Red Army. The statistical evidence about the Russian effort was, after all, concealed. Stalin was not willing to talk about the scale of Soviet losses and concealed it from his allies. Let us say for the sake of argument, as figures are almost impossible to pin down, that there were twenty-eight million Soviet dead from the war; this is one-seventh of the prewar Soviet population. To put it in perspective, in the siege of Leningrad, from 1941–1944, approximately 900,000 Russians perished. That is more than the total combined British and American dead for the whole war.

If you want to understand the way the Russians viewed World War II, the way Stalin viewed it, you have to appreciate the disproportionate magnitude of the Russian contribution. That was not fully perceived at the time. What was perceived in London was a series of Soviet demands in different areas of the world, many of which actually fit the parameters of Czarist foreign policy, such as the Baltic Sea, the Black Sea, or North Korea. These were areas of Russian influence under the Czars, but nevertheless Stalin's demands gradually added up in the British mind to something more sinister. And this is where another lesson of history comes in to play. Most policy-makers viewed what was happening in the late 1940s through the lens of the late 1930s. The pattern of aggression that they had failed to stop in the case of Hitler, they now saw being repeated in the Soviet demands. Thus, by the spring of 1947, there was a very clear sense within the Foreign Office of a totalitarian perspective on the Soviet Union and its foreign policy. They saw Stalin as doing what Hitler had tried to do. When Truman announced his famous doctrine in June 1947, he described a world divided into two ways of life: democracy and totalitarianism. In other words, Stalin was filling the shoes of Hitler. This increasingly became the perception and mindset in London and Washington. Any nuances of policy emanating from Moscow were filtered through this mindset.

For the Poles there were two critical issues over Poland: the drawing of postwar borders, and the organization of a Polish government. Defining Poland's borders was an issue that ran deep into European history. This was a tragic country that had a history of being carved up by more powerful countries. After World War I it existed as a free country with territorial borders that had been drawn at the expense of Germany and Russia.

Neither of those two countries found this acceptable. That placed Poland at the heart of World War II; it placed Poland at the heart of the Cold War as far as Stalin was concerned. For Churchill, this was the critical point of contention with the Soviets at the close of the war. And it was the one that he was least happy with in terms of his own role in the Allied negotiations. But he was in a no-win situation. The British government hosted the Polish government in exile during the war. Britain ostensibly went to war on behalf of Poland in 1939, and so the loss of Polish independence and freedom was something like the death of British honor when they conceded Poland to Stalin.

Churchill spent hours trying to settle the Polish Question on better terms. By the end he felt that the Polish government in exile was really quite obtuse about the geopolitical realities of the situation. What he wanted it to do was to accept a complete change in Poland's borders to the benefit of the Soviet Union, particularly, this meant allowing the Soviet Union to get back the old territories of the Ukraine. Eventually, Poland had to be moved westward, as Churchill showed graphically with movement of matches on the conference table at Tehran. He argued, however, that if territory had to be sacrificed, and traded with the Soviets, at least there should be some kind of coalition government in Poland. Churchill conceded that there would be communist predominance, but nevertheless pushed to get other political groups represented in the postwar Polish government. That was unrealistic to expect. For Stalin this was a non-negotiable issue. He was going to have complete control of Poland. But Churchill tried. At Yalta he pushed to the extent that he felt he could.

In the end Churchill conceded on Poland. The British extended diplomatic recognition to the Soviet controlled government with but a few token Russian concessions as to its composition. As a result, the London Poles were no longer the legal government of Poland. That is the tragedy, because these men fought against the Nazis all over Europe. They are buried so poignantly, for instance, in the Polish cemetery at Cassino in Italy. What happened to the Poles brings tears to one's eyes. But at war's end, they were deemed expendable diplomatically and morally. Churchill never forgot that; it was always with him. But, for both Churchill and Roosevelt, settling the Polish Question was but one part of the reality of constructing the larger postwar world order. Poland was a pawn, a small part of a larger picture. Churchill and Roosevelt were trying to bring about a larger rapprochement among the powers, which Poland somehow did not fit into.

The future of Germany was absolutely central to the Big Three after the war. In 1945, Germany was seen as the source of two devastating wars in a matter of thirty years. And the issue before the Allies was how to prevent that from happening again. To an extent that amazes us now, people in 1945–7 remained as worried about the German threat as the Russian. Or, as the Russians saw it from Moscow, they were as worried about the

German threat as they were about the American. The pressing question then was what to do with Germany, and that was what these powers could not agree upon—the stakes are just too high. To put it very simply, the British and the Americans fairly quickly came to the view that what was needed was to get Germany economically back on its feet. They understood that Germany was potentially the powerhouse of the European economy. At the end of the war Europe was ravaged. There was economic depression and there was political discontent throughout the continent. It was the view in London and Washington that all this was going to encourage communism. There was a huge swing to the left in Europe after the war. So the British and American policy became the restoration of the German economy as fast as possible. The Soviet view was that an economically strong Germany was going to be a militarily strong Germany. The Soviets, as well as the French, were convinced that Germany would turn its economic power into military might. These two countries, France and Russia, had suffered the most from German power over the previous thirty years. They both feared that a German economic giant would once more become a military giant. It was only gradually that the French came around to the British point of view.

In 1946–7, driven by economic necessity, the British and the Americans pushed their arguments. It should be remembered how bad things were. The British imposed bread rationing, which had not been done in Britain at any time during World War II. In 1947, however, the British imposed bread rationing at home because grain was being exported to feed the people in the British zone in occupied Germany. That was a situation that politically could not continue. Hugh Dalton, the British Chancellor of the Exchequer at the time, observed that despite having defeated Germany in the war, Britain now was paying reparations to Germany. Given that problem, which was both a domestic problem and a foreign policy issue, the British and Americans determined it was essential to build up the German economy. From Stalin's point of view this was a clear threat to the absolutely basic concerns of Soviet foreign policy.

What followed was a long series of crises that all centered on Germany. At the center of the Marshall Plan was Germany and German recovery. The introduction of a new currency, the *Deutsche Mark*, was about German recovery, and Stalin saw that as a threat. It precipitated Stalin's order for the Berlin Blockade. The Soviet blockade led to the British and American airlift and the crisis over access to Berlin helped the Truman administration to push the North Atlantic Treaty through Congress. Germany was at the very heart of this process of action and reaction. The German Question led by 1950 to a Cold War that none of the three countries had wanted.

Notes

1 See David B. Woolner, ed., *The Second Quebec Conference Revisited: Waging War, Formulating Peace: Canada, Great Britain, and the United States in 1944–1945* (New York: St. Martin's Press, 1998b) and David B. Woolner, Warren Kimball, and David Reynolds, (eds), *FDR's World: War, Peace, and Legacies* (New York: Palgrave Macmillan, 2008).

2 David Reynolds, *Origins of the Cold War in Europe: International Perspectives* (New Haven: Yale University Press, 1994); *In Command of History: Churchill Fighting and Writing the Second World War* (New York: Random House, 2005); *From World War to Cold War: Churchill, Roosevelt, and the International Histories of the 1940s* (New York: Oxford University Press, 2006); and Summits: Six Conferences That Changed History (London: Allen Lane, 2007).

3 See Vladimir Pechatnov, "The Big Three After World War II: New Documents on Soviet Thinking about Post War Relations with the United States and Great Britain," *Cold War International History Project*, Working Paper 13 (July 1995).

4 See David Engerman, "Ideology and the Origin of the Cold War, 1917–1962," in *The Cambridge History of The Cold War, Volume 1: Origins*, M. Leffler and O. A. Westad (eds) (New York: Cambridge University Press, 2010a).

5 Vladimir Pechatnov, "The Soviet Union and the World, 1944–1953," in *Cambridge History of the Cold War*, vol. 1, 95. See Vojtech Mastny, "Soviet Foreign Policy, 1954–1962," in *Cambridge History of Cold War*, vol.1.

6 Vladimir Pechatnov and C. Earl Edmondson, "The Russian Perspective," in *Debating the Origins of the Cold War: American and Russian Perspectives,* R. Levering et al. (eds) (Lanham: Rowman & Littlefield, 2002), 85.

7 Pechatnov and Edmondson, "The Russian Perspective," in *Origins of the Cold War*, 149.

8 The "secret protocol" divided Poland and other parts of Eastern Europe into spheres of influence.

9 Norman Naimark, "The Sovietization of Eastern Europe, 1944–1954," in *Cambridge History of the Cold War*, vol. 1.

10 George F. Kennan, "A Fateful Error," *New York Times*, February 5, 1997, A23.

11 John Lewis Gaddis, *The Long Peace: Inquiries into the History of the Cold War* (New York: Oxford University Press, 1987), chapter 2.

12 Reynolds, *Summits*, vol. 1, 133 and chapter 3.

13 Cordell Hull, *The Memoirs of Cordell Hull,* (New York: The Macmillan Company, 1948), vol. 1: chapters 26–7. The Reciprocal Trade Agreements Act was first passed in June of 1934. It granted the President the authority to raise or lower American tariffs by as much as 50 percent so long as this was achieved through a reciprocal reduction on the part of the other party.

14 Not surprisingly, this led to some major tensions with the British government over such questions as the future of the Empire and the global system of preferential tariff and exchange rates that the British had established in the early 1930s in response to the Great Depression.

15 Alan Henrikson, "FDR and the World Wide Arena," in *FDR's World: War, Peace and Legacies*.

16 The Lend Lease Act was passed on March 11, 1941. It gave the President the authority to determine which nations in the war might be vital to America's defense and hence eligible for American aid. Britain was the first recipient, but Lend Lease help was eventually extended to the Soviet Union, China, the Free French, and other allies.

17 See Michael Howard, *The Mediterranean Strategy in the Second World War* (New York: Praeger, 1967).

18 See David B. Woolner, "Coming to Grips with the German Problem: Roosevelt, Churchill and the Morgenthau Plan at the Second Quebec Conference," in Woolner, *The Second Quebec Conference Revisited* (1998a)

19 See David B. Woolner, "Epilogue: Reflections on Legacy and Leadership—the View from 2008," in *FDR's World: War, Peace, and Legacies*.

20 Franklin D. Roosevelt, Undelivered Jefferson Day Address, April 12, 1945, The President's Master Speech File, FDR Presidential Library and Museum, Hyde Park, New York.

21 See William T. R. Fox, *Superpowers: The United States, Britain, and the Soviet Union—Their responsibility for Peace* (New York: Harcourt, Brace and Company, 1944).

22 German Deputy Führer Rudolf Hess flew solo to Britain to negotiate peace with Britain. Hitler repudiated Hess and his putative peace mission; Churchill dismissed it as an act of madness.

CHAPTER THREE

Prelude to détente

US-Soviet relations progressed from nuclear confrontation to détente in the sixties and early seventies. Gordon Barrass provides an overview of Cold War developments in the 1960s, emphasizing the shift from the "Age of the bomb" to the "Age of the missile." He sets the stage for the consideration of this Cold War period from American, Soviet, and Chinese perspectives. James Thomson explains why the United States felt it was losing ground to the Soviets during the period. Stefan Halper describes how key events appeared from the viewpoint of Washington, DC. He places the failed Bay of Pigs, the Cuban Missile Crisis, and the Vietnam War in perspective and how détente set the stage for the appearance of Ronald Reagan. Vladimir Pechatnov describes the view from Moscow. He emphasizes the importance of the Sino-Soviet split as well as the implications of Soviet determination to attain strategic parity with the United States. Ying Rong offers the Chinese perspective on US-Soviet relations. He explains how the Chinese came to appreciate the opportunity to improve their security position relative to both the Americans and the Soviets through the 1960s and into the 1970s.

Cold War developments in the 1960s

Gordon Barrass

This is an overview of critical tense moments during the 1960s and how events shaped détente during the middle period of the Cold War.[1] In Chapter 1 Susan Eisenhower discusses the importance of the nuclear bomb that was tested by the Americans in 1952 and the Russians in 1953. That was the "Age of the bomb." What really began to transform the super-power confrontations in the late 1950s was the transition from the "Age of the bomb into the "Age of the missile." It was at this point in the Cold

War that the Soviets had their great successes. They were the first to put a satellite into space in 1957. Then, just before Kennedy met Khrushchev in Vienna in 1961, the Soviets put a man into space.

Despite Russia's technological successes the German problem remained, especially the intractable issue of the status of Berlin. It turned on the continuing Allied presence in Berlin, which the Russians felt was under-mining the stability of their East German regime; rightly so. Khrushchev, at the Vienna Summit in 1961, threatened President Kennedy with war unless the Allies began to pull out of Berlin. Kennedy faced him down eventually during that summer. The Americans did not withdraw. Khrushchev then ordered the erection of the wall that cut Berlin in two, dividing the western zone from the eastern zone and the German Democratic Republic (GDR). So, wanting to make sure no one thought he was weak, Khrushchev authorized the testing of the "Czar Bomba." This was the largest nuclear weapon that had ever been tested. Although Khrushchev had that satis-faction, he found it of little comfort. Having the largest thermonuclear bomb was of little strategic advantage because the Soviets did not have an arsenal of missiles capable of reaching America. The Russian leader was very worried that, although he had hardly any missiles that could get from the Soviet Union across to the United States, the Americans were progressing with the Minutemen and Polaris Missile programs. Soon, Khrushchev knew, the United States would have thousands of missiles that could hit the Soviet Union. Frustrated by this, Khrushchev found another path to countering the American advantage in missile delivery systems—basing Russian mid-range missiles in Cuba armed with nuclear warheads. These weapons could reach Washington, DC; indeed, they put virtually the entire United States within range of the best Russian missiles.

Khrushchev went ahead with a plan to secretly smuggle missiles onto the island of Cuba. The Americans, thanks to U-2 photography, spotted the preparations and this led to the Cuban Missile Crisis. Eventually the Russians agreed to remove the offending weapons from Cuba and the Americans promised not to attack Cuba, which resolved the crisis. After the trauma of the Cuban Missile Crisis, people desperately sought to bring more stability to East West relations. Kennedy and Khrushchev had planned to meet for a summit conference, but Kennedy was assassinated in 1963.[2] After Lyndon Johnson became president, very little progress was made between the United States and the Soviets on issues such as disarmament.

Colleagues became weary of Khrushchev's brinksmanship. He was ousted from power in October 1964, in favor of the more emollient and steady-handed Brezhnev who would serve their interest better. But at the same time, problems were developing elsewhere that soon impinged on the relations between the two countries. The Americans were becoming increasingly bogged down in Vietnam and the Russians used military force to suppress the "Prague Spring" in Czechoslovakia. One of the biggest concerns of the East and West at this time was that the Warsaw Pact's structure, strategies, and nuclear armaments virtually guaranteed the obliteration of Europe if war broke out in Central Europe. Both sides wanted to find a way of bringing more stability to their relations in Europe.

One of the things that increasingly worried Moscow was the resurgence of Germany. They were deeply concerned about the German economic miracle that restored West German power and prestige in Europe and around the world. Of even more concern to the Russians was the fact that the Germans were building one of the largest armed forces in Western Europe. In 1961, the Germans were expected within a few years to have a total of over 450,000 men under arms. Growing German economic and military power worried Moscow because West Germany had not been willing to recognize the postwar frontiers that had been agreed at Yalta and discussed at Potsdam. Further, the West Germans continued to refuse to acknowledge the German Democratic Republic in East Germany. Moscow began to feel that it had better come to terms with the West Germans sooner rather than later.

Problems for the Soviets extended further east, when in 1966 Chinese leader Mao Zedong unleashed what he called the "Great Proletarian Cultural Revolution." There was not very much that was cultural about Mao's revolution. Not only did he denounce American imperialism, but Mao also condemned Soviet revisionism. China's aggressive talk was harder on Russians than on the Americans. It led to Sino-Soviet conflicts along the Ussuri River, the frontier that separates the two countries in the Far East, and also clashes on the border in Central Asia. The Soviet Union began to build up forces facing China that, in a few years, were larger than those they had facing NATO in Central Europe.[3]

The Americans had a sudden boost of confidence in 1969, when they put the first man on the moon. At the same time that they were increasingly aware that the Russians had modernized their rocket forces and would soon have strategic nuclear forces that were capable of matching their own. So as they moved into and through the 1960s both sides had an increasing interest in trying to find a more stable relationship, which became known as détente.

One thing that was very notable during this period was that it was not just a question of getting arms control arrangements where you thought people had got equivalent numbers. Each side was terrified that the other side was thought to be stronger than they were. This feeling is encapsulated nicely in the observation that, "The truth of the matter is you only need five percent of your nuclear weapons to terrify the other side. You need ninety-five percent of them to reassure your own." Certainly we see elements of this in the politics of both sides during the sixties and seventies.

We understand quite well the Soviet view of détente. Yet, there remains the very important question of why the Americans at the time thought they were so weak. Because, after all, here was a country that had an economy that was clearly several times larger than that of the Soviet Union. As the world saw through the landing on the moon, they were technologically very advanced. Yet, the Americans were making assumptions about the Soviet Union being able to overtake the United States. If you look through the writings of Nixon and Kissinger on détente, they emphasize the need to reach some accommodation with the Russians because of the changes taking place in the world—including growing Soviet power relative to that of the United States.

America's decade of self-perceived weakness

James A. Thomson

I served in the US government in the White House and the Department of Defense during this period of the Cold War. Based on my experience, I believe it is quite easy to understand why America felt it was losing ground to the Soviet Union. There certainly was a very strong sense that we were getting weaker in comparison to the Soviets in many key areas, and the list of reasons is extensive. There was Vietnam; our army was decimated by the Vietnam War. There was the Soviet's achievement of strategic nuclear weapons parity, which we codified in a series of arms control agreements. The US economy was in the worst situation since the Great Depression, and that recession went on for several years. In the political realm, of course, there was the Watergate Affair, and the forced resignation of President Nixon. After Nixon we entered the presidency of Jimmy Carter, with what came to be known as a period of "malaise" in American society. So, when you examine the decade from 1968 to 1978, it is apparent that the United States did not feel as if it had the military or economic strength to take on the world. After 1978, all that changed, every dimension of America's perception of its strength improved, every single one.

The view from Washington

Stefan Halper

When John Kennedy arrived in the presidency, having declared a missile gap during the campaign, he soon found that in fact the United States had an advantage in missiles. Thus, his contention that the Eisenhower administration had allowed US missile capacity, including the number of warheads, to fall behind the Soviets was incorrect. Still, Kennedy felt that global pre-eminence was slipping away from Washington as the Soviets put the first man in space, suggesting a significant technological lead. The implication was that Soviet booster rocket engines were capable of carrying intercontinental ballistic missiles (ICBMs) to the continental United States. Growing concern, including a sense of heightened vulnerability, had become apparent in Congress, among the media and the public. Added to this were clusters of other knotty problems early in his term, few of which were going well from the administration's perspective. The President confronted the need to find an accommodation in Laos. Kennedy feared a withdrawal, though prudent, might imply a lack of resolve on Washington's part and give encouragement to further insurgency. Then, of course, there was the failed Bay of Pigs operation in Cuba, which was acutely embarrassing to Washington but, perhaps just as importantly, chilled his relations with the Joints Chief of Staff and the Central Intelligence Agency (CIA) whom, he felt, had provided misleading advice.

Following the Bay of Pigs failure, of course, was the disappointing Vienna Summit of June 1961. Khrushchev intimidated Kennedy, who found the Soviet Premier unfathomable. He later told Hugh Sidey of *Time* magazine,

> I never met a man like this, I talked about a nuclear exchange, how it would kill ten or seventy million people in ten minutes and he just looked at me as if to say, "So what?" My impression was that he didn't give a damn if it came that.[4]

Kennedy was deeply unsettled by the Vienna meetings which had been Khrushchev's objective. All of this meant, in Kennedy's mind, and certainly among his advisors, that he had to prevail against the Soviets in the Cuban Missile Crisis.[5] It also meant that Kennedy had to sustain Berlin's status as a free city in the face of Khrushchev's bellicose threats to negotiate a separate treaty with East Germany. And, it meant that Kennedy felt he had to demonstrate US resolve in Vietnam. Failing to prevail in these matters would put the US global enterprise in play by surrendering the momentum, which had sustained American primacy since World War II to Khrushchev and the Soviet Union—an eventuality Kennedy could not accept.

Beyond the strategic implications of Soviet progress in these issues was the vivid "red baiting" political reality of the time. The Kennedy presidency had been forged in the incendiary, anti-communist rhetoric of Joe McCarthy and the Red Scare. The "Junior Senator from Wisconsin" was abetted by the China lobby that, with allies in the media such as Henry Luce the *Time/Life* magazine publisher, church figures such as Cardinal Cushing of New York, and manufacturing moguls such as Arthur Kohlberg, advanced the notion of a monolithic communism that was directed by Beijing and Moscow. One of the challenges to the Kennedy administration was to unwind these ideas, which had blinded US policy-makers to the nuanced differences among the different strains of communism in the Soviet Union, China, and Southeast Asia. As became abundantly clear, the Soviets and Chinese had deep and abiding differences, which produced conflict along the Amur River and disputes over nuclear policy. The US failure to recognize or appreciate the Sino-Soviet split quickly enough led to flawed analysis of the Vietnam conflict. This not only compromised US strategy and tactics in Vietnam but also mis-positioned the United States as extraordinary events unfolded in Eastern Europe including the Soviet invasions of Budapest and Prague in 1968.[6] With 575,000 men on the ground in Vietnam, Washington had little scope to provide encouragement to the populations of either city; assistance was infeasible for political reasons given the budgetary demands of President Johnson's domestic programs, nor was military assistance possible for logistical reasons.

Richard Nixon entered office in 1969 and saw the opportunity to alter global power relations by taking advantage of Soviet-Chinese differences and China's increasing fear of a Soviet threat. In simple terms, he and Henry Kissinger saw global power as a "three legged stool" and proceeded to ally with the Chinese leg to isolate the Soviet leg. Their success brought a new era in which it was possible in 1972 for Nixon and Brezhnev to declare policies of peaceful coexistence, producing the Strategic Arms Limitation (SALT I) and Antiballistic Missile (ABM) Treaties. Thus, a policy, invested with a certain French perspective known as détente, replaced the previous era of cold hostility.

Later in the 1970s the Soviets ran into deep trouble in the Afghan War. The problem was not simply their investment in a war that had little prospect of military success, but also that Moscow was subject to global criticism for human rights violations in-country with a concomitant loss of credibility. The United States underscored its disapproval of Soviet policies by canceling American participation in the 1980 summer Olympics. Reagan and Thatcher then used the Afghan War to underpin an assault on Soviet values and civil society, characterizing the USSR as an "evil empire," headed toward the "ash heap of history." The imagery held, placing Moscow in a beleaguered international posture while suffering increasing internal dysfunction.

When the 1979 Solidarity movement emerged in Poland, Pope John Paul II provided a powerful platform for the expression of moral concern bringing the first successful resistance to Soviet authority in Eastern Europe. Strong international criticism of Moscow coupled with the real threat of Western economic sanctions effectively set aside the prospect of Soviet military intervention. Washington now concluded that the Soviet economy was now dysfunctional due to a sclerotic bureaucracy and the absence of a viable market mechanism. Widespread inefficiencies meant that Moscow could no longer compete with the West.

With the election of Ronald Reagan in 1980, détente had fallen from fashion. Reagan was determined to use what he saw as the American advantage to end the USSR as a going concern. America's deep pockets became the chosen instrument. The Strategic Defense Initiative, or "Star Wars" as it was derisively called, was thought by Moscow to neutralize important elements of the USSR missile force. Moreover, the expense associated with developing counter-measures was prohibitive. When Reagan first took office, I was on the White House staff. I remember a National Security Council meeting at which the service chiefs, members of the Joint Chiefs of Staff, reported one by one that the Soviets had overwhelming strength; they had more aircraft, more surface combatants, more submarines, more tanks, more battalions, and so on. With each report, the President said nothing. Eventually, the President turned to his old friend and new CIA director Bill Casey, and asked, "Bill, what do we have more of?" Casey responded, "We have more money." The President said, "Fine we'll use that." And that is what was done. Reagan had a capacity to focus like a laser. He saw the core of the issue, set it out very simply, and we more or less knew what we were doing from that point forward.

The view from Moscow

Vladimir Pechatnov

The period of détente is intriguing for historians as Soviet foreign policy was conducted in a new equilibrium of power.[7] We now know more about its origins since its decline and collapse in the 1970s, largely because new documentation is emerging from the Russian, American, and Chinese archives. What does the new archival material tell us about the origins of détente? First of all, the new evidence confirms the importance of structural changes in international relations during the 1960s. Among the most important were the emergence of nuclear parity between the United States and the USSR, the diffusion of power away from Washington and Moscow into other key areas, the Sino-Soviet split, and the rise of a more self-confident Western Europe. The French and the West Germans seemed particularly eager to operate more independently of the Americans, especially in developing their own relations with the Soviet Union. Second, the new data highlight the importance of specific political events that signaled shifts in the Cold War. In particular, the American disaster in Vietnam, which led to the rethinking of US strategy, and a growing American interest in rapprochement with both China and the Soviet Union.

Third, and even more surprising, the new evidence reveals the importance of more contingent factors in international relations. Thus, during the 1960s and early 1970s, we see the importance of domestic politics, especially in the American case, and the significance of the distinctive personalities of political leaders such as Brandt in West Germany, Nixon and Kissinger in the United States, and Brezhnev in the Soviet Union.

In the Soviet Union, détente was perceived as "crossing the Rubicon," if not the end to the Cold War. We now see in the documents that the Soviet leaders felt that they had finally caught up with the United States in the key strategic arms dimension and forced the Americans to recognize the legitimate security interests of the Soviet Union. The United States was seen as having given up its efforts to destabilize the Soviet system, to reverse the results of World War II, and as being ready to accept the Soviets as an equal power. At a closed meeting with his staff in the 1970s, Soviet Foreign Minister Andrei Gromyko observed, "Our foreign policy is now conducted in a qualitatively new environment of a genuine equilibrium. We have really become a world power, even if it took the hard work of two generations of Soviet people to reach that goal." For ordinary Soviets, the new global role of the Soviet Union was seen as a guarantee of national security. Superpower status became an increasingly important source of legitimacy for the Soviet system, which was facing increasing domestic difficulties. The growing security challenge from China was another powerful incentive for cooperation with the United States. Kremlin leaders also recognized that it was in the Soviet interest to develop American trade and economic assistance to alleviate mounting economic problems.

Détente seemed to have solved, or at least alleviated, three major post-World War II security concerns of the Soviet Union. All of which were of special importance to the Brezhnev-Gromyko generation that lived through World War II and were hardened by the experience. First, there was the series of treaties recognizing the postwar political and territorial status of Europe, such as the Helsinki Act, and treaties with Poland and the Federal Republic of Germany. Second, there was the stabilization of the German problem in 1971 with the Quadripartite Agreement on West Berlin. Finally, there was the reduced danger of nuclear war due to the creation of an arms control regime through new treaties. From the Soviet perspective, these were truly remarkable achievements. It is no wonder that they produced what Stalin used to call "dizziness from success."

Many in the Soviet political and military leadership misread détente as a decisive shift in the global correlation of forces in favor of the Soviet Union. They viewed it as a chance to fill the vacuum left by the retreat of American power after Vietnam. They sought further to weaken the US global position by expanding the sphere of Soviet influence in Africa, the Middle East, and Central America.[8] In 1971 the Politburo directed the Soviet foreign policy apparatus, "To seek, without disclosing it publicly, a weakening US role in international affairs, including its position in Western political-military alliances, as well as in strategically important regions of the world, Europe, Middle East, Asia." This new assertiveness was soon reinforced by the energy-driven economic crisis in the West, and by the huge inflow of petrol dollars in the Soviet treasury. It was also supported by the USSR's newly developed capability of projecting its power around the world. American diplomats registered with concern the new arrogance of their Soviet counterparts. Even the usually well-mannered and diplomatic Russian Foreign Minister, Georgy Kornienko, began telling his American colleagues that now they would have to get accustomed to living with the preponderance of power being held by the other side, as the Soviets had had to for so many years.

The main target of this new Soviet assertiveness was the developing world. By the end of the 1970s, Soviet military aid reached $30 billion going to almost thirty countries, although this aid brought more losses than profit to the USSR. Behind this surge was not internationalist ideology or security concerns, but rather it reflects the global zero sum game with the United States.[9] As one of the authors of Soviet Third World policy once remarked, "The more that can be taken away from Washington the better." This became a self-generating enterprise having very little connection with the real national interests of either country. This way of thinking, so natural for the Cold War mentality, often pushed to acquisitions, regardless of their true value or the capacity to digest them. Perceived by many Western experts as consistent grand strategy in the Third World, this expansion in reality was little more than a chaotic combination of group, agency, and even personal interests deprived of any genuine meaning and central goal. The former chief of the analytical branch of Soviet foreign intelligence, General Nikolai Leonov, confessed as much when he observed, "In Latin America and the Third World, the Soviet leadership did not have strategic plans backed up by sufficient human, technical, and material resources."

Third World expansion was the single most important blunder on the part of Soviet leadership during this period. It led ultimately to Soviet imperial overstretch and the deterioration of Soviet-American relations that produced the collapse of détente. Détente generated additional domestic problems for the Soviets. It led to an erosion of ideological controls in the milieu of expanding contact with the West, and a dissident human rights movement.

Western-Soviet cultural exchange agreements helped create the environment supporting détente. These cultural exchanges were a break-through, especially for Russians. It helped us to have a first-hand idea of what the world looked like from the other side. For example, Alexander Yakovlev, the future architect of perestroika as a senior advisor to Mikhail Gorbachev, was one of the first students to attend Columbia University in the 1950s as part of a cultural exchange. Later he remembered finding his time at Columbia a mind-boggling experience; he was never the same man again in his thinking. My more modest experience confirms the impact of living in America. I was at Columbia University for almost a year in 1976, and that made a lot of difference to my view of the United States. This kind of experience was important for many people holding middle and lower-level positions in the Soviet Union, who benefited from cultural exchange visits to America. I was also in the US Institute of the Russian Academy of Sciences, which was the Soviet think tank devoted to monitoring events in America during the Cold War. Most of us had cultural exchange experience, and this made a great deal of difference to our perspectives.

This still leaves us with a question, what was détente? Was it a natural face of the Cold War cycle, an inevitable period of relaxation of tensions? Or was it an aberration caused by unique combinations of circumstances never to be repeated? This question is still debated by the historians.

The view from Beijing

Ying Rong

China, during the 1960s, largely was forced to remain on the sidelines of the Cold War. It was in the very awkward position of being influenced rather than being able to influence the situation.[10] Beginning in 1968, however, China's one-sided strategy of alliance with the Soviet Union was no longer working in a manner acceptable to the Chinese. Ideological differences between the Chinese and the Soviets were now leading to problems in the state-to-state relationship. Also, the Cuban Missile Crisis led the Chinese to view its security situation as deteriorating.[11]

The origins of the growing split between China and the Soviet Union were very complicated. It involved ideological, historical, structural, and cultural contradictions. More importantly, there were conflicting interests involved and differences in the personalities of the leadership in both countries. These differences culminated in a point of no return in Sino-Soviet relations. Each regime saw the other as having betrayed communism. That is why China felt compelled to mobilize and unite "progressive forces" to fight American imperialism and Soviet revisionism. This explains why the Chinese began a new strategy, in which China sought to become a wedge between the Soviets and the Americans. In vivid terms, China resolved to fight with two fists: one fist targeted the Soviet Union, which to a certain extent now is gradually replacing the United States as its biggest security threat, and the second fist targeted the United States, which is still a threat but is no longer the only focus of Chinese security concerns.[12]

As the Chinese saying goes, "In crisis there are always opportunities." So, at this stage of the Cold War, China recognized opportunities to make productive shifts in its foreign policies toward both the Soviets and the Americans. This meant the Chinese began closely to examine its relationship and policies with the United States.[13] Coincidentally, the United States was reexamining its relationship with China, especially given China's troubled relationship with the Soviet Union at the time. Two examples illustrate how things were changing on the Chinese side. It has been widely reported in China that the Soviet leaders wanted to diffuse the tensions that had arisen between themselves and the Chinese leadership. So, the Soviet leaders tried to use the hotline between Moscow and Beijing to reestablish a direct dialogue with the Chinese leadership. Unfortunately, when the call from the Kremlin came through, a female operator in Beijing berated the "Revisionists." She screamed into the telephone that they had no right to talk to Chairman Mao and refused to make the connection to the Chinese leader. In the second example, the Chinese leadership tried to signal its willingness to become more open to the Americans and improve relations at a major public ceremony. They did this in the classic Chinese fashion of prominently placing an American journalist on the podium with the Chairman at the event. The picture of the American on the podium was published on the first page of *The People's Daily*. Unfortunately, this gesture was too delicate and the signal was not understood by the American administration.

Ideology was an important factor guiding Chinese maneuvering during this Cold War period, but this is often overexaggerated. When you examine the documentary record that has become available since the end of the Cold War, it is clear that ideology was not the most important factor. We have to look beyond ideology to other factors affecting shifts in the Chinese perspective.

When you examine the complex relationship between the Soviet Union and China, ideological differences were important. More important, for example, was China's emerging sense of its need for the development of comprehensive national strength in comparison to the United States and the Soviets. China realized it needed to combine diplomacy, soft power, with economic and military development, hard power, if it were to be secure. China increasingly saw its economic development as vital if it was going to be able to defend its territorial integrity and sovereignty. For that to happen, there needed to be a more stable and peaceful environment in international relations, such as détente was meant to foster. This explains subsequent Chinese efforts to develop and employ both soft and hard power in international affairs.

Notes

1   Gordon Barrass, *The Great Cold War: A Journey Through the Hall of Mirrors* (Stanford: Stanford Security Studies, 2009), chapters 11–13.

2   Michael R. Beschloss, *The Crisis Years: Kennedy and Khrushchev, 1960–1963* (New York: Edward Burlingame, 1991).

3   See Barrass, *The Great Cold* War, 154–6, Jonathan Haslam, *Russia's Cold War: From the October Revolution to the Fall of the Wall* (New Haven: Yale University Press, 2011), 191–93, Sergey Radchenko, "The Sino-Soviet Split," in the *Cambridge History of the Cold War, Volume 2: Crises and Détente*, M. Leffler and O. A. Westad (eds) (New York: Cambridge University Press, 2010b), and Odd Arne Westad, ed., *Brothers in Arms: The Rise and Fall of the Sino-Soviet Alliance, 1945–1963* (Stanford: Stanford University Press, 1998).

4   Quoted in Robert Dallek, *An Unfinished Life: John F. Kennedy, 1917–1963* (New York: Back Bay Books, 2004), 347.

5   See Alexandr A. Fursenko and Timothy Naftali, *One Hell of a Gamble: Khrushchev, Castro, and Kennedy: 1958–1964* (New York: Norton, 1997) and James G. Hershberg, "The Cuban Missile Crisis" in *Cambridge History of the Cold War*, vol. 2. New archival material is used by Sergo Mikoyan, *The Soviet Cuban Missile Crisis: Castro, Mikoyan, Kennedy, Khrushchev, and the Missiles of November*, ed. Svetlana Sayranskaya (Stanford: Stanford University Press, 2012) and Sheldon M. Stern, *The Cuban Missile Crisis in American Memory* (Stanford: Stanford University Press, 2012).

6   Haslam, *Russia's Cold War*, 245–50 and Anthony Kemp-Welch, "Eastern Europe: Stalinism to Solidarity," in *Cambridge History of the Cold War*, vol. 2: 222–30.

7   Svetlana Savranskaya and William Taubman, "Soviet Foreign Policy, 1962–1975," *Cambridge History of the Cold War*, vol. 2.

8   John Lewis Gaddis, *We Now Know: Rethinking Cold War History* (New York: Oxford University Press, 1997), chapter 6 and Christopher Andrew and Vasili Mitrokhin, *The World Was Going Our Way: The KGB and the Battle for the Third World* (New York Basic Books, 2005), chapter 1.

9   Michael Latham, "The Cold War in the Third World, 1963-1975," in *Cambridge History of the Cold War*, vol. 2 and Odd Arne Westad, *The Global Cold War: Third World Interventions and the Making of Our Times* (Cambridge: Cambridge University Press, 2005).

10   Lorenz Lüthi, "Chinese Foreign Policy, 1960–1979," in *The Cold War in East Asia, 1945–1991*, ed. Tsuyoshi Hasegawa (Stanford: Stanford University Press: 2011) and Sergey Radchenko, *Two Suns in the Heavens: The Sino-Soviet Struggle for Supremacy, 1962–1967* (Washington, DC: Woodrow Wilson Center Press, 2009).

11   On China's role in bringing the Cold War to its conclusion in the late 1980s and early 1990s see Chen Jian, "China and the Cold War After Mao," in *Cambridge History of the Cold War*, vol. 3, 186–200.

12 Chen Jian, *Mao's China and the Cold War* (Chapel Hill: University of North Carolina Press, 2001), chapter 9 and Radchenko, "The Sino-Soviet Split," in *Cambridge History of the Cold War*, vol. 2: 369–72.

13 See Yafeng Xia, *Negotiating With the Enemy: US-China Talks During the Cold War, 1949–1972* (Bloomington: Indiana University Press, 2006), chapters 6–8.

CHAPTER FOUR

From détente to dialogue

The Cold War between 1969 and 1989 featured events that exemplified the hopes and fears that permeated the relationship between the power blocs led by the Soviet Union and the United States. In the wake of the Cuban Missile Crisis, the superpowers stepped back from the brink of nuclear catastrophe and opened an extended, uneven process of stabilizing and improving relations, while simultaneously engaging in an arms race of escalating proportions. Détente offered the promise of a modus vivendi between the United States and the USSR. Its demise produced renewed military rivalry, which paradoxically led to an historic dialogue of the new generation of Cold War leaders: Gorbachev, Thatcher, and Reagan.[1]

The path from détente to dialogue is traced through the insider perspectives of American, British, and Soviet officials who served in their respective governments at the time. They provide a unique viewpoint on the game-changing movement from the rise and collapse of détente to the historic dialogue among Cold War leaders, which brought an end to the long era of East-West confrontation. John Warner was a senior official during the Nixon, Reagan, and Bush administrations and he served thereafter with distinction in the US Senate. Franklin Miller served on the National Security Council in the White House and at the Pentagon with the Department of Defense. They offer an insightful account of the development of the massive American program to enhance its strategic arms status, which eventually shifted to arms negotiations during the Reagan years. Lord Powell was Prime Minister Thatcher's Private Secretary and was a key foreign policy advisor. Sir Roderic Lyne served in the British Diplomatic Service and was the UK Ambassador to Russia. Powell and Lyne, as seasoned diplomats and keen observers, were well positioned to survey the tremendous tensions between the West and Soviet Union during the early Reagan administration. They witnessed the emergence of the relationships among Margaret Thatcher, Ronald Reagan, and Mikhail Gorbachev, which were so very crucial during this period. Alexander Likhotal, who worked with Gorbachev as the General Secretary's spokesperson and senior advisor, provides a detailed analysis of the transformative vision and actions of the Soviet leader. The distinguished broadcaster and former British Ambassador to the United States, Peter Jay closes the chapter by offering his opinion as to the exact date and time at which the Cold War ended.

Both sides had people working to prevent World War III

John Warner

I observed much of what was going on during the Cold War from 1969 on, initially as an undersecretary, then as the Secretary of the Navy, and finally as a US Senator. Richard Nixon and Henry Kissinger were influential in shifting American strategic thinking as the Cold War moved into the 1970s. The best example of their contribution was when Nixon went to China, which Kissinger had arranged during his secret trip to Beijing in July 1971. This was an unexpected wake-up call to the Soviet Union. It signaled to the Soviet Union that henceforth they had to worry about Sino-American rapprochement as an important feature of the Cold War.

Every morning we got up in the Department of Defense, the five years I was there, and had our intelligence briefing at around 7:30 in the morning. We started with the overnight positioning of the Soviet submarines. They were ranging off the Atlantic coast distances anywhere from 200 to 300 miles. The armaments on a single submarine could have obliterated the nation's capital, the Pentagon, and everything in an instant. Those were the tensions under which we were living. At the same time, we were heavily engaged in the war in Vietnam. The American public was at a total state of unrest about Vietnam, and in a state of apprehension about the Cold War. Against that background, I will emphasize two major points about this period.

First, those of us serving in the US Department of Defense (DOD) held a set of unwritten, core understandings about the Soviet Union's defense structure. We understood how military decisions were made in the Soviet Union. They were done very carefully, very methodically, and were consistently reviewed with the utmost care from the bottom to the top of the command system. There were those outside of the DOD who were concerned about the "Doctrine of the HairTrigger," but we had confidence in the Soviet command and control system. They also had confidence in ours. We at DOD recognized that when tensions between the United States and the USSR rose too high, steps had to be taken to alleviate them so as to avoid a global catastrophe. And we did just that.

For example, we were intensely spying on the Soviets, and they were spying on us. This led to naval incidents on the high seas between our ships, which were potentially disastrous. By this time the Soviet Navy was largely comparable in size to our own. We both had very capable surface ships, and superb submarine forces. From time-to-time, in the course of our respective spying operations, US and Soviet ships would come too close and would literally rub the paint off one another. At such times there was always the chance that someone at the helm of one of the ships involved could have made a mistake that would have triggered, not instantly perhaps, but methodically a greater confrontation. The Soviets and we recognized that this situation could not continue; the dangers were simply unacceptable. Over the course of eighteen months we produced an agreement between the US Navy and the Soviet Navy, which is still in effect today and used as a model by other nations. President Nixon, very thoughtfully, asked me to join his delegation for his trip to visit Russia when he concluded strategic treaties with the Soviet Union. The day before his public signing ceremonies with Brezhnev, I signed the Incidents at Sea Agreement of 1972 on behalf of the United States. These events were public, historic examples of how, during the Cold War, we had maintained communications with the Soviet Union and could—and did—achieve binding agreements in the interests of global security. Most important were the treaties, signed by Nixon, with his valued national security advisor, Henry Kissinger, by his side, which contributed to a lessening of tensions, confrontations, and the possibility of active military operations.

The second major point to be emphasized is that, while I served in the Defense Department, we were dedicated to maintaining a balance in strategic weapons among the branches of our military forces, especially between the missile systems of the Navy and the Air Force. As the Secretary of the Navy, I dealt constantly with the Secretary of the Air Force on these matters. Later, during my Senate years, the strategic balance became even more important. I worked with President Reagan on the Strategic Defense Initiative (SDI), nicknamed "Star Wars." In my view, it was the combination of the SDI, and our willingness to spend whatever money we had for defense, that drove the Soviets to the negotiating table, which began the process for a negotiated settlement to end the Cold War.

It is worth emphasizing that Ronald Reagan was a man of great foresight. He came from a career in films, and some people wondered if the new president was just going to be an actor. Well, he really was a superb actor and he had an ability to project himself. People listened to what he said. When Reagan went to Berlin in June 1987, and implored Mr. Gorbachev to "Tear down this wall," more seasoned minds around him counseled the president to drop the demand from the speech. He refused to do so. Reagan was resolved to confront the Soviets abroad, and strengthen national defense at home. I well recall how he reinstituted the B-1 Bomber

Program that President Carter had canceled. Frankly, in my judgment, the B-1 Bomber itself was not a great addition to our strategic arsenal, but Reagan conducted a magnificent campaign to promote it. He revved-up the American public to build the B-1 Bomber, which kept the defense economy going, and laid the foundation for the B-2 Bomber Program, which was a very effective weapon.

Thinking about who deserves the most credit for preserving peace on the Western side during the Cold War, I must give that to Sir Winston Churchill. Churchill possessed the spirit, wisdom, and foresight that eventually permeated most of the thinking of the US government.

At the same time, on the American side, tremendous credit must be extended to the superb individuals who served on the staff of the National Security Council (NSC) in the White House. Throughout the Cold War, the NSC was one of the more effective arms of the federal branch of our government. Because of the NSC, American presidents had good advice in most instances. Based on my experience with the Soviets during negotiations for the Incidents at Sea Agreement, I was impressed by the Russian defense staff as well. On both sides there were experienced and wise people working and "communicating" to prevent circumstances that could have triggered actual military confrontation that could escalate into a World War III scenario.

The underlying policies during that era were adeptly described years later in President Reagan's use of the phrase "peace through strength." Today, the Western nations—NATO—continue to adhere to that doctrine.

We needed to find ways to restore American strength

Franklin C. Miller

As a young American naval officer serving at sea from 1972 to 1975, I participated in several of the incidents to which Senator Warner referred earlier. These were very dangerous confrontations and I am glad that when he served as Secretary of the Navy, John Warner put an end to them. These incidents between the Russian and American Navies took place at a time when the United States felt particularly defensive. Initially our orders were to stay out of the way of Soviet ships at sea. This reflected the crisis of confidence within the US government at the time. We were acutely concerned in the 1970s about the Russian strategic buildup, such as their deployment of the SS-20 missiles in Europe. American officials generally believed that we were on the defensive in the Cold War. They began to search for ways to rebuild American confidence and strength, both at home and abroad in four areas.

The first area was the restoration of strategic weapons equilibrium with the Soviets. Several strategic weapons modernization programs, such as those for the MX Missile and B-1 Bomber, were bogged down in Congress. This was at a time when we knew the Russians were increasing their strategic forces, which deeply concerned us.

The second area requiring attention was the restoration of relationships with our allies in Europe and elsewhere. Dr. James Schlesinger, the former Secretary of Defense in the Ford administration, promoted this most effectively. Schlesinger argued that the Western Alliance was critical to American national security. In his view, the United States could not survive as a free democracy if we tried to go it alone. We had to have the European democracies and Japan with us. Strengthening America's alliance relationships, particularly our special relationship with Britain, was something I emphasized throughout my career in government.

The third area of tremendous importance in rebuilding American confidence and strength was the enhancement of our strategic intelligence. We needed to better understand what the other side was thinking. During my first decade in government, we were constantly worried about maintaining nuclear deterrence. Effective nuclear deterrence required that you affect the thinking of the other side. If you did not understand what the other side was doing, you were probably going down the wrong road. Unfortunately, our intelligence was not particularly good sometimes, and we worked hard to improve it. It was vital to improve our information about Soviet intentions and then, based on this intelligence, to signal to them that we knew what they were doing. For example, in the early 1980s we discovered that the Soviet leadership, for reasons we found inexplicable, appeared to believe it could fight and win a nuclear war. Our intelligence indicated they secretly were building deep underground bunkers outside Moscow. So we signaled them that it was not going to work. We let them know that we knew what they were doing. This signaling was accomplished by publishing an article about it in the annual Pentagon report *Soviet Military Power*. As our strategic intelligence improved, we found ourselves better able to revise nuclear planning in line with Soviet strategy and tactics. Thus, we completely revised our nuclear strategy during this critical period.

The fourth area in which the United States sought to enhance its security posture vis-à-vis the Soviets was in arms control. This area was vital, and not just in the context of limiting the number of nuclear weapons on both sides. It was also about stabilizing the situation. It was about setting limits on the kind of weapons being developed and deployed so as better to assure stability. Therefore, the bilateral negotiations that produced the Strategic Arms Limitations Treaty (START I) in 1972, focused on freezing the number and types of strategic ballistic missile launchers and warheads. We wanted to provide the Russians with an incentive to put more of their warheads at sea, on submarine-launched ballistic missile systems (SLBMs), because that was a more stable force. We wanted them to place more warheads on bombers, because bombers were relatively slow moving delivery systems, as compared to faster moving systems, such as ICBMs. It was a tremendously challenging period. We were simultaneously refining our strategic plans for an Armageddon that we hoped would never come, and working with the other side to stabilize the forces with which Armageddon might be waged.

Things changed when Ronald Reagan was elected President of the United States in 1980. When Reagan came in to office, he often repeated the slogan "Peace through Strength," and it was deeply felt. It meant rebuilding American confidence by rebuilding the American armed forces, and purging the last vestiges of the post-Vietnam syndrome from them. He sought to rebuild our strategic forces to the point that we felt confident in the US capability to deter the Soviet Union. It also was about reaching out in some fairly radical ways to the Soviets, such as endorsing the idea of reducing to zero the presence of long-range nuclear forces in Europe. Initially it seemed a completely ridiculous idea. But, the Intermediate Range Nuclear Forces Treaty, signed by Reagan and Gorbachev in 1987, did exactly that. It was an historic landmark in the Cold War, as it abolished an entire class of weapons. What Reagan brought to the Cold War was patience and strength in dealing with the Soviets. Furthermore, he revived through his remarkable relationship with Mrs. Thatcher, the "special relationship" with the United Kingdom that was so important to us all.

The Americans who ultimately contributed the most to ending the Cold War peacefully were President George H. W. Bush, and his national security advisor, Brent Scowcroft. That is because of the deft way they managed the breakup of the Soviet empire, and how they handled the transition from Gorbachev to Yeltsin. This was accomplished while simultaneously holding the NATO alliance together and, working with Prime Minister Thatcher, steering through the German reunification process. All the while, Bush and Scowcroft found a way to dramatically reduce nuclear weapons in Europe. What they accomplished, and how they did it, truly was remarkable.

Détente had unintended consequences

Sir Roderic Lyne

The British were the back markers in détente. That was a good role to play because you need to have somebody with their foot on the brakes when you have other people pushing on the accelerator. For example, when Gromyko first started floating the idea of a European security conference, we were the most skeptical among the Europeans. We held out against this until Prime Minister Harold Wilson changed the British position.

I first served in Moscow in 1971. That was one year after the autumn of 1970, when we expelled 105 Soviet spies, thereby setting a new world record for expulsions at one go. That cemented the British position as the back marker of the Cold War. So, when I arrived in Moscow, I found that we were a pariah state. Our only friends in Moscow were the Chinese. Whenever we met Chinese diplomats at parties, they would approach us with glee, rubbing their hands together and say, "One-hundred and five! Congratulations. We are Public Enemy Number One, and now you are Public Enemy Number Two!"

The Soviet-Chinese tensions during the Cold War sometimes assumed some very colorful features. I was visiting Blagoveshchensk a couple of years ago. I was drinking vodka as one does, and gazing across the Amur River at China. One of my Russian hosts told me that, in the high days of the border dispute, the Chinese put up massive placards with pictures of Chairman Mao on their side of the river, facing Blagoveshchensk. Their communist brethren in Russia responded by building massive walls, so that none of the population of Blagoveshchensk could see Chairman Mao's face. Then they added a refinement. At the riverbank, the Russians built a long row of latrines for their border guards. They built the latrines, however, with no backs on the side that faced China.

I was in Moscow at the time Henry Kissinger made his secret trips, unbeknownst even to the American ambassador, to negotiate Nixon's first visit. That was the beginning of the big arms control agreements. This also was the time when the Germans were pushing ahead with *Ostpolitik*. We could not get into the détente game at that time, but we joined it later.

Why did we do it? What was the point of détente? It was clearly driven by our fear of nuclear war and the feeling that you had to talk to the other side if you were ever going to diminish the threat of war. This meant we had to get into arms control. I do not think, as much as I would like to believe it now, that détente was driven by a deeply subtle plan to undermine the Soviet Union. But it had that unintended consequence. Because one of the results of détente was that it gradually weakened the level of ideological control that the Communist Party and the Komitet Gosudarstvennoy Bezopasnosti (Committee for State Security) (KGB) had over the Soviet Union. It allowed more information to get into the USSR. Throughout Russian history the control of information was seen by those in power as a vital tool to cement their hold on the country. Unfortunately, we see this remains somewhat the case in Russia today.

So, ultimately détente was a good thing. When we did get involved, we became rather enthusiastic players at the Helsinki Conference. Despite our earlier suspicions about the Conference on Security and Cooperation process, we found the Helsinki Final Act ended up as something that was very much to our advantage, not least because of the provisions for vastly expanded distribution of Western information around the Soviet Union. It became a large crack in the wall that developed into a fissure.

I watched the Soviet succession crisis of the 1980s from New York, where I was posted until 1986. So, I missed all the funerals. But, even at that distance from Moscow it was apparent that Soviet leadership had fossilized. We were just waiting until fossilization came to an end. We were waiting for the generational change, which came with Gorbachev. I believe the interesting thing about Gorbachev was that it took at least a year after he came to power before it was generally perceived in the chancelleries of the West that this man was really different, and that we needed a different approach to him. Some of that history has now been rewritten, but before I was posted to Moscow in 1987, I spent time at Chatham House as research fellow. We were studying what Gorbachev was doing and how we were handling him. And in a way, our initial analysis of Gorbachev was not wrong. We originally thought that this man, as a communist sitting on top of the vast Soviet nuclear arsenal, was still dangerous and threatening to us. What he was trying to do was to make the communist system work better and become more effective. Therefore, from our perspective, this made him more threatening in the competition between East and West. It was not until Margaret Thatcher and Charles Powell visited Moscow in 1987, that things began to move in a really different direction.

Gorbachev did not set out to break communism. He still believes to this day in the reform of socialism, and he was out to do precisely that. It was only after a while that it became apparent in the course of what he was doing, that we were going to be dealing with a very different kind of Soviet Union where there were possibilities. And that was really where Margaret Thatcher began to play a massively important role.

I worked for Lord Carrington, the foreign secretary. I remember that one of the bones of contention between Carrington and Thatcher was that she would not let him go to Moscow to talk to the Russians, which he was very keen to do. She was very reluctant to be a party to arms control that only considered the military balance. The state of the Russian economy also featured in her thinking.

When you looked at the Soviet Union from the point of view from its economy, it did not appear as formidable. I first had a tiny glimpse of this in 1961–2, when I was there as a schoolboy. It was obvious to me that ultimately this system was not going to work. We in the West always held the stronger hand economically. Although we did not fully appreciate how much stronger it was at the time. Still, if you have the much stronger hand, it actually makes sense to negotiate, as we showed in Helsinki. I think it was the failure of the Soviet economy that ultimately led to the collapse of the Soviet Union. They found it impossible to maintain an economy that was permanently geared to the military-industrial complex.

By the time that Thatcher and Reagan came into office, Soviet expansion had happened. It was no longer actually increasing by that point, and they were beginning to suffer quite badly from imperial overstretch. So, in the early 1980s we perhaps did not read the state of their economy quite right.

At the time I began service at the British Embassy in Moscow in 1987, we did not know that the Soviet Union was going toward the breakdown. Clearly, Gorbachev thought he knew what he was doing at that time. He was trying to reform the economy, but without changing the model. If he had a new model in mind, however, I think it was somewhere between Canada and Sweden. He had been to Canada and that was a visit that had a very big impact on him. Beyond what he saw first-hand in Canada, Gorbachev spent time with Alexander Yakovlev the Soviet Ambassador. Yakovlev was in something like exile in Canada due to his reformist views. He wanted to see the USSR move toward a new economic model. By 1989, Yakovlev and the other liberal economists around Gorbachev were telling him that reforming the communist economy was not enough. The entire economic model had to be changed. By the end of Gorbachev's regime, these liberals broke with him. Their differences with Gorbachev were not just about the economic model. They were also about the powerbase of the government. I think Gorbachev was very sensitive to the fact that his powerbase was still the Communist Party of the Soviet Union. And, Gorbachev felt he still needed the KGB's support up to a point. He knew that he was going to be in a lot of trouble if the KGB turned against him, which they ultimately did. So Gorbachev was constrained as a leader.

Eventually things got out of hand for Gorbachev. Change took off and became a rather uncontrolled process. It was fascinating to watch it at close hand. But, you did not have a real sense that Gorbachev knew where they were going. Was it inevitably going to lead to the breakdown of the Soviet Union? Well, when you start to reform an authoritarian system, it does become a very dangerous process, one that is very hard to stop. Plus the fact that Gorbachev could not get the economy really to work properly. That was ultimately the cause of his undoing.

To understand Gorbachev, and how he tried to meet the tremendous challenges he faced, one needs to appreciate what distinguished him from his predecessors. Yuri Andropov, whom Gorbachev succeeded as First Secretary of the Communist Party, may very well have known the truth about the sorry state of the Soviet system. But, Andropov did not state it in public. The dramatic thing about Gorbachev at the beginning was not the slogans, and it was not even the prescriptions. It was the fact that, for the first time, a Soviet leader told his people that their economy was falling further and further behind the rest of the world. And that it would continue to do so unless they took dramatic action. This was just a sharp gear change from everything they had been told before. It took enormous courage, and Gorbachev did it again and again. He did it at great lengths,

PHOTO 4.1 *Thatcher and Ronald Reagan at No. 10 Downing Street during visit to Britain in June 1984 (Courtesy of Churchill Archives)*

probably excessive lengths. That to me was the first really dramatic shift in Gorbachev. He told the truth in a way that nobody else had done before.

I suspect that probably a lot of people inside the KGB Center knew the truth over the years. The sea change with Gorbachev was in telling the truth to the Soviet people, which had not happened before. By that I mean that at least the partial truth would have been told within layers of the Communist Party. But to actually go out in public and deliver the message that we are not catching up with the West, we are not overtaking the United States; we are falling further and further behind. It was a dramatic message.

Thatcher, Reagan, and Gorbachev

Lord Powell of Bayswater

I will provide, based on my close association with Margaret Thatcher, an overview of what she thought of détente. Her view, which President Reagan shared, was that détente was a product of weakness. It was the weakness of American society, particularly in the 1970s. There were the problems of Watergate and Vietnam, as well as the weak Carter presidency. The Central Intelligence Agency had been rendered virtually ineffective by congressional investigations and ill-conceived reforms. In Britain, of course, it was the time of great inflation, the winter of discontent, the threeday workweek, and the rundown of our economy.

While that was happening in the United States and the United Kingdom, on the Soviet side it was a time of relative resurgence. They deployed the SS-20 Missiles in Eastern Europe with little fear of our reaction. There was the steady expansion of Soviet influence around the fringes, as they used surrogates in Africa and Central America. The Soviets actively pursued efforts to disorient and divide West Europe and the European allies. As a result, the West was not fit psychologically, militarily, or economically to resist Soviet expansion. Détente was the only alternative available in the 1970s for dealing with the extension of Soviet power. In the eyes of Margaret Thatcher and Ronald Reagan, the steady erosion of Western interests, which was on an endless downward course, was intolerable. They both came to power with the determination to change that equation. So, they took a pretty dim view of détente.

It has been said that I had something to do with stiffening Margaret Thatcher's spine. But that is quite simply not true. Whenever I see Mr. Gorbachev these days, I am always told, "All right. You are a friend, but we know that you were the man who made Margaret Thatcher so difficult." I always say, "Well heck, this was the last thing I was trying to do. She did not need any help being difficult." Then Gorbachev says, "No, no, our intelligence services told us that you were the man who made her so difficult."

Reagan and Thatcher were concerned about the military balance that favored the Soviet Union. But it was the continuing expansion of communism, the Soviet's belief that communism should be extended, which I think fired both of them up most. Ronald Reagan and Margaret Thatcher made a very conscious decision to do something about it. Both knew that it was necessary to build a platform of strength from which to the deal with the Soviet Union. They set forth to remold their respective societies through economic reform, thereby restoring national confidence. This effort was the only way, as they saw it, to successfully confront the Soviet challenge.

It started, of course, in rhetorical terms where we had all the talk about the "evil empire" and the "Iron Lady." This was when Margaret Thatcher was fond of quoting Franklin D. Roosevelt: "We, and all others who believe in freedom as deeply as we do, would rather die on our feet than live on our knees." There was that sort of feisty rhetoric. But, it went far beyond rhetoric. There was the building up of military budgets, much more in the United States than Britain, but in some degree in Britain too. At the core of it all was the determination that we had to be able to demonstrate strength as the basis for dealing with the Soviet Union. This is illustrated by one of my favorite stories about President Reagan. At an early meeting with his National Security Council, Reagan was presented with a very thick folder. He asked what it was. He then was told: "This is your strategy for the Cold War Mr. President." To which he replied "I don't need this strategy, I've got one already." So they asked the President, "What is your strategy?" He said, "My strategy is much slimmer than yours. Mine is we win they lose."

The rapid succession of funerals for Soviet leaders, we called them "working funerals," between 1982 and 1985, offered excellent opportunities for bilateral meetings with other heads of government, without having to travel further than Moscow. Unfortunately we ran out of these opportunities after Mr. Chernenko.

There were two phases in the 1980s. The first half of the eighties, during which the platform of strength was being built up, was obviously a very bad time for détente. Intermediate nuclear forces were being deployed in Europe, modernization of strategic nuclear forces was being discussed, and arms control negotiations in Geneva were broken off. The successful deployment of intermediate-range missiles in Europe was a crucial moment in the final stage of the Cold War. This action made clear that the West European countries, slowly and with some reluctance, would stand up to the Soviets. These weapons were deployed despite all the pressures mounted against doing so. Not to do so would likely have delayed the end of the Cold War.

President Reagan announced the SDI and Margaret Thatcher was a cautious early supporter. She focused on the importance of doing the research for SDI, which in her mind encompassed testing, but not deployment. She felt any deployment of SDI was a matter of negotiation under the Anti-Ballistic Missile Treaty, but nonetheless she was a supporter and became a more fervent one as the years went by.

In 1984 we held a seminar on the future policy for the Cold War, which I think produced some rather interesting results. One was the determination to get in touch with the next generation of Soviet leadership. The people who we identified at that time as potentially the future Soviet leader were Gorbachev, Romanov, and Grishin. We proceeded to extend invitations to them to visit Britain. Very fortunately, it was Gorbachev who agreed to visit us. Otherwise things might well have taken a rather different course. At the same time, we determined that we would reach out to the East European countries. We sought to build a cautious relationship with them, so as to begin to work on detaching them from the Soviet orbit. We had to be very careful about it so as not to provoke the Soviets in response.

The upshot of this was the visit of Mr. Gorbachev to the Prime Minister's residence at Chequers in December 1984. It was indeed a rather dramatic moment as he came into the Great Hall of Chequers. It was in December, and there was a huge fire burning in the fireplace. From the very first second, you could see that Gorbachev was something completely different from the Soviet leaders with whom we had dealt up until that point. He was quite young and as he entered the room he bounced on the balls of his feet. He grinned and was cheerful. He acted from the first like a Western-style politician.

All through lunch he and Margaret Thatcher argued about the relative merits of their systems. She told him what a rotten system communism was and he responded in kind.[2] After lunch they met in the library for very nearly three hours. It was noticeable instantly that Gorbachev did not need advisors, although his assistant, Mr. Yakovlev, was sitting in the room. He did not need much in the way of notes. Gorbachev occasionally produced a paper to refer to some statistics. And at the end of that meeting Margaret Thatcher used the phrase, "This is a man I can do business with." She conveyed this to President Reagan in a message the next day, and in person about three weeks later in a meeting at Camp David. It is fair to say that she realized at that moment an opportunity to actually engage sensibly with the Soviet Union. But there would be a lot work to be done.

The Prime Minister was not starry eyed about Gorbachev. She did not think he was going to give it all up and bring the Soviet Union crashing down. But, she could see a way forward with him that was not evident before. Thatcher built very meticulously on that relationship over the next five or six years, in the course of a series of meetings in Moscow and in Britain among other places. But, of course, we could not really deliver on our own. We needed the Americans to deliver on the substance. Thatcher had a big role in convincing Ronald Reagan about Gorbachev. In this she was going against the advice of quite a number of his close advisors at the time. So, Thatcher worked to convince Reagan that Gorbachev was someone upon whom they could depend. She persuaded the President to reengage with the Soviet Union by meeting with Gorbachev, first in Geneva, and later in Moscow.

As to the dynamics of the Thatcher-Reagan relationship, it was simple adoration on her side. They had actually met a couple of times before either of them became, respectively, president and prime minister. It was quite an interesting example for British politicians. Reagan on his first visit to London asked to see the current prime minister and was told that would not be possible. Instead, he was taken to see the foreign secretary.

All Reagan remembers about that meeting is that the foreign secretary did not even bother to get up from his desk, but waved Reagan toward a chair and spent ten minutes with him before passing him on. Margaret Thatcher, who then was in opposition, met him on that visit and they had a long conversation. She then met Reagan again, after she had become leader of the Conservative Party. They found, from the first, that they had very similar views on the basic issues of everything from lower taxes to the evils of communism, to the importance of strong defense, and so on.

Now, in a way it is curious because in character they were completely opposite. President Reagan was relaxed, rather like a chairman of the board. A US Senate majority leader once said that Reagan would have made a hell of a monarch. Whereas, Margaret Thatcher was extremely busy, great on the detail, and so on. I remember sitting in bilateral meetings when Margaret Thatcher was going on about the finer details of the ABM Treaty. You could see President Reagan's eyes looking toward the clock to see how far it was to lunch. But the fact is that there was an emotional, intellectual, and political bond between them, which I think was absolutely crucial. The importance of personal relationships very often is exaggerated in politics. But in this case, it is hard to exaggerate the solidarity between President Reagan and Margaret Thatcher. I think it was an absolutely crucial element in bringing the Cold War to a conclusion.

Mikhail Gorbachev was essentially a humane man, and that was almost the most important thing about him. It was quite clear from the late 80s anyway that he was not going to use force in Eastern Europe; he was not going to use force in East Germany to prevent the democratization of the area. I am not saying he necessarily wanted it or welcomed it, but he was never going to use force to stop it. Even in the Baltics, I believe he teetered on the brink of using force, but he did not do so. That to me was the crucial element in bringing the Cold War to an end peaceably. Gorbachev was prepared to accept that this was no longer a time when it would be right for the Soviet Union to use force for those purposes.

One could argue that one of the problems with Russia today is that the West virtually raped Gorbachev in 1989 and 1990. He made all the concessions. He was forced to step back on everything: on Berlin, and on the democratization of Eastern Europe. In return from us he got very little, especially in terms of economic assistance. This left Gorbachev really to the mercy of the ultra-right extremist backlash, which was followed by his dethronement by Yeltsin. I know a lot of people would take the view that it was not our job to keep Gorbachev in his position, and I agree with that. I think, however, that maybe Russia today would be run in a slightly different way if that whole process had been handled a little more gently, and a little more slowly.

Finally, are we absolutely certain that the Cold War is finished? I sometimes think that we declared victory a bit too early in 1990 at the

PHOTO 4.2 *Thatcher and Gorbachev during visit to Britain in 1987 (Courtesy of Graham Wiltshire)*

Paris Conference. When one thinks about the former Soviet Republics that remain in the orbit of Russia, such as Georgia, and what happened there in 2008, one must wonder whether the Cold War really is over.

Gorbachev wanted a reform but brought a revolution

Alexander Likhotal

It was in March 1985 when I first heard of Mikhail Gorbachev. I was at a ski resort, and during the television announcement of Chernenko's death, I heard Gorbachev's name mentioned. During this period, I was a scholar and academic who was not very much interested in practical domestic politics. So I was not familiar with Gorbachev as a rising figure in the Communist Party of the Soviet Union (CPSU). In fact, as the broadcast played the music from *Swan Lake*, which at that time meant that something important had happened, I first thought that it was Gorbachev who had died. I was puzzled as to why such a fuss was being made over the death of a rank-and-file member of the Politburo. Years later, when I told Gorbachev about this, he laughed quite a lot. But, his ascension to power, and appointment as Chernenko's successor as the General Secretary of the CPSU, brought an absolutely new situation for the country.

Then, in April 1985, I watched on television Gorbachev's first trip to Leningrad, now St. Petersburg. Suddenly, here was a new energetic leader spontaneously speaking, not in the usual Orwellian language, but in a very straightforward manner. He spoke about the problems that we faced and how to deal with them. I was shocked, as were all those who understood, that this was not merely the facade of change. Gorbachev instituted a long series of reforms. These led in March 1988 to the free election for the Supreme Soviet, which was the parliament at that time. This was something that was unprecedented in our history. And not just for the Soviet period, never before had there been free elections. Then, just a couple of months later, the television started broadcasting live from the sessions of the Parliament. For the first time the Soviet people could see genuine legislative debate, with all of its collisions of opinion and arguments among different groups. It was an exhilarating gulp of fresh air at the time.

Despite the uncertainty during the period, we were not gloomy about the future. We were all much younger then, and that made a difference in our views, which were more optimistic than those of the older generation. At the same time, I think that we should be realistic about the changes Gorbachev pursued. Today many people look back and say, "Gorbachev was no revolutionary. He did not seek radically to transform the Soviet Union." They seem somehow surprised that Gorbachev wanted to preserve the system, to reform it, and to make socialism with a human face. It is true. That was his goal. To me, however, there is nothing surprising in this. When have we ever seen a leader of the regime that wants to have a revolution? It is obvious that Gorbachev did not want to bring about a revolution; he wanted a reform. The difference between revolution and reform was well stated by the British statesman Robert Bulwer-Lytton who noted, "A reform is a correction of abuses; a revolution is a transfer of power." Obviously a leader of the country is not interested, and never can be interested, in the transfer of power. Thus, Gorbachev wanted to reform the Soviet Union. The real question is how deep he wanted to go with it. Today many people argue that Gorbachev pursued reform because he did not have a choice. He did have a choice. I contend that, even if Gorbachev did not have a plan for change, he nevertheless had a vision of where he wanted to go. He wanted to bring reform and freedom to the country.

The main element of this position dated back to his younger years as a university student. Beginning at that point we can see the tremendous capacity of a human being to refine his worldview. During his years as a law student at Moscow University, Gorbachev's roommate and closest friend was Zdenek Mlynar. Mlynar was a Czech who later was one of the leaders of the Prague Spring in 1968. Both men were dedicated young communists. When Stalin died in 1953, they both cried. They did not see how the country and communism could go ahead without him.[3] Gorbachev later wrote his thesis about Stalin and dedicated the work to him.

Therefore in his youth and early career, Gorbachev was conventional in his view of the Soviet system and its role in international affairs. Then came the events in Czechoslovakia in 1968, which culminated in the Soviet invasion and occupation of Prague. Gorbachev realized exactly what happened in 1968, and it affected him. He traveled to Prague two years later, and there he experienced the situation first-hand. He was struck by how the Czech people looked at him as a representative of the Soviet Union. Before the Soviet invasion, there was a lot of friendship toward the Soviet people. But, after that, everything dramatically changed. As the military occupiers of Czechoslovakia, Gorbachev found the Soviets were disliked. He realized that the Soviet Union could not go on in this way.

Gorbachev was appointed as chairman of Chernenko's Funeral Commission in 1985. The man who would be designated to succeed a deceased party leader usually held this position. So that night, when Gorbachev returned home he talked to Raisa, his wife, about the future. He said, "It is now clear I will be elected the next Secretary General. Do you understand what it means?" Raisa said, "Yes, I do." "Do you understand," Gorbachev asked, "that we cannot live like we lived before?" She said, "Yes, I do." Gorbachev went on, "Do you understand it will require a lot of sacrifices?" And Raisa said, "Yes, I do." That was the beginning of what became great change in the Soviet Union.

Little attention was paid to Gorbachev's thinking at the time. Eventually, however, he decided that Soviet force would not be used against the upheavals in Eastern Europe. But, Gorbachev's thinking about change in Soviet policy in Eastern Europe was clear as early as March 1985. During the days surrounding Chernenko's funeral, Gorbachev met with the leaders of every communist party in Eastern Europe. During these conversations, he told every one of them, "You are responsible for your own country. Do not expect us to get involved." Nobody believed him at that time. History, however, proved that Gorbachev really spoke his mind, and his position became clear over time. He believed that a country could not be free if it enslaved other nations. This led to the cancellation of the Brezhnev Doctrine, when Gorbachev refused to intervene in the Polish crisis in 1980–1981. The next step obviously was to recognize the freedom of other nations to leave the Soviet Union.

It is true that between 1989 and 1991, there were violent military actions taken against demonstrations in Georgia, Azerbaijan, and Lithuania. The extent to which Gorbachev was involved in ordering the use of violence in these instances is subject to dispute. This, however, must be remembered: Russia impacted world and European history twice in the twentieth century. The first time was when Lenin released and materialized the spirit of communism in Europe. This led to much bloodshed in Europe and around the world, producing several million casualties. On the other hand, it was Gorbachev who practically alone dematerialized the spirit of communism. He did this almost single handedly and with so little bloodshed that it is absolutely incomparable. I am not saying the death of even a single person can be ignored, but in historical terms, it was practically a bloodless revolution.

Economic considerations, of course, played a role in Gorbachev's decision to reform the Soviet Union. Some even argue that it was Reagan's threats to bankrupt the USSR with a new arms race, featuring his Star Wars initiative, which drove Gorbachev to become a reformer. This is very much an exaggeration. It should be remembered that the arms race was not new in 1985. It had been going on for years. President Reagan tried to deal with four different Soviet leaders, from Brezhnev to Chernenko, and was unable to make any progress. It took Gorbachev's coming to office for real change to begin. The role of the Star Wars in the arms race is largely exaggerated. Both the United States and the USSR already were making similar efforts in the development of strategic defense systems. But, the cost of doing so was not comparable. For example, because labor in the Soviet Union was so cheap, the cost of countering US arms race programs was many times less expensive for the USSR than the United States. Of course, Gorbachev understood the weight of the arms race on the Soviet economy; he knew it bled the economy white. Seventy percent of the engineers in the Soviet Union at the time were employed in the military industrial complex. The production of civilian goods and services was practically ignored. Gorbachev inherited an intolerable situation and set out to change it. This he did long before Star Wars arose as an issue.

Something else needs to be considered in assessing how US threats of a new arms race affected Gorbachev. He was well aware that after World War II, after twenty-eight million of its people were lost during this war, the Soviet Union was ready to pay any price to counter threats, either real or imagined, to its security. National security always remained the driving force for Soviet leadership, and in this Gorbachev was no different. He simply had a more comprehensive view than his predecessors of the true nature of Soviet national security, and what it would take to assure it.

Gorbachev wanted to change both domestic and foreign policy. He sought to reform the Soviet Union and to bring freedom to the country. There is a big difference between the reform of the Soviet Union and Eastern Europe. The Soviet Union was trying to reform the system. The East European countries struggled for independence, which is very different. For Gorbachev everything started with domestic reform. Eventually, however, he clearly saw this would not be possible without changing foreign policy through international cooperation. He found he could not reform the USSR without stopping the arms race, and ending support for the so-called friendly regimes in the developing world, which were consuming a huge part of the budget. Unless foreign policy problems were dealt with, it would not be possible to solve domestic problems. That is why Gorbachev found himself fighting on domestic and international fronts simultaneously. He was determined to proceed with both domestic and international reform programs.

The situation when I joined Gorbachev's staff in 1989 obviously was acute. There were several different factions inside the Communist Party. Unfortunately, it turned out that Gorbachev did not have time to resolve these divisions. Events took over, everything accelerated very quickly, and he lost control. Gorbachev was, perhaps, just a little bit overconfident. When he left for his vacation in August 1991, Gorbachev was absolutely sure that he would be able to keep the situation under control.

The American Ambassador at the time, Jack Matlock, informed Gorbachev about intelligence the United States possessed indicating that a coup d'état was being planned in the country. Gorbachev received this information directly from Matlock. Although he did not brush the Ambassador's warning aside, Gorbachev did not pay much attention to it. He well knew who his opponents were within the Communist Party, such as the Prime Minister, Pavlov. But there had already been several revolts by certain leaders during plenum sessions of the Central Committee of the Communist Party. And each time, Gorbachev prevailed over the opposition of the old guard of the Communist Party. At one session of the Central Committee he even said to his opponents, "Okay, either I resign or you resign." And 40 members of the Central Committee were forced into resignation as a result of this session. That is why Gorbachev believed that he knew all the people involved. And he thought that he would be able to tackle that challenge.

It is interesting to note, however, that Gorbachev did not know how far things had gone. Just on the verge of the coup, which occurred on 18 August, Gorbachev met with several aides. He informed them that, after he returned from vacation, he planned to sign a treaty to create a new Soviet Union. Gorbachev did not know, as was disclosed many years later, that the KGB was taping this and other of his conversations.

The relationship between Ronald Reagan and Mikhail Gorbachev started very excitingly at the Geneva Conference in 1985. I was not present at that conference. I know of it from conversations with Gorbachev and people who were at the meeting. After having spoken to President Reagan at their first meeting for just over an hour, Gorbachev came back to his staff. The staff, of course, were very curious and they asked Gorbachev about his impression of the American President. He said, "What a dinosaur." As I understand it, President Reagan had a similar experience with his staff. When Reagan's people asked for his impression of Gorbachev, Reagan responded, "He's a diehard Bolshevik."

Things changed. At the Reykjavik Summit in 1986 Reagan said, "Call me Ronald." Gorbachev and Reagan, thereafter, were on a first name basis. I would say that there was something supernatural in the relationship between the two leaders. They came to so much mutual sympathy and understanding. This makes sense, of course, if you take into account all the responsibilities that were on both of them. The final act of trust was when Ronald Reagan wrote his last letter to Gorbachev. This final letter was written after Reagan had been diagnosed with Alzheimer's disease and it explained the situation. The letter was delivered well before Reagan's situation went public. It took a lot of courage for Reagan to write Gorbachev this letter. It demonstrated Reagan's tremendous trust of Gorbachev, his former partner in ending the Cold War.

With President George Bush, it was not easy at the very beginning. The Bush administration, after assuming office, took a pause in US-Soviet relations to reassess the relationship. In the end, the Bush-Gorbachev relationship was nevertheless very fruitful. Eventually they developed mutual trust. On his eightieth birthday, George Bush invited Mikhail Gorbachev to join him in the parachute jump from an airplane. Now that was a gesture of trust.

Mikhail Gorbachev developed a very special relationship with Margaret Thatcher, and it continues to this day. Whenever Gorbachev visited London he met with the late Prime Minister and their meetings were very emotional. Raisa, the late wife of Gorbachev, said that while they were having dinner in the course of their meeting in December 1987 the conversation turned to the utility of nuclear weapons. At that point, the discussion grew heated and emotional. Raisa saw that her husband and Mrs. Thatcher were approaching the issue from such different perspectives that they fell into silence. Thatcher was on one side of the table and Gorbachev was on the other, not talking to one another anymore. Raisa thought everything was finished, the meeting was over. But then Gorbachev said, "Mrs. Thatcher, I am not charged by the Politburo to convert you into a communist. I hope you do not expect to convert me into a conservative. And I think we still have things to discuss." This ended the tension and the conversation resumed anew.

I admire both Mikhail Gorbachev and Margaret Thatcher for their contrasting characters. I have observed them preparing for public appearances together since they left office. I remember on one occasion in particular that Thatcher appeared to be very nervous before speaking. She was pacing back and forth, from one corner of the room to the other, as she prepared for the lecture. Gorbachev was in the same room, sitting quietly, and drinking tea. He was totally relaxed. Thatcher remarked, "I have always known, Mikhail, that you have nerves of steel."

The behavior of both the East and the West in conducting the arms race during this period of the Cold War is an important issue. During the 1980s there was, for example, the issue of the deployment in Europe of intermediate range missiles, such as the Soviet SS20 and the American Pershing. At that time I was part of the so-called Group of Five. This was the coordinating body for Soviet disarmament negotiations. It served to coordinate five agencies directly concerned with disarmament: the Ministry of Foreign Affairs, the Armed Forces General Staff, the KGB, the Central Committee of the Communist Party, and the Ministry of Defense. It was much more difficult to come to an agreement during these coordination sessions than during the negotiations with the American partners. When I talked to negotiators from the American side, they agreed that this was also the case for them. They had similar committees in the United States. They too found it much more difficult to come to an agreement with each other than with us. To a certain extent, the development and deployment of new weapons systems was justified on both sides by what each perceived were the activities of their adversaries. Yet, the reality of the situation was often different from such claims.

How is it that the Berlin Wall fell and German unification followed so swiftly? Well, today many people are certainly claiming credit for these stunning events. Perhaps my experience at the twentieth anniversary of the dismantling of the Wall is instructive. During the ceremony, suddenly it came to my mind that it had become too crowded there. Too many people were claiming authorship of the historic event. I thought that there are, nonetheless, a few people who do not make such claims. These are Mikhail Gorbachev, George Bush, Margaret Thatcher, Helmut Kohl, and Ronald Reagan. They themselves never claim credit for the fall of the Berlin Wall and the end of the Cold War. Why not? In my judgment it is because people such as these do not need to remind anybody about their role. The role they played in history is clear. But, unfortunately, there are many other people who seek to elbow their way into history to claim they were an important part of the process.

How did the Berlin Wall fall, Germany reunify, and the Cold War end? To whom do we give credit? In reality, there is no single hero who ended the Cold War; there are two. The heroes in this process are the Russian and German nations. It was the people of Russia and Germany that ended the Cold War. The Russians came to understand that Germany had reformed itself completely. It was no longer a threat to Russian security. The German people, for their part, absolutely demanded to be united. The German politicians came to understand that there were only two ways to react to the people's demands: either to stand against them or accept them. Luckily, all the leaders involved accepted these changes.

In understanding Gorbachev, and what he attempted to do with perestroika and glasnost, it is useful to examine his relationship with Yuri Andropov, his predecessor as leader of the Soviet Union. The relationship was quite close. This was the relationship of colleagues, between a senior member of the Politburo and a new member of the Politburo. To a certain extent, Andropov took care of Gorbachev. It was Andropov, for example, who proposed bringing Gorbachev to Moscow in 1979. Andropov, as the former head of the KGB, had accurate information about the reality of the situation within the Soviet Union. Based on his conversations with Gorbachev, it is clear Andropov understood that reform of the system was inevitable. Unfortunately, he was not ready to take this reform himself. Andropov was already too old, and his health too fragile, for that undertaking.

It has been said that the Soviet economic system did not function well by the 1980s, when Gorbachev rose to power after Andropov's death. I would say this is an underestimation. The Soviet economic system did not function at all. And it could not function. Beginning in the 1960s, the tremendous revolution in technology and economics posed challenges to the world that required modernization. This challenge continued through the end of the century. The West modernized to meet the challenge. But the Soviet economy missed the point where it could have joined this modernization path. This was what Gorbachev faced when he assumed power. His first slogan was: "Acceleration." He discovered, however, that the Soviet economic machine was standing still, and "acceleration" could not work. The machine had to be restarted to get it moving again. And that is what Gorbachev set out to do.

Finally, defining the beginning and the end of the Cold War, although it appears to be a simple task, is difficult because it involves politics, ideology, and a wide variety of conflicting interests. It depends, of course, on what you mean when you refer to the "Cold War." If you mean that the Cold War started with the imposition of Soviet domination and rule in Eastern Europe, then the Cold War was over when this dominance was lifted from Eastern Europe in 1988–90. If you mean by the Cold War, the superpower relationship, the balance of power, and the so-called MAD (Mutually Assured Destruction) component of this relationship, then obviously it ended at Malta in December 1989. This was the conference at which George Bush and Mikhail Gorbachev shook hands and just declared, "We are not adversaries anymore."

Every historic event exists in some historic continuum. Therefore, as it is very difficult to say when exactly the Cold War started, it is also very difficult to say when it ended. In my judgment, it ended when perestroika was started in the Soviet Union. To be more specific, for the Soviet Union the Cold War ended at the Nineteenth Party Conference in July 1988. There it was announced that a free, competitive system of the elections would be introduced in the Soviet Union. That triggered the future chain of events that brought the Cold War to its conclusion. There are those who contend Gorbachev contributed to this historic turn of events only through his inaction. That is absolutely not correct. Gorbachev, by waging perestroika inside the Soviet Union, created the conditions in which the regimes of Eastern Europe were doomed to disappear.

On the end of the Cold War

Peter Jay

It is only a mild exaggeration to assert that we know the year, day, and hour when the Cold War ended. It ended on the day, year, and hour when Mikhail Gorbachev told Erich Honecker that he would not send Soviet tanks into the streets of Berlin to save the East German regime. This signaled to the entire world that the end of the Cold War was inevitable, predictable, and obvious, because one side of the war was unilaterally capitulating. The Russians no longer would defend the communist regimes within the Soviet Empire.

The Soviet Empire survived by imposing fear. It took all the brutality of Stalin to establish enough fear to maintain that regime for a very long time. The moment Gorbachev publically admitted that he no longer would use military force against those who step out of line, everybody knew the game was over. Gorbachev, himself, might not have known it at the time. But even so, he understood that the Soviet Union could no longer be held together by force and fear. Gorbachev's recognition of that fact is why I believe overwhelming credit for ending the Cold War, and the bloodless way it ended, belongs to Mikhail Gorbachev.

Notes

1   On détente and its collapse see Jussi Hanhimäki, *The Rise and Fall of Détente: American Foreign Policy and the Transformation of the Cold War* (Herndon: Potomac Books, 2012, chapter 8, and Olav Njolstad, "The Collapse of Superpower Détente, 1975–1980," in *The Cambridge History of the Cold War, Volume 3: Endings*, M. Leffler and O. A. Westad (eds) (New York: University Press, 2010c).

2   Margaret Thatcher, *The Downing Street Years* (New York: Harper Collins, 1993), 459–63 and Mikhail Gorbachev, *Memoirs* (New York: Doubleday, 1995), 160–1.

3   Mikhail Gorbachev and Zdeněk Mlynář, *Conversations with Gorbachev: On Perestroika, the Prague Spring, and the Crossroads of Socialism* (New York: Columbia University Press, 2002), chapter 1.

CHAPTER FIVE

In the shadow of the bomb: The technology of the Cold War

The Cold War exercised a profound effect on the relationship between science, technology, and the national security state. Historians, scientists, technologists, and policy-makers in this chapter provide an analysis of the role of science and technology in the conduct and conclusion of the Cold

PHOTO 5.1 *American atomic bomb test at Bikini Atoll in July 1946 (Courtesy of Churchill Archives Centre)*

War. Beyond a detailed discussion of the vast array of important technological developments during the era, these experts offer a variety of opinions
as to which technology advancements—nuclear and thermonuclear, ICBMs,
attack submarines, satellites, the transistor, carbon fiber, to name a few,
most affected the Cold War and its dénouement. The technological fruits
of the military-industrial complex and the "Wizards of Armageddon," on
both sides, propelled and shaped the immensely expensive strategic arms
race—distorting national economies and constraining domestic policy
choices. The nature and operation of national and international scientific
communities were transformed, and were transformative, as they operated
in the shadow of the bomb during the Cold War.[1]

Waqar Zaidi reviews the spectrum of perspectives offered by historians regarding science, technology, and the Cold War. Thom Mason,
describes the development of US national laboratories during World War
II, and assesses their importance in the Cold War and its aftermath. James
Thomson surveys science, technology, and strategic arms as they shaped
the Cold War and transformed warfare doctrine. Franklin Miller provides
the policy-maker's perspective on science, technology, and the Cold War.
Miller's essay focuses on how certain strategic technologies influenced the
conduct of the Cold War. In response to Miller's emphasis on the importance of missile technology as a feature of Cold War strategy, Anthony
Kelly explains the critical importance of the development of carbon fiber
technology in assuring the efficacy of US and Soviet mutual deterrence.
Graham Farmelo analyzes the impact of the Cold War on science and
scientists. As an historian of science, he focuses particularly on how the
imperatives of the national security state affected the relationship between
scientists and their government.

An historian's perspective on technology and the Cold War

Waqar Zaidi

Historians have not agreed upon a single grand narrative about technology
and the Cold War. We have differing views, not necessarily mutually
exclusive, but certainly requiring more exploration and articulation.
Historians are only really just beginning to get to grips with this issue.
There are several reasons as to why historians have been unable to pick a
singular Cold War technology as the most important for the war, or focus
on a singular narrative about technology and the Cold War.

First, our picture of the Cold War has radically expanded over the past
twenty years. We have moved away from thinking of the Cold War just in

military terms and now consider its cultural, economic, and social aspects. Thus, when we think about technology and the Cold War, we have to think about those aspects as well. We have also moved from a Eurocentric view, which saw Europe as the primary battleground of the Cold War, to one that recognizes the global nature of the Cold War. The problem before us now is to fit, for example, the American interventions in Vietnam and Korea and the Soviet interventions in say Afghanistan and Ethiopia into a single narrative. This is deeply challenging for historians, even before we recognize the need to include the Cold War activities of their allies—the British in the Middle East and the Cubans in Angola for example.

One way in which historians have successfully managed to incorporate all this global activity into one framework has been with the notion of a clash of ideologies. Unfortunately, this narrative has not really left much room for a technological grand narrative. We have many vignettes of the role of technology in various Cold War conflicts, such as the American ideology of technological war and its evolution during the Vietnam War. I am referring, for example, to US Secretary of Defense Robert McNamara and his technocratic view of warfare. Another example is that of US Congressman Charlie Wilson's advocacy of the provision of stinger missiles to the Mujahideen in their struggle against the Soviet Army in Afghanistan. Yet, even in these vignettes our understanding remains incomplete. How many people know, for example, that the humble mule was an essential component of the stinger system as it was used to transport the missiles into the war zone? The CIA spent a considerable amount of time and effort importing mules into Pakistan in the mid-1980s.

A second reason for the lack of consensus among Cold War historians is due to the intrinsic relationship between how we think about technology and our understanding of the Cold War, how it was conducted, and why it eventually ended. From one perspective, for example, the most significant Cold War technology was the telecommunications satellite, because it allowed many countries to join into a process of globalization that undermined isolated communist regimes. According to this view, the masses in the Communist bloc were isolated from the West going into the 1980s, but due to satellite telecommunication technology, these populations could see that they were losing economically and culturally to the West. This view of technology is attached to a very particular perspective of the end of the Cold War and its aftermath. American-led globalization, according to this view, eventually led to perestroika, glasnost, and the end of the Cold War. So in the broader arc of history, the Cold War was a retarding episode in the larger process of technology driven globalization. Not everyone subscribes to this view, however. Many historians choose instead to emphasize particular policy choices made by the United States or the Soviet leadership, the growing acuteness of the Soviet Union's economic problems, or processes at the periphery of the global Cold War system. For them modern mass communications technologies were much less important to the final resolution of the Cold War.

Nuclear weapons are often important for those historians seeking to understand why the Cold War remained Cold, rather than degenerating into a shooting war between the two superpowers. Aviation and rocket technology, meanwhile, has sometimes been emphasized by those trying to understand the sheer global reach of the Cold War. Allied to these was the significance of the idea of modern technology—particularly the American belief that it could rely on modern technological development to make up for its manpower deficit vis-à-vis the Soviet Union. Yet once again there are counter-perspectives that do not rely heavily on technology in their explanations—for example those emphasizing the role of Third World conflicts in explaining the lack of direct hot wars between the superpowers, or those focused on power or ideological vacuums in explaining the globalization of the Cold War.

Some historians who have sought to explain what drew nation states toward the United States rather than the USSR, and the attraction of American culture, have emphasized the importance of consumerism and capitalism. Here one sees the importance of computer technology and electronics, which so advantaged the US economy as compared to the Soviet.

Finally, there is another story that historians have told, which is the growth of large, complex technologies and the development of "Big Science." Allied to this has been the view that the Cold War led to an intertwining of military industry and science. Yet historians here are faced with the awkward fact, not yet adequately addressed in their histories, that this type of "Big Science" had its roots in the decades prior to World War II, and that even then private corporations were working closely with governments on massive modern technological projects. An example closer to the Cold War is the Manhattan Bomb Project. The Manhattan Project was a very intimate intertwining of the military, industry, and science. We tend predominantly to think about the physicists when we consider the Manhattan Project. But, it should be remembered that it was the project management expertise of companies such as DuPont, which enabled this enterprise to be completed so effectively. And DuPont, of course, had its unique project management expertise because of the development of nylon in the 1930s. The importance of these connections between the military, science, and industry is what President Eisenhower was partially alluding to in his famous speech on the military-industrial complex.

Government-sponsored research and the Cold War

Thom Mason

Oak Ridge National Laboratory was created in 1946, following the Rutherford era and around the time of the Moscow celebration of the founding of the Soviet Academy of Science. Formed out of some of the facilities of the Manhattan Project, it then was known by the code designation X10. As is true of many scientific and technical institutions around the world, the American national laboratories were a creation of the Cold War. It is not at all obvious that these institutions would have necessarily come into being without it. After the Manhattan Project had been successful and the bomb was developed, it was obvious that the atomic production facilities would continue to operate. After all, the material required for the construction of a bomb had been exhausted in the two nuclear weapons that had been deployed against Japan. Some sort of production complex was needed for construction of additional weapons. As the war wound down, there was a great deal of discussion about everyone going home and returning to the science that they had left before the war. While that happened in many cases, the science had been transformed by the new insights and capabilities developed during the war.

New laboratories emerged in the United States during and following the war to meet the scientific and technical requirements of national security. These included, in addition to Oak Ridge and Los Alamos, a number of laboratories that were not part of the Manhattan Project, such as Argonne, which evolved from the project's metallurgical laboratory, and Brookhaven. It is interesting to consider why that happened. In my view, the reasons are that the impact of technology during World War II had a qualitative difference from prior history. Certainly there were historical precedents in the development of technological advantage in warfare, such as longbows at Agincourt and the introduction of gunpowder. And there had also been examples of military objectives driving research, such as the Royal Navy's interest in longitude. But what you had in the wartime examples of the atomic bomb and radar was unique. These were developed in highly concentrated programs dedicated to very specific operational ends. Each was based on extensive prewar fundamental research, which in a very short time was converted to wartime applied science. Both are rather startling examples of what could occur when a modern society mobilized its scientific resources in a different sort of way. It showed the kind of outcomes that were achievable and of great relevance in terms of military superiority.

Something of a new vision of the relationship between government and science was in the air. Thus, in July 1945, Vannevar Bush wrote *Science, the Endless Frontier*, which called for the US government to accept new responsibilities for promoting the flow of new scientific knowledge and the development of scientific talent. Bush essentially laid out a greatly expanded role for government in research.[2] Prior to that, research was largely a philanthropic activity that existed in parallel with education. There was not really a large government role in scientific research. Bush's report paved the way for what we now view as the modern infrastructure of scientific research, including the creation of the Atomic Energy Commission (AEC), the National Science Foundation (NSF), the Defense Advanced Research Project Agency (DARPA), and the National Aeronautics and Space Administration (NASA). In 1949, Bush published a book on the role of science in the preservation of democracy that made the New York Times Best Seller List.[3] In this influential book *Modern Arms and Free Men*, Bush wrote of World War II as a war of applied science, which had drawn so heavily on the accumulated stock of fundamental scientific knowledge that it was all but exhausted when the fighting stopped. Bush discussed the weapons developed during and immediately after World War II in the context of the unfolding Cold War. He expressed a great concern for the need to replenish this stock of basic scientific knowledge and promoted the creation of national institutions such as the NSF toward that end.

The national laboratories and other scientific institutions that emerged in the postwar United States often undertook fundamental research that had little, if anything, to do with military technologies. I am referring, for example, to the work on particle accelerators and what became known as high-energy physics. From the work of the new scientific institutions emerged a range of tools for technical innovation and public investment, from the transistor, to computing technology, to GPS (global positioning satellites). These tools fueled the economic engine that eventually gave Western economies the tremendous competitive advantage that was such an important part of the conclusion of the Cold War.

Much of the work that eventually produced this economic advantage, however, was not explicitly undertaken to that end. The Cold War effort to replenish the depleted stock of basic scientific information was aimed at supporting the applied science required to develop advanced weapons systems, such as the hydrogen bomb. It nevertheless had the unintended consequence of providing the broader technological innovation that arose to profoundly transform our lives. For example, the X-10 site at Oak Ridge National Lab during the war was devoted to research on the properties of plutonium. The very specific purpose of this work was to develop the process for separating plutonium produced in the first engineered nuclear reactor as part of the effort to build the atomic bomb. In the period immediately after the war, however, the same research reactor was used to produce the very first medical isotopes, which were first shipped from the Lab in 1946. Clifford Shull conducted Nobel Prize-winning work at Oak Ridge, working with Ernest Wollan to develop the neutron scattering technique that is used to study materials.[4] Lab researchers, in an effort to understand the effects of radiation on humans using mice as a mammalian proxy, led to the discovery of the Y chromosome in mammals. These scientific findings, which eventually saved lives in their medical applications and led to better understanding of the composition of human life, were not the intended purpose for constructing the X10 facility. But they were a profound, if unintended, consequence of it.

This is the legacy of science in the shadow of the bomb. At the close of World War II, there was an appreciation of the strong link between science and technology and its impact on military and economic competitiveness. But a true appreciation of the power of this link was only possible fifty years later. It can be seen in the outcome of the Cold War. And it can only be appreciated when we consider, as is shown in economic models, that roughly one-half of the real growth in GDP since the war's end was driven by new technology. I do not think anyone could have anticipated the transformation in life this has brought to the world.

Strategic weapons systems and the Cold War

James A. Thomson

This appraisal of the role of strategic weapons is based on my years of service during the Cold War in the US Department of Defense at the Pentagon, the National Security Council at the White House, and at the Rand Corporation. The strategic context in this period of time was that the Soviet Union was perceived to have achieved strategic parity with the United States and that had been codified in the SALT talks. It was a widely accepted point of view that the two sides had reached a nuclear standoff in strategic weapons. This had two consequences from a strategic perspective inside the US government. One was to find a way to shore up nuclear deterrence, to make it more credible, particularly to shore up what was called "extended deterrence." That was the deterrence we were extending to Europe. This involved developing new systems and targeting doctrines. The second consequence was the need to create options for conventional deterrence, so that there would be an equality of some kind between the NATO and Warsaw Pact forces.

Germany was the focal point of the Cold War. This was the place where Soviet military forces were concentrated in huge numbers. It was believed that this tremendous superiority put a heavy political weight on West

Germany. That weight could affect German behavior over the long run. American decision-makers, among others in the West, perceived it to be very important to do something about this situation, since arms control had not succeeded. There were many assessments made in those years, especially between 1968 and 1977. In these the central argument was that there was a new numerical significant disadvantage for NATO and we needed to find ways to offset it. Ultimately, the answer was sought in technology.

My nominee for the most important technological development during the Cold War is the p-n junction and the transistor. The p-n junction and transistors were developed at Bell Labs in the United States. These discoveries, in conjunction with developments in solid-state physics, made electronics smaller immediately. This initiated a long period of research and development, mainly focused in the private but also within government laboratories. This work made solid-state devices faster and smaller, which brought the miniaturization of electronic components. Those who used transistors in laboratories during the 1970s know that they were not rugged. When the temperature got too hot in the lab, the transistors would malfunction. So there was also the issue of ruggedness of these solid-state devices. For that reason their defense applications proceeded more slowly than civilian applications because the defense environment is one of significant physical stress due to intense temperature changes and the like. The technology, however, kept improving.

In 1962, US General Bernard Schriever held a conference called "Project Forecast" to talk about what technological developments would be crucial for the future. Schriever promoted the idea that it would be possible to develop weapons with zero Circular Error Probable (CEP). Schriever's goal was the development of a weapon that could be delivered from a very great distance exactly on its target, not just near it. So he set the Air Force laboratories to work on this task. This work primarily proceeded at the research level, although during the Vietnam War, some systems were adapted for use in the field. Thus, in the later stages of the Vietnam War, we had the first deployment of systems that had rugged, solid-state devices, namely the AIM7 and the Sidewinder missiles. Also deployed were laser-guided bombs, and antitank guided missiles that required humans to direct them to their targets.

The key convergence happened in 1977, when a review panel examined all of the different electronic guidance programs and concluded it was now possible to build very small CEP weapons. The panel recommended that the United States drive in that direction. The director of defense research and engineering, William Perry, saw the real possibilities here. William Perry created, along with Harold Brown, what we called the "Offset Strategy."[5] From that point forward, we worked to offset the Soviet advantage in conventional forces with technologically sophisticated and highly lethal weapons. Eventually, this became a "system of systems" with the code name "Assault Breaker." Assault Breaker was designed to integrate surveil-lance intelligence systems, munitions with precision guidance, and air and ground-launched cruise missiles into a network devoted to attacks deep into the enemy rear. There were additional technological developments during this period that proved very important to offset strategy, but which were not originally intended for this purpose. Among these were the development of global positioning satellites and stealth aircraft, which gave us a different kind of delivery platform. This was nothing short of a military technical revolution.[6] In 1978 William Perry testified before Congress and said:

> Precision-guided weapons, I believe, have the potential of revolutionizing warfare. More importantly, if we effectively exploit the lead we have in this field, we can greatly enhance our ability to deter war without having to compete tank for tank, missile for missile with the Soviet Union. We will effectively shift the competition to a technological area where we have a fundamental long-term advantage. The objective of our precision guided weapon systems is to give us the following capabilities: to be able to see all high value targets on the battlefield at any time; to be able to make a direct hit on any target we can see, and to be able to destroy any target we can hit.[7]

As research and development in support of the Offset Strategy proceeded during the Carter administration, news leaks of tests of these new weapons systems occurred. Such leaks continued in the Reagan administration. It is clear to me that the Soviets were watching this research and development activity very closely. In 1984 the Chief of the Soviet General Staff, Marshall Ogarkov said:

> Rapid changes in the development of the conventional means of destruction and the emergence in the developed countries of automated reconnaissance and strike complexes, longrange, highaccuracy terminally guided combat systems, unmanned flying machines, and qualitatively new electronic control systems make many types of weapons global and make it possible to sharply increase (by at least an order of magnitude) the destructive potential of conventional weapons, bringing them closer, so to speak, to weapons of mass destruction in terms of effectiveness.[8]

That is how the Soviets saw the development of advanced conventional weaponry—they saw it as a revolution in warfare. We thought research and development was going to be hard. And it was. The Soviets began to assume as early as the mid-1980s that we had attained this transformation. But, we did not get there until later. This was the point that Star Wars connected to the strategic arms race. We held a series of meetings with the Soviets at the RAND Corporation between 1986 and 1988. We talked about a lot of different aspects of strategic arms, including strategic defense. I recall Soviet experts and generals saying to me,

> Look, we know this SDI thing can't work. It's impossible. The computational power required is too much. You just can't do that. But we worry about the technological development that it will create. A new round of technological development will get adapted into other stuff that you're building, and that it will as a consequence further offset what we've built up. We cannot keep up with that.

So my view about the SDI and the Cold War is simply that SDI symbolized an American technological advantage that deeply concerned the Soviets.

What most people today fail fully to appreciate is that, due to technological research and development fueled by the Cold War, there has been a tremendous shift in the nature of warfare. This is the so-called Revolution in Military Affairs (RMA) as it became known in the 1990s. People began hearing about the RMA in the 1990s, as we first saw the nascent capability of its first weapons during the Gulf War of 1991. Subsequently, we watched the significant capability of the new weapons systems used in the opening phase of the Iraq War in 2003. The revolution in military technology continues, and new weapons capabilities will continue to be deployed.

Thus, these revolutionary technologies produce weapons capabilities that are excellent at defeating armies in the field. But, they do not solve all problems. They, in particular, do not solve the fundamental problem of warfare, which is how to get people to accept a new political order. Military force only makes possible political compromise. It does not solve it. The problem of these magic weapons is that it makes you fall into the trap of believing that warfare is simply a military technical matter and not a political one.

Strategic technologies and Cold War stability

Franklin C. Miller

From a policy-making perspective, there were two technological developments that were fundamental to the nature, conduct, and outcome of the Cold War. The first, of course, is the development of the nuclear weapon. The nuclear weapon fundamentally changed the nature of warfare. Before the nuclear weapon was invented, governments would always depend on their generals' assertions, which were often boasts, lies, or miscalculations that they could produce a winning campaign strategy and accomplish a military victory. The nuclear weapon gave the party about to be vanquished the ability to turn the victor's gains into ashes. As the American strategist,

Bernard Brodie, wrote in the late 1940s, the nuclear weapon now created a situation where the purpose of governments was not to win wars, but to prevent them.[9] Nuclear proliferation is bad, of course, and the nuclear weapon is not in any circumstances a universal deterrent. When you look at the period from 1945 to the end of the Cold War, however, nuclear and thermonuclear weapons induced tremendous caution among government leaders in the United States and the USSR.

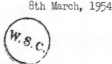

8th March, 1954

Most Secret and
  Confidential.

My dear Friend,

     Thank you for your letter. I am honoured by the kind personal things you say.

     There is no difference between us upon the major issues which overhang the world, namely, resistance to Communism, the unity of the free nations, the concentration of the English-speaking world, United Europe and NATO. All these will and must increase if we are to come through the anxious years and perhaps decades which lie ahead of hopeful but puzzled mankind.

     On the day that the Soviets discovered and developed the Atomic Bomb the consequences of war became far more terrible. But that brief tremendous phase now lies in the past.

     An incomparably graver situation is presented by the public statement of Mr.Sterling Cole at Chicago on February 17. I have discussed these with my expert advisers. They tell me that the 175 ft. displacement of the ocean bed at Eniwetok Atoll may well have involved a pulverisation of the earth's surface three or four times as deep. This in practice would of course make all protection, except for small Staff groups, impossible. You can imagine what my thoughts are about London. I am told that several million people would certainly be obliterated by four or five of the latest H bombs. In a few more years these could be delivered by rocket without even hazarding the life of a pilot. New York and your other great cities have immeasurable perils too, though distance is a valuable advantage at least as long as pilots are used.

Another ....

PHOTO 5.2 *Most Secret letter from Churchill to Eisenhower in March 1954 (Courtesy of Churchill Archives Centre)*

It is somewhat remarkable that, on a European continent which was punctuated by war every ten to fifteen years going back far as the fifteenth century, there was no war in Europe after World War II. Consider what the Cold War might have been like had there not been nuclear weapons in the hands of the Soviet Union, the United Kingdom, and the United States. War changed dramatically as a result of the development of nuclear weapons, and the long European peace from 1945 to the present is, in large part, the byproduct.

The second technological development, which I think was absolutely fundamental to the Cold War, but that is almost completely unrecognized, is the Trident II Submarine Launch Ballistic Missile. Since December 7, 1941, when the Japanese struck Pearl Harbor, one of the elements of the American psyche has been the fear of another surprise attack on the United States. In the early 1960s the Soviets began to develop long-range missiles. The bulk of the American's deterrent force was based on strategic bombers. Russian long-range missiles directly threatened the US bomber force because their airbases now could be destroyed rapidly, and with very little warning of an incoming attack. In response to this Soviet strategic threat, the United States moved to develop its own long-range, land-based missiles. By the late 1960s, however, the Soviets had developed and were deploying advanced strategic missiles that rendered the American land-based missiles vulnerable. The United States needed to develop a safe, secure, and reliable deterrent. Submarine-based ballistic missiles, which could be launched from under the sea, was America's response to the Soviet threat to deterrence. Beginning with the Polaris missile program, American nuclear strategists spent an enormous amount of time developing a strategy and a technology whereby deterrence was restored through a missile delivery system, which is both invulnerable and extremely precise. What they worked to develop was a submarine-launched missile that threatened those assets most valued by the Soviet leadership. In the 1990s, they attained this goal with the development of the Trident II ballistic missile.

Entering the 1990s, Soviet nuclear strategy was devoted to creating a situation where US strategic nuclear forces were vulnerable to a preemptive strike that would render a retaliatory response ineffective. For example, they hardened in underground facilities those assets most valued by the Soviet leadership. The Trident II ballistic missile rendered such efforts futile and broke the back of the Soviet nuclear strategy. It was a game-changing Cold War technology, which undergirded nuclear deterrence in a way that overwhelmed Soviet capabilities.

Sometimes technologies emerged during the Cold War that caused considerable consternation and misunderstandings among policy-makers and the general public. For example, there is the case of the enhanced radiation weapon known as the neutron bomb. This weapon was designed to defeat Soviet armored forces. It was supposed to be a more lethal anti-tank weapon because of the enhanced radiation. The reduced blast effect, as compared to a tactical nuclear weapon, was an additional benefit. The controversy over this innovative weapon arose because of the way it was portrayed in the mass media. The press presented the neutron bomb as a weapon that, by its very nature, was more likely to be used than any other nuclear weapon. Eventually, this contributed to such an outcry in the United States and Europe that the Carter administration canceled the enhanced radiation weapon program. One of the fundamental misconceptions of the common press treatment of nuclear deterrence is that if a weapon produces a smaller explosion, then political leaders are more likely to use it. In my experience, political leaders understand what it means to cross the nuclear threshold, regardless of the explosive effect of the weapon. Had there been a Soviet invasion of Western Europe, which thankfully there was not, the US Army and NATO Armies would have used weapons that would have created much greater collateral destruction than that caused by enhanced radiation weapons.

In my nearly three decades of service at the Pentagon and in the White House, the discussions of nuclear and other strategic weapons were extensive and extended. Throughout my career, whenever we were in sessions with the most senior civilian and military leaders of government, the deliberations were reasoned and thoughtful. I am aware that there are those who question the extent to which governmental and political leaders truly understood the complex issues surrounding strategic weapons and their lethality. But, that is desperately unfair to the civil servants, public officials, politicians, and military with whom I served over the span of a long career. All of the officials with whom I engaged in these desperately serious matters, upon which the survival of nations depended, consistently deliberated in a serious and careful manner.

Carbon-fiber technology transformed strategic nuclear weapons

Anthony Kelly

The nuclear bomb is essentially a World War II thing. The Cold War, from where I stood in defense work for a time, was about mutual deterrence with nuclear weapons. You cannot deter unless you can deliver that weapon. The most important thing in delivering the weapon was the development of the rocket. The rocket did not play a large part in World War II. The Americans and the Russians developed, first of all, a solid fuel for rockets. You can send rockets to the moon with liquid firing, but you cannot on the battlefield have a liquid-fueled rocket. Thus, a solid-fuelled rocket was developed.

That rocket had to be delivered over very large distances if the United States and the Soviets were to deter one another. One of the most important elements in accomplishing this feat is the weight of the casing. When the Polaris program started, the range of the Polaris Missile was limited by the fact that the rocket motor case was made of steel. The Americans first, and then the Russians, realized that because you only use a rocket carrying a weapon once, all you had to do was have a cylinder that would not burst during flight. They realized that you could make that kind of casing with glass fiber. Therefore, glass fiber replaced steel, and the Polaris Missile delivered a significant strategic advantage, given the extended distances it thereby could cover.

It is true that the Russians in their tests exploded a much bigger hydrogen bomb than the Americans. But this gave them little or no strategic advantage because they could not deliver it. The Americans held the strategic advantage in nuclear weapons because they could deliver those they developed. The reason the Americans were ahead was that in the West we developed carbon fiber. Carbon fiber replaced glass fiber in the rocket motor casing and made the whole intercontinental ballistic exchange of weapons possible. Carbon fibers were developed simultaneously in the United States and the United Kingdom in the early 1960s. This made carbon-fiber technology a crucial Cold War development. It made mutual deterrence possible because rockets could be thrown distances that could not be attained with steel casings. That is also why carbon fibers are replacing aluminum in modern aircraft, and is what justifies considering carbon fiber as a most important strategic technology during the Cold War.

The Cold War's effect on science and scientists

Graham Farmelo

The German-born British scientist Rudolph Peierls has asserted that the Cold War began two weeks after the end of World War II. The occasion to which he referred was the anniversary of the founding of the Russian Academy of Sciences by Peter the Great. In May 1945, scientists all over the developed world received invitations from Moscow to attend the celebrations. General Leslie Groves, director of the Manhattan Project, put his foot down. He did not want any scientists from the United States, and anyone privy to the secrets of the Manhattan Project, to attend that conference. As a result, the leading physiologist A. V. Hill believed, Winston Churchill vetoed the participation of most of the leading British scientists, including physicists who had worked loyally on the war effort and were now looking forward to reestablishing contact with friends in the Soviet Union, then a

British ally. The British scientists were angry that their trip was canceled, especially as Churchill gave a patently fictional excuse that they might be needed in continuing war with Japan.[10] I know from my own work that Britain's leading theoretical physicist at that time, Paul Dirac, was apoplectic. His wife said she had never seen him angrier, except perhaps when Cambridge University withdrew his parking permit.[11] That particular event provides some sense of the background to the application of nuclear technology in the Cold War—the British scientists who had abandoned their academic work to work for the government saw how unpleasant it was to be pushed around by their ungrateful leaders.

In the late 1920s and early 1930s, Ernest Rutherford of the Cavendish Laboratory was the world's leading nuclear physicist. He was doing "fundamental physics"—curiosity-driven science, done primarily not to be of material benefit to society, but to increase human understanding of how the universe works. Through his enormous energy and penetrating intellect Rutherford prosecuted what you might call a kind of romantic science. This was science that was very open, international, transcending the individual politics of the scientists concerned. And, it was a science undertaken with a curiously English disdain for industrial application and industrial money—unless those funds took the form of a check to fund his science.

The first third of the twentieth century was one of the best possible times to be alive as a physicist. They were developing principles that overthrew Newton's laws in the understanding of subatomic quantum mechanics. Thanks largely to Rutherford's preeminent genius, the scientists at the Cavendish Laboratory made remarkable progress in discovering the content and inner workings of the atomic nucleus. The roster of those who passed through Cavendish is virtually unprecedented in laboratory work. Among Rutherford's boys and associates at that time working in Cambridge were such renowned physicists as Patrick Blackett, James Chadwick, John Cockcroft, Paul Dirac, Rudolf Peierls, Peter Kapitsa, Igor Tamm, and Ernest Walton. These people were seized with the energy and the idealism that Rutherford brought to physics. In 1938, however, a year after Rutherford's death, and just before the outbreak of World War II, fate paid one of the cruelest tricks it has played on the human race: nuclear fission was discovered in laboratories in Hitler's Berlin. This finding gave some inkling for how nuclear energy, which Rutherford had long believed was unlikely to be harnessed in the coming few decades, might be released—possibly to form a weapon.

At this time at Birmingham in the United Kingdom, Otto Frisch and Rudolf Peierls, who were technically "enemy aliens," invented the first theoretical mechanism for a nuclear bomb. They were working in a lab alongside people doing much more sensitive defense work, on radar, the technology that was perhaps most critical in winning the war. Frisch and Peierls were then confronted with the horror of deciding whether or not to share this discovery, which could produce a bomb of unprecedented power. Terrified of the Nazis and the eminence of the scientists working behind the Nazi lines, Frisch and Peierls wrote a classic memorandum for government officials, describing how an atomic bomb could be produced and the effects it would have if it were used. Much of the subsequent British work on the atomic bomb, and the Manhattan Project that produced the first weapon, was ultimately based on the research of Frisch and Peierls. The project became perhaps the most intense concentration of scientific and technological effort in human history and it produced the bomb within a timeframe that most scientists had earlier believed impossible.

That was the background to Winston Churchill's refusal to allow British scientists to visit the USSR in May 1945, when the United States was preparing to test its first nuclear weapon. With the Nazis defeated and the war likely to end soon, the scientists felt the visit to the USSR was an opportunity to go back to that era of science in which they had thrived. The scientists found Churchill's veto of their visit deeply offensive, mainly because of the implication of their untrustworthiness. Dirac himself tore up his contract as an advisor to the government. Blackett was motivated, partly by this, to become perhaps the most vocal critic of Allied nuclear policy.

So the postwar physics agenda was set. The community did not go back, as many physicists expected, to the world of fundamental research with which they were familiar before the war. Instead, what emerged was a new world of "Big Science," in which fundamental physics was done on a huge scale, with generous funding from governments, which had now seen curiosity-driven research could have important consequences for the military. Contrary to the prewar romantic notion of science being so totally international, postwar science was to be deeply fragmented.

The most critical technological development in the Cold War was the hydrogen bomb because it completely changed the landscape of weaponry. The atomic bomb, one can argue, in its destructive power was comparable to the worst of the devastation wrought by the B-29's bombings of Tokyo at the end of the war. The hydrogen bomb, however, raised the stakes to a much higher level. It convinced Churchill that he had completely underestimated the potential of nuclear weapons to change the nature of war.

Meanwhile, the Soviets were quick to build their own bomb, aided with first-rate intelligence from agents in Britain and the United States. The brilliant Soviet physicist Pytor Kapitsa, however, stood on the sideline during the making of the Russian atomic bomb, mainly because he was alienated and could not bear to work for Stalin's henchman, Beria—who had been placed in charge of the program. To my knowledge, Kapitsa was the first person to work privately on a strategic defense initiative to render nuclear weapons unusable.

In the United States, the terrain is well known. Robert Oppenheimer, who led the scientists in the Manhattan Project, went from being a famous and acclaimed scientific figure to a broken man because of his opposition to building the hydrogen bomb. Eventually, Oppenheimer was humiliated by a kangaroo court that inquired into his loyalty and his security clearance was withdrawn. He was superseded as the US government's leading advisor on nuclear weapons by the brilliant and opportunistic Edward Teller. Teller, because of his abrasive personality and unrelenting devotion to weapons development, became the person many physicists loved to hate.[12] He continually urged the US government to develop ever more powerful nuclear weapons in order to stay ahead of the Soviets. The booming American economy funded the nuclear program, with many fundamental physicists participating in its development. The program benefitted from the services of the theoretical physics community, led so effectively by Robert Oppenheimer in Berkeley before he joined the Manhattan Project.

Britain was almost bankrupt after the end of the war. But Attlee's government was determined to have its own atomic bomb despite the appalling state of their finances and the virtual absence of assistance from the Americans. The three people who did most to deliver the weapon were William Penney, Christopher Hinton, and John Cockcroft, the "Atomic Knights," as they would become known in Whitehall. John Cockcroft was one of very few scientists who made the transition from working in fundamental physics to applied weapons work. He was a trained engineer as well as a brilliant physicist. He had the background, training, and personality traits required to navigate his way around the extremely difficult postwar political terrain. In 1946, he helped lead the establishment of the Atomic Energy Research Establishment (AERE) at Harwell in Britain. He served as the head of AERE and became one of Britain's nuclear leaders. For much of that time, because of the McMahon Act,[13] America did not assist Britain in the development of its nuclear program—a policy deeply frustrating and hurtful to the British government and to the British scientists who had helped to get the Manhattan Project off the ground.

The state of fundamental physics in Britain declined significantly and after the war it languished, especially in the eyes of those who had seen it in its prewar heyday. This is apparent, for example, when Britain's leading young theoretical physicist, Freeman Dyson, decamped to the United States where he became a United States citizen in 1957. Dirac left Britain to live in the United States after retiring from Cambridge University in 1969.

The British government seemed to have lost much of its faith in research into sub-nuclear physics. And it appeared that Britain was unlikely ever again to be home of the very best research into experimental work into the fundamental nature of matter. By the end of the 1930s, America had largely taken the lead in this kind of research. To participate in the field, the British scientists were compelled to become research collaborators at places such as

CERN, and many of the physicists became active in international organizations such as Pugwash.[14]

Imagine what Rutherford would have thought, had he seen what happened to his beloved fundamental physics just 20 years after his death. He would have seen its transformation from a subject with apparently no practical applications into a field employing thousands of people all over the world in applied research, development, and production. He would find a world in physics slowly became the source for nuclear power, and then very rapidly became the source of devastating armament. The fundamental physicists had lost their innocence and purity, and had been forced to get into the world of public engagement.

The government papers in the United Kingdom and the United States reveal that the discussions of the biggest issues of nuclear warfare have been poor. The way in which information about the epidemiology or civil engineering associated with a nuclear blast, for example, was used indicates a very limited amount of rational discourse between experts and government officials. It appears as if government officials handled expert advice on nuclear matters in a desultory way. During election campaigns these matters were rarely discussed publicly in ways that do our democracy credit. The superficiality of these debates, offered without many of the subtleties offered by scientific and technical experts, is especially worrisome. Even today it seems to me that there is much too little public debate on nuclear weapons, yet the threat of the huge arsenals remains. The world will, I believe, be fortunate if another fifty years pass without these bombs being used.

The dark consequences of the large-scale transformation from fundamental to applied physics remain with us today. When you read the press, look at the mass media, and examine the websites, society's overwhelming concern now appears to be global warming. You also see concern about infectious diseases and terrorism, all legitimate points. But it is the nuclear weapons, still poised for use, pretty much around the Cold War capacity, that could completely end human civilization. That, I submit, is the unromantic technological legacy of Rutherford's romantic pursuit of science.

Notes

1   See David Reynolds, "Science, Technology, and the Cold War," in *The Cambridge History of the Cold War, Volume 3: Endings*, M. Leffler and O. A. Westad (eds) (New York: Cambridge University Press, 2010c).

2   Vannevar Bush, Science, *The Endless Frontier: A Report to the President on a Program for Postwar Scientific Research* (Washington, DC: US Government Printing Office, 1945).

3 Vannevar Bush, *Modern Arms and Free Men: A Discussion of the Role of Science in Preserving Democracy* (New York: Simon & Schuster, 1949).

4 T. E. Mason et al., "The early development of neutron scattering: science in the wings of the Manhattan Project," *Acta Crystallogr A.* January 1, 2013; 69 (Pt. 1): 37–44.

5 Harold Brown, *Thinking About National Security: Defense and Foreign Policy in a Dangerous World* (Boulder: Westview Press, 1983).

6 Thomas Mahnken, *Technology and the American Way of War Since 1945* (New York: Columbia University Press, 2008), chapter 4.

7 William Perry, "Testimony to the US Senate Armed Services Committee," *Hearing on Department of Defense Appropriations for FY1977, Part 8: Research and Development* (February 28, March 7, 9, 14, 16, and 21, 1978), 5598.

8 As quoted in Mahnken, *Technology and the American Way of War*, 130.

9 Bernard Brodie, ed., *The Absolute Weapon: Atomic Power and World Order* (New York: Harcourt, Brace and Company, 1946).

10 Most of the documents concerned with the UK government's handling of this matter are in the UK National Archives at Kew, notably in CAB 123/147 and PREM 3/139/7.

11 See Graham Farmelo, *The Strangest Man: The Hidden Life of Paul Dirac, Mystic of the Atom* (New York: Basic Books, 2009).

12 See Gregg Herken, *Brotherhood of the Bomb: The Tangled Lives and Loyalties of Robert Oppenheimer, Ernest Lawrence, and Edward Teller* (New York: Henry Holt, 2002).

13 The McMahon Act of 1946 established the Atomic Energy Commission to direct civilian as well as military use for nuclear power. The law, however, soon fell prey to Cold War priorities and the American nuclear programs predominantly focused on weapons research, development, and production.

14 CERN is the high-energy physics research laboratory for the European Organization for Nuclear Research located in Switzerland. The Pugwash Conferences are international meetings of scientists to assess the dangers of weapons of mass destruction.

CHAPTER SIX

Coming in from the cold: Intelligence in the Cold War

Intelligence played a significant part in the conduct and resolution of the Cold War. Christopher Andrew offers an overview of the gaps in Cold War intelligence research and identifies areas that need to be addressed if we are better to appreciate the contribution of espionage to foreign relations and security policy-making. With an emphasis on the British standpoint, Gordon Barrass examines the nature of Cold War intelligence operations focusing on the critical nature of analysis. Mark Kramer surveys the subject from the standpoint of the Soviet bloc and describes the critical importance of recent access to the intelligence archives of former Warsaw-Pact countries. From personal experience and reflection, Rear Admiral Roger LaneNott discusses the critical role of submarines in Cold War intelligence operations. Finally, Air Marshal Chris Nickols, Chief of Defense Intelligence in the United Kingdom, compares intelligence capabilities then and now. He raises disturbing questions about the capability of effectively gathering and analyzing intelligence in the post-Cold War world of international terrorism.

Intelligence and the Cold War in context

Christopher Andrew

At the beginning of the Cold War, Cambridge University had a rather cosmopolitan record of intelligence recruitment. The KGB considered its five leading Cambridge graduates, recruited in the mid-1930s and still in place after World War II, the ablest group of foreign agents it ever recruited.[1] Many of its foreign intelligence officers also enjoyed Hollywood westerns;

among them the box office hit *The Magnificent Seven*. Within the KGB the Cambridge spies were sometimes known as "The Magnificent Five." The careers of similar bright young graduates of US universities recruited by Soviet intelligence have been less intensively studied.

We now know far more about the role of intelligence during the Cold War than we did when the Cold War ended.[2] Much more research, however, is needed. Three major areas for further investigation immediately come to mind. The first is signals intelligence (SIGINT). It is unimaginable that any historian would nowadays write a book on World War II that failed to mention SIGINT. By contrast, most books about the Cold War ignore SIGINT altogether. Signals intelligence is, of course, an extremely difficult area of research, though the US National Security Agency (NSA) website[3] indicates a number of research opportunities.

At the center of the transatlantic special relationship rests a UK/USA signals intelligence alliance, for which there is no peacetime precedent in the history of international relations. Yet the alliance curiously passes unmentioned even in most histories of British-American relations. The recent declassification of the 1946 agreement is likely to ensure that it is omitted no longer.

The first great Cold War successes of the UK/USA signals intelligence alliance were the VENONA decrypts of Soviet intelligence cables. The declassification of these decrypts in 1996 has transformed our understanding of Soviet intelligence penetration of the United States. Thanks in part to the extensive assistance given to Soviet codebreakers by KGB penetration of embassies in Moscow and foreign ministries abroad (of which the material exfiltrated by Mitrokhin from KGB archives provides numerous examples), Soviet SIGINT had a series of Cold War successes. Because of the penetration of their cipher systems, at several stages during the Cold War, France and Italy were among a number of powers unwittingly conducting something akin to open diplomacy with the Soviet Union.

A second priority area for research is covert action (operations to influence the course of events by methods ranging from planting stories in the media to paramilitary operations). Just as the history of intelligence collection in the Cold War has been distorted by the neglect of SIGINT, so the history of covert action has been distorted by over-concentration on the US experience. No history of American Cold War policy in the Third World, for example, omits the role of the Central Intelligence Agency (CIA). By contrast, covert action by the KGB passes almost unmentioned in most histories of both Soviet foreign relations and developing countries. The result has been a curiously lopsided account of the secret Cold War in the Third World—the intelligence equivalent of the sound of one-hand clapping. The admirable history of the Cold War by John Gaddis, for example, refers to CIA operations in Chile, Cuba, and Iran, but makes no reference to the even more extensive KGB covert action in the same countries (amply documented in the Mitrokhin material from KGB archives).[4]

A third important area needing further research is the use (and non-use) of intelligence by policy-makers—a topic often conspicuously absent from political biographies. Winston Churchill, whose passion for intelligence is now well known, is a rare exception to this rule. It is usually forgotten, however, that as wartime prime minister Churchill had much less direct contact with MI5 than his postwar Labour successor, Clement Attlee. At Attlee's request, he had more personal meetings with the director general of MI5 than any other twentieth-century prime minister. Little research has so far been done on the early Cold War fear amongst Labour Party leaders that communists had penetrated their organization. In 1961, Hugh Gaitskell, Attlee's successor as leader of the Labour Party, George Brown, the deputy leader, and Patrick GordonWalker, later Labour foreign secretary, took the decision to give MI5 lists of sixteen Labour MPs who they believed were secret communists and of nine other possible communists on Labour benches. MI5 politely refused to discuss these lists with the Labour leadership on the grounds that to do so would break the prohibition against its involvement in party politics.

Though there are still many gaps in our knowledge of the use made of intelligence by British and American policy-makers, there are even greater gaps in our knowledge of its use by policy-makers in most other states. The task of assessing the influence of intelligence on, for example, German chancellors and French presidents has barely begun. Assessing that influence consists of far more than evaluating their response to individual items of intelligence. Historians of the Cold War have also to consider the broader question of how far intelligence raised or lowered the level of policy-makers' threat perception. President Eisenhower once said that intelligence on what the Soviets did *not* have was often as important to him as information on what they did. Of how many other Western policy-makers was that true?

The more we learn about the role of intelligence during the Cold War, the more it becomes apparent how much we still do not know. It is significant perhaps that the best-known intelligence officer of the Cold War remains a fictional character, James Bond, rather than an actual intelligence practitioner. Among the most enduring legacies of the intelligence Cold War are the fictional images which it generated, vividly illustrated when Bond accompanied the Queen to the opening of the 2012 London Olympics.

A Western perspective on intelligence during the Cold War

Gordon Barrass

When World War II came to an end, it really was quite remarkable how little we in the West knew about the Soviet Union. The first thing we learned was just how much they knew about us. Through various spies who were being exposed in the mid- to late 1940s, it became clear that the Russians had been spying in America on a massive scale from the moment that the Americans became their allies in World War II. As it turns out, we now know they had started espionage operations in the United States long before that. In the case of Britain, they had gotten some of their most valuable intelligence on nuclear matters from members of the Cambridge Five, and a lot more valuable information thereafter.

So we start the Cold War period with the West knowing remarkably little about the Soviet Union, and the Soviet Union determined that we should not know much about it. Trying to find Russians or East Europeans who were willing to provide information to the West was an immensely difficult task. The Russians were masters of intelligence and counter-intelligence; they operated on a scale that was just beyond our comprehension. So really we made little headway in the early period except through an ability to intercept various communications, but not break their major current codes. The Americans decided that if it was going to be so difficult to recruit good agents, they should invest heavily in what they called intelligence technology.

The U-2 overflights of the Soviet Union provided convincing evidence that there was no bomber gap in Moscow's advantage and they began to indicate there was no missile gap either.[5] But it was the American ability to develop satellites that not only could look down and see what was going on the ground, but later could also begin to intercept communications from space. Over the years the Americans, working with the British, really did manage to put together a comprehensive picture of the things that worried them most, which was the Soviet military forces and their capabilities.

It is fair to say that by the 1970s, the White House knew as much about Soviet missiles as the Soviet Politburo. It can also be said that the Americans may, in some cases, have known about just as much as did the Soviet Ministry of Defense itself. This was very important information for them. What they were able to do bit-by-bit, piecing fragments of information together, looking at photographs, linking with things they were listening to, was to put together this overall picture. So the West knew about Soviet capabilities, but the big unresolved question, the one that everyone wanted the answer to, was what were their intentions? And that was a particularly hard issue to address.

Fortunately, during the Cold War, the West did succeed in recruiting a number of first-rate agents, not only from the Soviet Union, but also from Eastern Europe. I would like to mention one or two of them to give a flavor of their contribution.

The first was a Soviet military intelligence colonel, Petyr Semyonovich Popov, who was recruited by the Americans in Vienna around 1955. His great value was that he was able to pass on information about Soviet military activities in Eastern Europe. The number of NATO troops was minimal in Europe at that time, and they feared a Soviet offensive. Thanks to Popov and the ability of western intelligence agencies to monitor Soviet communications, it was possible for the West to have a certain degree of assurance that nothing was going to happen in the near future.

Then later on, an extraordinary man, Colonel Oleg Penkovsky, offered his services to the British and the Americans. This was in 1961, and he was able to provide highly convincing documentary material about the Soviet rocket forces that so concerned the West. This material allowed us to determine that the Soviet's had fewer missiles than had been thought. This intelligence really helped Kennedy face down Khrushchev during the Cuban Crisis. The detailed manuals that Penkovsky had produced about Soviet missiles enabled the Americans accurately to assess the length of time necessary to prepare the weapons for launching. This enabled them to understand that there was still time to negotiate a way out of the crisis. Penkovsky's material was an extraordinary contribution to Western policy.

For nearly a decade beginning in 1972, the Americans received top-secret documents from Polish colonel Ryszard Kuklinski, who worked with the Soviet general staff on Warsaw Pact war plans. Kuklinski passed on to the CIA documents containing the Warsaw Pact plans for conducting military operations in Central Europe in the event of a war with NATO. The Russians had always been terrified that if a conflict started in Central Europe, it quickly would escalate into a nuclear conflict. Their tactics and strategy shifted in the 70s. Still determined to avoid war if possible, the Russians decided it was best to develop the capacity to overwhelm NATO forces so fast that the conflict did not have the time to go nuclear. NATO learned, thanks to the documents provided by Kuklinski, that the Warsaw bloc would open their offensive with a massive attack of 2,000 aircraft, followed by a force of two million men on a front extending from Norway down to Turkey.

During the Reagan administration, the Americans and NATO countered this strategy by investing heavily in new conventional weapons and with a buildup of conventional forces. Strategies were developed by NATO, which basically checkmated the Russians in Europe. President Reagan made it clear that the Americans would spend whatever was necessary to prevail in a conventional arms race. All of this led Mikhail Gorbachev and his military colleagues to realize, not only that they could not win an arms race, but also that it increasingly was futile for them to try. That is when the Russians began to show serious interest in arms limitation control negotiations—first on missiles, then on conventional forces—which eventually were successful and so important to ending the Cold War.

The other person whose intelligence played an important part in ending the Cold War by providing intelligence to Western officials was KGB Colonel Oleg Gordievsky. In 1974 Gordievsky began working for the British Secret Intelligence Service (MI6) as a penetration agent inside the KGB. During his decade of work for MI6 Gordievsky was an extraordinary source of information, which proved of great assistance to British Prime Minister Margaret Thatcher. Due to Gordievsky, Thatcher had an understanding of Soviet insecurity and paranoia long before anyone else.

Gordievsky's knowledge about the thinking of Soviet leaders enabled Thatcher to adjust her diplomatic strategy and tactics with several Soviet leaders, especially with Gorbachev. For example, he was the source of extensive information given to Thatcher as she was preparing to go to Moscow to attend the funeral of General Secretary Yuri Andropov in February 1983. In Moscow she met Andropov's successor, Konstantin Chernenko. Thatcher repeatedly emphasized the need for peace in her conversations with the new Soviet leader. The Soviets were astounded by this turn of events. They did not expect the famous Iron Lady, renowned as a Cold Warrior of the first order, quite suddenly to speak so incessantly about peace and improving relations with the Soviet Union. Thatcher, nonetheless, managed to get through to the Russians. For their part, the Russians began to think differently about the way in which it might be possible to come to some accommodation with the West.

Gordievsky also played a highly constructive role during the subsequent meetings in London between Prime Minister Thatcher and Mikhail Gorbachev shortly before he became the leader of the Soviet Union. Gordievsky in his memoirs mentions that he had assistance from some of his "friends" in MI6 in preparing the briefings he delivered to Gorbachev in advance of the Soviet leader's first visit to London. These friends from MI6 helped Gordievsky craft a fine portrait of Mrs. Thatcher that was appealing to Mr. Gorbachev.[6] At the same time, Gordievsky provided the British with details of Gorbachev's approach to these preliminary meetings. This greatly facilitated the talks between the two leaders, and that was a very good use of intelligence by a policy-maker. Above all, Gordievsky showed Thatcher and others that the Soviet leadership was increasingly nervous about what they saw as a rising threat of aggressive action against them.[7] When this concern was brought to the attention of President Reagan, he came better to understand the Russians. Eventually Reagan embraced a more positive approach to the Soviets and increased his efforts to bring the Cold War to an end.

The French also had a very valuable agent known as "Farewell," whose real name was Vladimir Vetrov. Colonel Vetrov produced a huge amount of intelligence showing how the KGB and the GRU were plundering the West of scientific secrets of one sort or another. He also showed how weak the Soviets were in many critical areas of technology. This was something that the Americans exploited mercilessly, including in shaping President Reagan's approach to the Strategic Defense Initiative (SDI) known as "Star Wars."

Soviet-bloc intelligence had a significant impact on the Cold War and not all of the effects were bad for the West. The vast East German intelligence penetration of the West German government, for example, sometimes led the communists to make some sound judgments about their adversary. And this proved to be mutually beneficial. The East German Communists hated the West German Social Democratic Party (SDP), led by Willy Brandt. Their intelligence penetration of the SDP, however, allowed the East Germans eventually to appreciate how thinking within the SDP was evolving. That is to say, despite the fact that the SDP was an anathema to the Communists, the East Germans began to realize that there was a willingness on the part of West German Chancellor Brandt to open negotiations with them and to try to resolve standing issues between them.

The intelligence the East Germans gathered played an important part in facilitating the negotiation of the Moscow Treaty of 1970 and the treaties that were linked to it. The risks associated with how much the East Germans knew were always greatest on the military side, because they knew so much about NATO. This depth of knowledge helped calm tensions, but if a war had taken place it could have had catastrophic consequences for NATO.

Starting in the early 70s the Russians became deeply concerned about the increasing accuracy and effectiveness of American conventional weapons. They were especially anxious about the development of what came to be known as "assault breaker" weapons, which were under development for use by aircraft against Soviet-bloc armored forces. The Russians feared that such weapons could efficiently and quickly destroy their tanks with bombs that released hundreds of mini-bombs. They recognized that this technology, if perfected, could really transform the nature of conventional war in Europe. They understood that, in the event of war in Central Europe, this technology could checkmate their plans to overwhelm NATO with a massive assault of conventional forces. That is why the Russians put so much of their intelligence resources into finding out about US efforts to develop these particular weapons.

It seems that as early as 1975 Soviet intelligence obtained a film about the new weapons under development. This film caused the Soviets to become very concerned. The Soviets did not realize, however, that the film had been very carefully edited; it was intended to promote the sale of the weapons to the American armed forces. So, for example, the film showed an aircraft soaring over a battlefield releasing a single bomb, which then deployed hundreds of mini-bombs. These hit hundreds of tanks that exploded into flames. What the Soviets did not understand was that exercise was staged. In reality, the tanks were sitting on the bottom of a canyon and were not moving. Wires holding the bombs were strung across the top of the canyon right above the stationary tanks. The bombs were hand-made and cost a fortune, but the filmed demonstration gave the appearance of authenticity in its staged effects.

This could be taken as yet another example of what people at the time called "the Russians getting it wrong." The Russians, however, had another way of looking at these situations. Their approach was that if a perceived threat arose, such as the development of the new assault breaker weapons, it was better to overestimate rather than to underestimate it. In that way they would proceed to develop counter-measures for threats in a timely fashion. Thus, although in a sense they got it wrong, they also got it right. Because later, one could see from the way the Russians were changing their military maneuvers that they were less vulnerable to these weapons.

I once heard an American admiral say that he thought it was terrible that they had lost their naval codes to the Russians. But, of course, one of the things that the Russians learned from this intelligence was how good American and British submarines were in targeting them. Therefore, when you look at the longer-term history of the Soviet Navy during the Cold War, one can understand why the Russians decided to deploy their submarines that carried ballistic missiles in bastions—in the Barents Sea in the west and the Sea of Okhotsk in the east. They were nervous about what Western submarines could do to them. Nevertheless, that was a small silver lining in the clouds created by the successful penetration of NATO's naval codes by Soviet intelligence.

This gives some of the flavor of the importance of intelligence during the Cold War. The task of judging what the Russians were doing was made particularly difficult because the West was not only concerned with their capabilities—which were not too difficult to establish. It was concerned as well with their intentions, and that was always hard to judge. Judging their intentions proved especially important because, as we now know, the Russians were extremely scared of nuclear war. But that is the last thing they wanted us to know. What they did constantly was to act amazingly tough and firm about their determination to fight and win a nuclear war. They sought endlessly to convince us that their war fighting capacities were greater than those of the West. This made it very hard for analysts to judge what was going on with the Russians. It made those agents we developed inside their system extremely valuable. The very good agents we had helped us understand Soviet and East European thinking.

The Soviet-bloc perspective on intelligence during the Cold War

Mark Kramer

I will provide a brief overview of Soviet and Warsaw Pact foreign intelligence as a dimension of the Cold War. In the mid-1980s, Christopher Andrew and David Dilks described foreign intelligence as "the missing dimension" of historical scholarship.[8] They were correct in observing that intelligence has rarely played much of a role in studies of the Cold War.

The good thing is there is now a lot more information about intelligence available for both East and West. I will go through some of the activities and different forms of intelligence gathering in the Soviet bloc, and then briefly discuss intelligence as it was conducted by the Warsaw Pact countries. I will then focus on the relationship between intelligence and policy-making as it affected the Cold War. For even in those instances when intelligence did not necessarily affect policy-making directly, it may have had a broader impact on the Cold War.

Beyond what was captured by Western governments, very little information was available about Soviet-bloc foreign intelligence until around 1990. Occasionally there were important defectors who brought out material. Oleg Gordievsky was the most notable Soviet defector prior to the end of the Cold War, and several other intelligence officials defected from Bulgaria, Czechoslovakia, East Germany, Poland, and Romania. Still, even with defectors, there was by and large very little information about Eastern-bloc foreign intelligence operations available before the end of the Cold War.

In the post-Cold War period, especially after the collapse of the Soviet Union, an immense amount of information has become available. Most of the countries in Eastern Europe now have made their foreign intelligence archives accessible to a significant degree. In addition to their own files, the KGB archives of the former Baltic states of the Soviet Union (Estonia, Latvia, Lithuania) contain copies of some documents relating to the activities of the central Soviet intelligence services—documents that are still classified in Moscow. Although the Soviet foreign intelligence documents stored in the Baltic archives tend to be limited in range, they remain extremely useful.

On the other end of the spectrum, the Russian Foreign Intelligence Service (SVR) archive, which houses the voluminous files of the Soviet KGB foreign intelligence services, is wholly inaccessible. Nonetheless, some important materials from the SVR archive have become available despite the archive's efforts to keep everything sealed. Vasili Mitrokhin, who served as a foreign intelligence archivist, brought out a large cache of transcribed documents right after the Soviet Union collapsed.[9] Christopher Andrew has published two extremely valuable books based on the Mitrokhin materials.[10] In addition to the items excerpted in the books, Mitrokhin provided some very useful documents to the Cold War International History Project (CWIHP) shortly before he died, and these are now posted on the CWIHP website. Although all these items together constitute only a relatively small fraction of what Mitrokhin brought out of Russia (the full collection of Russian transcripts is in the possession of Britain's Secret Intelligence Service, which has declined to release them), they are extraordinarily useful.

More recently, Alexander Vassiliev spirited his notebooks out of Moscow. Vassiliev, a former KGB intelligence officer who was given access to materials in the mid-1990s regarding Soviet espionage in the United States during the Stalin era, brought out transcriptions in eleven notebooks. These are all available now in both the original Russian and full translation. These pertain to notorious spies like Alger Hiss, Julius Rosenberg, Lauchlin Currie, Lawrence Duggan, and others who were mentioned in the Venona papers (decrypted Soviet foreign intelligence communications that were intercepted by US intelligence agencies) as well as to some who were not mentioned in Venona (e.g., Engelbert Broda, Russell McNutt).

Ryszard Kukliński, who served as a colonel on the Polish general staff, provided a trove of crucial Warsaw Pact documents to the CIA. Colonel Kukliński was the chief aide to General Wojciech Jaruzelski during the Solidarity crisis of 1980–1 and had been working for the CIA for nearly a decade before that. He had to flee in November 1981, some five weeks before martial law was imposed in Poland, but until that time he provided more than 45,000 pages of documents of great value to the West.[11] Other crucial sources are the foreign intelligence documents that have been captured in various countries, especially in the Middle East, and the memoirs of various spies and spymasters from former Soviet-bloc countries. The memoirs have to be used with great caution because many of them are unreliable and hyperbolic. However, if used with due circumspection, they can reveal important information and convey the mentality and perspective of Soviet-bloc intelligence officers.

The Soviet bloc's foreign intelligence efforts were coordinated by the KGB through various channels, both bilateral and multilateral. The East European agencies often had separate roles or designations and were given some leeway, but they invariably performed in strict coordination with the KGB. This was also true, to varying degrees, of intelligence services in other communist countries such as Mongolia and Cuba.

The Soviet-bloc state security organizations included both internal security and foreign intelligence. By far the largest share of their resources and personnel (roughly 85 percent) was allocated to internal security. But these organizations were huge compared to their Western counterparts, and even though only a relatively small proportion of what they did pertained to foreign intelligence, it still represented a very large foreign intelligence apparatus. That is why the Eastern-bloc agencies were very aggressive in their foreign intelligence operations. Increasing centralization of Soviet-bloc intelligence gathering and covert operations took place in the 70s and 80s. This is well documented in some of the documents brought out by Kukliński, but it is now even clearer in many documents available in the East European countries, especially those found in the Czech foreign intelligence archive. Vast quantities of Czechoslovak foreign intelligence documents from the Communist era have been posted in an online archive over the past decade, with a very good search engine.[12] Under legislation adopted in 2004, other Communist-era intelligence documents are accessible at both the Czech foreign intelligence archive (*Archiv Úřadu pro zahraniční styky a informace*, or AÚZSI) and the Czech security services archive (*Archiv bezpečnostních složek*, or ABS). Along with the former KGB archives in the Baltic countries and the former Stasi (state security) archive in Germany, the Czech ABS is the most open of the former Soviet-bloc intelligence archives.

Cooperation and allocation of Warsaw Pact intelligence assignments were usually spelled out in bilateral and multilateral agreements signed with the Soviet Union. Efforts have been under way in the East European countries over the past several years to collect and make available the agreements that were signed, and these can now be viewed by scholars. The documents include many common features stipulated by the KGB, but they also contain some specific allocations of assignments. The only exception was in the case of Romania, where the foreign intelligence service ended most of its cooperation with the Soviet Union after the mid-1960s.

The impact of Soviet and East European foreign intelligence gathering on policy-making at times is difficult to determine. This is true even in Western countries, where knowledge of information about how policy is made is much better known and far more widely available. In the former Soviet-bloc countries, little was known about the role of intelligence in the policy-making process until quite recently. Even now, especially with regard to the Soviet Politburo, information about decision-making is still not as readily available as we would like. Although the decision-making process is still murky in many respects, one thing that can be said is that the role of intelligence in the process varied depending on the circumstances and individual leaders in question. One can certainly see instances in which foreign intelligence had no impact on policy-making. For example, in the lead up to the German attack on the Soviet Union in June 1941, the Soviet dictator Josef Stalin received excellent intelligence from numerous sources about the impending German onslaught. Yet he took no measures to prepare for the invasion. On the contrary, he regarded the intelligence as essentially disinformation that was deliberately trying to provoke some Soviet action. So, he disregarded it, even though it was the best intelligence one could possibly hope for.

In other instances, however, foreign intelligence operations clearly made a big difference. The aggressive espionage that the Stalin-era foreign intelligence service undertook to penetrate the US nuclear weapons program during World War II certainly did help the Soviet Union's own subsequent program. To be sure, the Soviet Union would have built a bomb even without that foreign espionage, but the information provided by Soviet spies accelerated the USSR's postwar nuclear bomb program, perhaps as much as a couple of years. So again, there are cases in which one can clearly point to an impact on policy-making, but it varies from case to case. It would be equally incorrect to say either that foreign intelligence *always* had a large impact or that it *never* had much of an impact.

The East German case is an interesting one because the East German intelligence service (Stasi) extensively penetrated the West German government, gaining access not only to West German secrets but also to sensitive NATO information. Even a cursory review of documents stored in the former Stasi archive, which is now headed by a German federal commissioner who oversees the Stasi files, makes this abundantly clear. The senior and mid-ranking West German officials who from time to time surface as having worked for East German intelligence were important, but in some ways the East Germans learned even more from secretaries and janitors. These custodial and clerical employees were usually less conspicuous and were able to make off with far more valuable documents. It is quite astounding to work in the Stasi archive now and see what secretaries were able to turn over to the East Germans, such as top-secret military plans and the personal notebooks of officials. One can also get a very good sense of other Eastern-bloc foreign intelligence services from the Stasi archive. For example, materials in the East German archives reveal the depressing fact that every agent the CIA had in Cuba during the Cold War was a double agent.

Through espionage against West Germany, the Stasi gained a formidable capacity to penetrate NATO headquarters during the Cold War. East German officials and diplomats enjoyed ready access through West Germany to Western intelligence and NATO offices. Ironically, in some ways this penetration proved helpful to the West because the East Germans learned about the nature of NATO's military planning and could see that, contrary to Soviet fears and Eastern-bloc propaganda, NATO was not planning to launch an attack. On the contrary, NATO was truly a defensive alliance.

In other instances though, Eastern-bloc foreign intelligence clearly was harmful by allowing Warsaw Pact countries to take easier counter-measures against possible Western action. So-called foreign intelligence "games," which actually involved life-or-death stakes, were a standard feature of the Cold War. These dangerous competitions brought out shows of bravado on the part of the Eastern-bloc and Western foreign intelligence services. Many of these pitted the Soviet and US intelligence services against each other, but some of the smaller Warsaw Pact agencies also got involved.

Extensive directorates were set up in each of the Soviet-bloc foreign intelligence services to analyze intelligence. Timely analysis of intelligence was an enormous part of their work. Gathering intelligence is one thing, but making good use of it for policy-making is quite another. Although our lack of access to the SVR archives prevents any definitive judgments, the large number of documents available in other repositories indicates that Soviet-bloc foreign intelligence services were often highly capable in their analysis but at times were stymied by policy-makers from above.

East European covert operations were given the designations of "special tasks" and "active measures" (or the slang "wet affairs"). Both the Soviet Union and most of the East European countries were involved in arming and training Middle Eastern and Latin American terrorists. The state security archives of these countries contain vast quantities of documents that reveal this support in exquisite detail. The Soviet-bloc intelligence services also conducted sabotage and jamming operations against the different Western radio stations such as Radio Free Europe and the BBC. This included bombings as well as efforts to plant spies inside the organizations. Soviet-bloc covert warfare against Western shortwave broadcasters continued until the late 1980s.

The Soviet Union, the East European countries, Cuba, and Vietnam were voracious consumers of open sources in the West. The Soviet embassy in Washington, DC is an excellent example. The US Defense Department in the 1980s produced a publication called *Soviet Military Power*. The Soviet embassy would order up to 100 copies of this publication even though the information by and large was readily available elsewhere. They just wanted to see what was being made available.

Even though the Soviet and East European intelligence services avidly gathered open sources, they often were very skeptical of the information they contained. Their suspicions resulted in some duplication of intelligence-gathering efforts because they relied on espionage to produce information that was already fully available had they not distrusted the open sources.

It is difficult to make any set judgments about how intelligence from either open or covert sources affected Soviet policy-makers. In some cases it is impossible to know the impact of intelligence. There are, however, some specific instances in which it can be traced. Take, for example, the case of the development of new Soviet ICBMs and the US strategic defense system. In this instance, intelligence gathered about what would be feasible, what sorts of countermeasures could be taken, and so forth often had very little impact on the way strategic forces were configured. Deployments of new Soviet missiles were shaped more by the interaction between the Soviet defense industry and commanders of the strategic missile forces under the supervision of the Soviet general staff. Detailed foreign intelligence might tell military commanders one thing, but the information did not have much effect on actual policy because the commanders already knew what they wanted to do.

As I have already mentioned, the impact of foreign intelligence activities on East European and Soviet policy-making, especially with regard to NATO tactics and strategy, was of great importance. I mentioned both negative effects and more favorable effects. The favorable effects include the extent to which sound intelligence allayed concerns about any impending war and let policy-makers know that NATO was not about to undertake a surprise attack.

Finally, there is the question of the overall impact of intelligence on the Cold War. What we find applies to the US side just as much as it applies to Soviet and Warsaw Pact intentions. The Soviet Union had various means of detecting imminent attack and readiness for war. Although Soviet technology in most areas consistently lagged behind that of the United States, Soviet military commanders were able to rely on extraordinarily sophisticated means of intelligence gathering, especially for overhead and electronic reconnaissance. These reconnaissance platforms played a crucial role in showing that NATO was not preparing for an imminent attack or ready to go to war.

By the same token, various means of detecting the size and configuration of Soviet military forces were important for the United States in getting a handle on the size and configuration of Soviet Warsaw Pact forces. This was also true for the other side. From a variety of means (electronic intercepts, reconnaissance, human sources) Soviet intelligence agencies learned a great deal about the readiness level and configuration of US strategic nuclear forces and of NATO forces deployed in Europe against the Warsaw Pact. Although technical means were valuable in revealing the complexion of Western forces, human intelligence was the best source of information about NATO's military plans and intentions. Even if the impact of this information on Soviet decision-making was limited, it did at least partly allay the more outlandish of Moscow's concerns.

On the other hand, foreign intelligence operations at times had negative effects on the Cold War. The Soviet Union's extensive espionage and covert operations created suspicions in Western policy-making circles about Soviet intentions. Spying often created tensions in East-West relations. Spy scandals periodically emerged, and different Western countries would expel Soviet spies or vice versa. These tended to blow over relatively quickly, but they engendered some nagging doubts about long-term Soviet intentions.

For example, one can very clearly see the tensions caused when disclosures began to emerge in the United States, particularly in the late 40s and early 50s, about the scale of Soviet espionage in the United States during World War II. Deep tension arose from revelations of Soviet spying in the US nuclear weapons program. Subsequently, distrust arose when US officials learned that Soviet spies had successfully penetrated high levels of the US government. Things became especially tense when US decryption analysts discovered that the Soviet foreign intelligence agencies had agents working in US intelligence and counter-intelligence agencies. As the magnitude of the Soviet espionage networks in the United States gradually became apparent, these revelations colored the Truman administration's perception of Soviet intentions. The emergence of McCarthyism was related to fears engendered by Soviet spying in the United States.

Finally, of course, tensions were sparked by Soviet and East European covert warfare, the so-called "active measures." Periodically, information would come to light about "special tasks," such as the assassination of Georgi Markov in London or of Soviet funding and training of terrorists in different areas of the world. Whenever this happened, Cold War tensions were bound to increase.

Thus, intelligence activities had a dual impact on the Cold War. Disclosures of NATO's defensive stance had a stabilizing impact on the Soviet bloc's role in the Cold War, but revelations of Soviet-bloc espionage and covet operations produced greater tension—tension that persisted throughout the Cold War and even after.

Submarine intelligence and the Cold War

Rear Admiral Roger Lane-Nott

To put my remarks into context I was born a month before the Potsdam Conference. When the Cuban Missile Crisis was resolved in October 1962, I was playing on a highly successful rugby team at school. The following September I joined the Royal Navy at Dartmouth. As it turned out, my naval career was shaped by the series of UK/US agreements in the late 1950s and early 1960s. These agreements eventually made submarine-launched missiles (SLBMs) the key weapons in Britain's nuclear deterrence force.

In 1960 Prime Minister Macmillan and President Eisenhower agreed to base U.S. strategic submarines (SSBNs) at Holy Loch in Scotland. They also established an early warning system for Soviet missiles in North Yorkshire. Then there was the agreement to partner in the Skybolt missile project. This program would have made an air-launched missile known as the Skybolt the key weapon in our deterrent force. The United States decided to cancel the Skybolt Project. Subsequently, over a less than friendly negotiating period in the Bahamas in December 1962, Britain was offered and accepted the Polaris missile.[13] This weapon was designed to launch from a submarine. The Royal Air Force, of course, was furious, which always pleases the Royal Navy. A former Chief of the Air Staff wrote in protest that it was really appalling that a couple of ministers and a zoologist, Sir Solly Zuckermann, had to skip off to the Bahamas without a single member of the Chiefs of Staff Committee, and commit to a military monstrosity on the purely political issue of nuclear independence.

On 15 February 1968, Britain's first Resolution Class submarine successfully fired its first Polaris missile. Thus opened the Royal Navy's critical role in providing our independent nuclear deterrent, as well as our sea-based mission in support of NATO for the remainder of the Cold War. It is worth remembering that the United Kingdom has undertaken continuous at sea deterrence without a break, twenty-four hours a day, seven days a week with four Polaris and four Trident submarines continuously since May 1968. That goes on today, and if you read *The Times* you know that we are seeking in this extremely difficult financial time to procure four Trident replacements in the next few years.

Intelligence, along with communications was the key element to the effective operation of our Polaris submarines. Submariners by nature are aggressive. Early in the Cold War we tended to engage enemy submarines when we found them. Tactics changed, and it took the development of a new breed of submariners to fulfill the deterrent mission. What was now called for were submariners who could be relied upon to move away from the enemy submarine when contact was established, and then to follow the Russian ship without being detected. The essential elements of Polaris and Trident II submarines are to remain undetected, to remain in constant communication, and to maintain immediate readiness to fire. But to do that, you need good and timely intelligence; you need to know in advance where these things are likely to happen.

That is where the nuclear-powered hunter-killer submarines (SSNs) came in play. Because in addition to doing all of the other things that you would expect a submarine to do, they were chocked up with numerous sensors of different types. They were deployed all around the world to provide the best positive intelligence picture for our nuclear-powered ballistic missile carrying submarines, the SSBNs. They had a role of protecting the SSBNs, but at the same time seeking out opposing Soviet SSBNs and collecting intelligence about them.

It is worth considering the Russian developments in submarines at this point. They produced in 1967 a Yankee Class, which carried sixteen SS-N-6 missiles with a range of about 1,800 kilometers. Then they produced the Charlie Class, which had a SS-N-7 missile system with a range of only thirty-five kilometers. It was targeted specifically at the American carrier groups. The Russian Charlie Class submarines used to sit behind the carrier groups in an attempt to creep up and target them. Some of the incidents that we had trying to keep them away from American carrier groups were fascinating.

The first effective Russian fast-attack submarine (SSN) was the Victor Class. In 1971 they produced an SSBN, the Delta Class. These submarines had twelve SS-N-8 missiles, with a range to 6,700 kilometers. This meant that the Russians no longer had to move out into the Atlantic to be within range of their targets. They could remain in home waters and still be an effective threat. Now the Russian submarines could stay in the Barents Sea. Or, they could go "Up North" and maneuver under ice. The Delta Class submarines had a couple of SSNs riding shotgun for them. That made the whole business of tracking where the Russian SSBNs were going a completely new deal.

As the Cold War progressed, our intelligence confirmed the Russians significantly were improving their submarines. This concerned us deeply. They started to produce a hunter-killer SSN, the Alpha Class after 1971. This submarine could do forty-five knots, which is nearly fifty miles an hour underwater. It could dive deeper than what we had anticipated in the design of all NATO torpedo systems. In the late 1970s, the Russians introduced their Akula Class of SSN. This brought them closer to the capability of the British Trafalgar Class and to the Americans' Los Angeles Class of SSNs. So, all of the new Soviet SSNs and SSBNs were challenges that intelligence had exposed, but did not really resolve for us.

Naval competition between the NATO and Soviet Union Navies was not restricted to the submarine fleets during the Cold War. In 1962, for example, the American aircraft carrier *USS Wasp* sailed into the Baltic. Although the Americans were just going into international waters, the Soviets saw this move as provocative as they considered the Baltic Sea their backyard. It was not long thereafter that the Russians started deploying their fleet in significant numbers in the Mediterranean. By 1967, during the Six-Day War, they had more than sixty units operating in the Mediterranean. It took us a while to work all this out.

In a democracy, of course, it is necessary to release at least a certain amount of information about submarine capability. Not least to convince taxpayers that the money invested in the spectacularly expensive machines is well spent. Admiral Gorshkov, Commander-in-Chief of the Soviet Navy during the massive naval buildup during the Brezhnev era, was under no such obligations.

NATO and its navies nevertheless needed to know the operational capabilities of the Soviet fleet. It was critical that we had the best possible information about them so that due preparation could be made in the event of war. Specifically, with regard to their growing submarine fleet, we needed a wide range of information. We required intelligence as to their operating capability, such as the speed, diving depth, endurance, and sonar capability of their SSNs and SSBNs. And we needed to know the range of their missiles. We had to know the habitual operating patterns of Russian submarines at sea. It was essential to accurately determine their ability to detect our submarines and, even more importantly, how we could detect them.

Such information one might think could be derived from various sources, such as agents on the ground, spy planes, or satellites eavesdropping, and signals intelligence. But few methods of intelligence gathering proved more effective than actually going up and visiting the Russians in their home areas. Since the late 1940s, therefore, the West had dispatched submarines to the main Soviet ports: Vladivostok on the Sea of Japan, Leningrad in the Baltic, and Murmansk in the Barents Sea. These submarines, in addition to performing general intelligence gathering duties, could also register any sudden deployment of Soviet submarine fleets that might signal war.

"Up North" to the Royal Navy Submarine Service meant the Barents Sea. There were various incidents during the Cold War that exemplify the dangers associated with such close patrolling under extremely difficult operating conditions. When the Americans first went up "Up North" in 1949, they had a disaster when the spy submarine *Cochino* caught fire. Another submarine had to come to rescue people from the stricken boat. Prime Minister Churchill personally was involved in the operation order when the British first went "Up North" in 1952. One can imagine how difficult this was to undertake in a diesel submarine. But things improved dramatically over the years, especially when nuclear-powered submarines became available for service. Still, the patrols in diesel boats were a real challenge. Nobody really knew how the Russians would respond when they discovered our submarines operating so close to their territorial waters. As it turned out, when the Russians detected our submarines they used aggressive anti-submarine tactics. In some instances our submarines were involved in accidents and collisions in which Russian ships chopped off bits of hull and towed arrays and so forth.

These patrols were meant to be a challenge for the submarine commanders. A lot of the time you were at periscope depth, often in what we call "black lighting," which meant all the lights were turned off in the control room so that you could see through the periscope. There were dangers created by short periods of daylight, ice flow, and shallow water; all this affected operations.

Many submarine commanders believed it was their job, and forgot about the niceties of international law, to drive straight into Soviet territorial waters all intent on getting the best possible intelligence. If that meant you had to be up stream of a target barge when a Russian missile test was being conducted—so be it. That attitude prevailed right through my time. It was imperative, when on station, to absorb just as much visual, acoustic, electronic, and signals intelligence as possible. On our typical seventy-day patrol, we would return with forty-five large bags of records for analysis. Russian-speaking intelligence experts were on board during the cruise to assist with tactical analysis. This was essential to assure that the vessel was in the right place to ensure that the best intelligence was gathered.

It took the Soviets a long time to realize that we were tracking their submarines with communications intelligence (COMINT) and the sound surveillance system (SOSUS) network. We were very good at using our electronic intelligence and sonar surveillance to follow Russian submarines without their knowing we were doing so. For example, in my submarine I once picked up a Russian submarine as it came out of the Kola Inlet. Then, without being detected or ever losing contact with it, I returned with the Russian submarine to the Kola Inlet eighty-four days later. This surveillance capability forced the Soviets to change their tactics and hold their submarine fleets closer to home bases.

Eventually, of course, the Russians did catch on to what we were doing. I remember watching the BBC's *Panorama* segment on *The Deep Cold War*, and as far as I am concerned, the BBC compromised SOSUS in that program. We had been relying on SOSUS for quite a long time and it shows the relevance of real-time intelligence. The Walker family of spies in the United States gave away a great deal of information over a number of years. In the United Kingdom, we had Harry Houghton, Ethel Gee, and the Portland Spy Group, which gave the Russians our hull-mounted sonar system.[14]

During the Cold War, the Warsaw-bloc intelligence penetration of NATO brought other problems as well. For example, all submarine plans within NATO during my time there, and up until the early 1990s, were promulgated through what were known as "NATO Subnotes." These were notices somewhat like an aircraft's flight plan. In the United Kingdom, and I am sure the United States did the same, we worked on the principle that every NATO Subnote was ending up in Russian hands and therefore we took appropriate action.

Then there was the problem of transmitting the intelligence we gathered and analyzed to our submarines in time for it to be useful during their operations at sea. In 1976, when I was in the fleet headquarters running special submarine operations, we reckoned real time was twenty minutes. That was the time in which you got a piece of intelligence, whether it came from an aircraft or some other form of surveillance, and you were able to turn that around and relay it to our submarines. Remember, we were transmitting on teletypes on very low-frequency radio to submarines at that time. Assuming they were at periscope depth or had a wire out to receive it, twenty minutes was a pretty amazing timescale to get a piece of information that the submarine could use when they were chasing another submarine. Now we consider it grossly appalling if it takes twenty minutes to get intelligence to submarines; today communication is instantaneous. That, of course, puts pressure on the submarine to receive those communications without revealing its position to the enemy—who is always listening.

When it comes to the detection and surveillance of Russian submarines a lot of people think that we going around pinging away like World War II surface ships. We do not; our detection is entirely passive. With the whole business of spectrum analysis and frequency analysis, passive information has moved on in leaps and bounds over the last thirty or forty years. So, any form of communications intelligence is very important—but it has to be communicated securely and quickly. The problem is that we are almost into too much information. You have got to get that information, decide what is relevant, and determine what it means.

At the danger of being patronizing, many people understand submarines and their operations based on the film *The Hunt for Red October* with Sean Connery. There were elements of what went in that film that are vaguely true. The author of the book upon which the film is based, Tom Clancy wrote: "The submariner's trade required more than skill. It required instinct, and an artist's touch; monomaniacal confidence, and aggressiveness of a professional boxer."[15] That is true to a certain extent, and I think that the intelligence that we brought back through aggressive, close-in submarine operations was absolutely vital in a whole variety of ways. More often than not, it provided the final piece in the jigsaw about what you might have heard, or known, or got from other forms of intelligence about a missile system. But, this cannot compare to having actually seen or heard the missile launching—that is the sort of information that cannot be beat.

Cold War intelligence in perspective: Then and now

Air Marshal Chris Nickols

The current Chief of Defense Intelligence is a graduate of the University of Cambridge and he is still on our side. This is perhaps because nobody has yet made him a better offer. That, of course, brings up a very serious point. Who these days would make him a serious offer? Things have changed dramatically since the end of the Cold War in the field of intelligence. I was recently at a joint intelligence committee meeting as I am a member. Now, obviously I cannot tell you what we discussed or what we decided. I can tell you that we did not discuss Russia. And it brings up the point, of course, that nowadays it is not so clear as to who is a friend and who is an enemy. It is not so much black and white as it is that we are looking at a whole area of grays. This illustrates the importance of understanding the difference between then and now in appreciating the Cold War legacy.

There is no point in looking at the Cold War unless we try and learn the lessons that are the most relevant to the present. It is useless unless our examination of history helps today's practitioners in the intelligence community to achieve their goals in a changing world.

My background in the Cold War was relatively short. I served as a tactical reconnaissance pilot in what was then West Germany from 1980 to 1989. This was really what many would call the peak of the Cold War. For those of us in Germany, it was all about training and practice. Unlike submariners, who were actually doing it for real, we could not engage the enemy. We could not fly over East Germany in our tactical aircraft. But that did not make it any less real to us. It actually was very real to those of us who were there. That is something that we need to remember these days. I hope to convey a sense of how real the threat of going to war was to us at the time. I spent my first year in Germany as a pilot in a squadron of Jaguar aircraft. There were twenty pilots assigned to that squadron. In that single year we lost three aircraft in crashes, and in two of those accidents the pilots died. That was because we were constantly training so hard. So it was very real to those of us who served at the time.

I currently serve as the Chief of Defense Intelligence for the United Kingdom. For the vast majority of the analysts on the defense intelligence staff with whom I serve, the Cold War is history. Many were barely even born when the Cold War ended, let alone when we were all in the middle of it. And so this point about learning from history for the current day is very, very relevant to my staff. But we need to remember that they see it as history, not as something that happened to them when they were younger.

I am a great believer in the principle that we need to see threats very much through the lens of capability and intent or capability multiplied by intent. I think doing so focuses on the key lessons that must be learned about threats and potential threats from enemies.

It is now apparent that we knew a great deal about Soviet capability during the Cold War. In fact in some areas, we probably knew more than many of the Russians did. Their capability was relatively easy to measure once satellites and U-2 aircraft were in our armory. It was relatively easy to measure because the capability we were talking about was mass military capability. It was how many tanks and what could those tanks do, how big were their armies and all of that. So that was quite easy.

We also thought we knew a lot about their intent, because that is what the Cold War was all about. And I think, of course, what history is teaching us now is perhaps we did not know quite as much about intent as we thought we did at the time. But certainly where I was serving at the tactical level, if you were in our forces in West Germany or in the Northern Atlantic, we thought we knew what their intent was, that was for sure.

Both capability and intent have become incredibly more difficult to assess in the time period between the end of the Cold War and now. Capability is still in some areas relatively easy to measure. When we are trying to measure the military capability of another country, generally we can do that quite well. But, in the majority of cases, that is not actually the threat with which we are most concerned these days. Now, when we examine the capabilities of the groups that we are the most likely to confront in armed conflict, it is terrorist organizations of various types. We most always find it far more difficult to measure their capability than that of nation states. It is also the case that in many areas of threat, we are looking for intelligence from within closed societies. All of this continues, despite improvements in our intelligence capabilities, to make it quite difficult to accurately assess the capability of those groups, which arguably constitute the greatest danger to our security.

If discerning capability is more difficult in this day and age, then intent sometimes is almost impossible. Yes, we think we know what the intentions are of major international terrorist groups, such as Al Qaeda. But when it comes to the highest levels of these terrorist organizations, we get mixed signals. We tend to receive inconsistent and conflicting intelligence. Getting mixed signals from the senior people in organizations really should not be any surprise to us—whether or not the organizations are official, such as governments, or unofficial such as terrorist groups. Officials in organizations of whatever kind are giving mixed signals to their own people all the time. So it should not surprise us that we are getting conflicting evidence and have to work through that.

I would not go as far as to assert that all of this makes intelligence gathering and analysis more difficult today than it was during the Cold War. I think that would be a rather naive thing to say. But it certainly is no easier. Intelligence analysis remains as difficult despite the fact that technology has moved on enormously in the twenty years since the close of the Cold War. We have hugely improved technology, not only for collection, but also for analysis.

Against that, as I mentioned earlier, many of the most important targets for intelligence collection have become much more difficult to identify and penetrate. Further, the environment in which we collect information about threats is filled with tremendous background noise. It is very challenging to sort through it all. A classic example of that, of course, is in the SIGINT area. Modern technology has allowed communications to such a vast global audience that the amount of information out there is enormous. Sifting through this vast sea of noise and focusing on your target is hugely difficult.

In the current situation there also is the issue of whom you can trust now that the Cold War is at an end. My basic point is that even when you work with some people and trust them, they nevertheless have problems that affect us all. And that would even go at home in the United Kingdom or in the United States. The issue that is on everybody's mind at the moment is terrorism and counter-terrorism. There is virtually no country in this world that could actually look you in the eye and say they do not have an internal terrorist problem. We certainly do in the United Kingdom. So it is not just a matter of whom you trust; it is the fact that the intelligence community may have to be looking over a much wider area than we have traditionally done. That is the issue—global problems require global solutions. We collaborate today with many countries that during the Cold War we would never have imagined working with. This demands us to think about new ways of sharing intelligence and working together.

Finally, there is this question of balance among the various methods of collection. We now are starting to see a different balance in the importance of satellite imagery, SIGINT, and human intelligence, whether it is at the tactical or the strategic level. We still need all of those, but the balance between them and the importance of each shift almost day to day. The important thing to us in the intelligence business these days is the fusion of the intelligence from all of those sources; we strive to get the best picture we can.

Notes

1   The Cambridge spies have been identified as Anthony Blunt, Guy Burgess, John Cairncross, Donald Maclean, and Kim Philby. See Christopher Andrew and Oleg Gordievsky, *KGB: The Inside Story of its Operations from Lenin to Gorbachev* (New York: Harper Collins Publishers, 1990), 216–17.

2   Christopher Andrew, "Intelligence in the Cold War," in *The Cambridge History of the Cold War, Volume II: Crises and Détente*, M. Leffler and O. A. Westad (eds) (New York: Cambridge University Press, 2010b).

3   National Security Agency/Central Security Service, http://www.nsa.gov.

4   See Christopher Andrew and Vasili Mitrokhin, *The World Was Going Our Way: The KGB and the Battle for the Third World* (New York: Basic Books, 2005) and John Lewis Gaddis, *We Now Know: Rethinking Cold War History* (Oxford: Clarendon Press, 1997), chapter 6.

5   Gordon Barrass, *Great Cold War: A Journey Through the Hall of Mirrors* (Stanford: Stanford Security Studies, 2009), 113.

6   Oleg Gordievsky, *Next Stop Execution* (New York: Macmillan, 1995) and Christopher Andrew, *Defend the Realm: The Authorized History of MI5* (New York: Alfred A. Knopf, 2009), chapter 9.

7   Andrew and Gordievsky, *KGB*, 2 and 599–601.

8   Christopher Andrew and David N. Dilks (eds), *The Missing Dimension: Governments and Intelligence Communities in the Twentieth Century* (London: Macmillian, 1984).

9   See Christopher Anrew and Vasili Mitrokin, *The Mitrokhin Archive* (London: Allen Lane-Penguin Press, 1999).

10 Christopher Andrew and Oleg Gordievsky (eds), *Instructions from the Centre: Top Secret Files on KGB Foreign Operations, 1975–1985* (London:

Hodder & Stoughton, 1991), and Christopher Andrew and Oleg Gordievsky (eds), *More Instructions from the Centre: Top Secret Files on KGB Global Operations, 1975–1985* (London: Frank Cass, 1992).

11   Mark Kramer, "Colonel Kuklinski and the Polish Crisis, 1980–81," *Cold War International History Project Bulletin*, Issue No. 11 (Winter 1998), 48–60; and Mark Kramer, *The Kukliński Files and the Polish Crisis of 1980–1981: An Analysis of the Newly Released CIA Documents*, CWIHP Working Paper No. 59 (Washington, DC: Cold War International History Project, March 2009).

12   The archive is located at http://www.abscr.cz/cs/elektronicky-archiv

13   See David Reynolds, *From World War to Cold War: Churchill, Roosevelt, and the International History of the 1940s* (New York: Oxford University Press, 2006), 322.

14   See Andrew and Gordievsky, *KGB*, 442–44.

15   *The Hunt for Red October* (New York: Berkley Books, 1985), 81–82.

CHAPTER SEVEN

Ending the Cold War: Uncertainties and breakthroughs in Europe

The fall of the Berlin Wall and its aftermath had great significance in the final stage of the Cold War. These authors witnessed the momentous events from the Helsinki Final Act to German unification, which culminated in the sudden, and in many ways unanticipated, ending of the Cold War.

PHOTO 7.1 *Piece of the Berlin Wall (Courtesy of Churchill Archives Centre)*

They offer first-hand insights into the dramatic period of transformation in European affairs that precipitated and followed the withdrawal of Soviet military forces from Eastern Europe. Consideration is given to whether or not the destruction of the Wall was inevitable, or if it should more properly be credited to the vision and actions of Ronald Reagan and Mikhail Gorbachev. The progression of certain key episodes before the fall of the Berlin Wall is delineated, as is the significance of the reactions of Mikhail Gorbachev and Western leaders, such as Helmut Kohl, Margaret Thatcher, and George H. W. Bush, to the rapidity with which German reunification followed the collapse of the Wall.[1]

Lord Watson offers a first-hand description of the events in East Germany surrounding the collapse of the Berlin Wall. For Watson the peaceful ending to the division of Germany was virtually miraculous. Hella Pick witnessed most of the crucial activities that contributed to the fall of the Berlin Wall. She focuses on the importance of the Helsinki Final Agreement and key developments in Poland, such as the visit of Pope John Paul II and the Polish Solidarity Movement. Alexander Likhotal analyzes how the force of events in Eastern Europe compelled the Soviet leadership to overcome its fear of Germany and to accept the inevitability of German unification. Sir Christopher Mallaby offers a British diplomat's perspective of the context, meaning, and legacy of the collapse of the Berlin Wall. From the West German viewpoint, Hermann von Richthofen emphasizes the diplomatic maneuvering between Helmut Kohl, the Chancellor of the Federal Republic of Germany (FRG), and Gorbachev that brought about the peaceful unification of Germany.

A broadcaster's perspective on the collapse of the Berlin Wall

Lord Watson of Richmond

The fall of the Berlin Wall which, if it does not mark the actual end of the Cold War, has come to symbolize the end of the Cold War. The rapid unification of Germany that followed now seems quite inevitable. Until the Wall was opened, however, the prospect of a unified Germany in the near future was seen as both unwise and unlikely.[2] In 1985, I attended a British-German Conference at the Königswinter, a small town on the Rhine near Bonn. There was session in the morning, which I remember vividly, in which we were discussing the consequences of what was happening with Solidarity in Poland. During the coffee break, I spoke to a British Member of Parliament and found we were both a bit frustrated by the panel discussion. This was because the group was having a conversation about the nonintervention of

Soviet forces to suppress Solidarity in Poland, but seemed to be ignoring that the logic of nonintervention must eventually lead, in the end, to Berlin. So, after the coffee break, I ventured this suggestion: I said that surely we were looking at things that would happen, if the Soviets did not ultimately change their minds and return to maintaining their order with tanks, that something would change in Berlin. When I said this, I remember vividly that the person from the German delegation looked at me with sheer horror. When we broke for lunch he came up to me and said,

> How could you be so irresponsible? You've opened Pandora's box and everybody is going to look into it! They're going to be very frightened by the prospect of German unity. You've set things back by mentioning this at a Königswinter conference.

I was not in Berlin when the Wall came down. I was sitting in my home in Richmond watching it unfold on television. I was overcome with the most extraordinary sense of frustration, having been so involved in Berlin during my career, and having been interested in German affairs. So it struck me, "Why in the hell wasn't I there?" It was too late to do anything about it that evening. The next morning, as I followed the continuing wall-to-wall coverage of events in Berlin, I resolved to get to Berlin somehow. I rang my old employers in the BBC and tried to persuade them to let me do a program about the collapse of the Wall. I reminded them of my extensive professional experience in Germany and explained that I was absolutely compelled to get to Berlin to tell the story. They responded that my compulsion to cover the story was all very well, but the BBC already had excellent correspondents in Berlin. I was informed that my services were not needed, "Thank you very much and goodbye."

Undeterred, I proceeded to contact Roger Bolton by telephone. Roger was an old friend from BBC days and in charge of Thames Television. "Roger," I said, "I've got to do something about this. I must cover the Berlin Wall story." "Well," he said, "it's no good talking about it. You've got exactly twenty-five minutes before I go into the program meeting here at Thames to do an outline of four programs of one hour each. I'll do my best to get you the budget." I have to say, I was filled with a sense of hopelessness really. But I sat down and wrote out a series of programs by hand, which I called: "The Germans: Who Are They Now?" I faxed the outline to Roger and he rang me back about an hour later. He said, "I don't know how this has happened, but you got the budget."

We proceeded to film for three months, with two camera crews, throughout East and West Germany. We tried to measure what was happening in the wake of the sudden fall of the Berlin Wall. What happened in 1989 and 1990 was somewhat miraculous. There was a touch of Pentecost about it. Somehow there was the touch of an angel's wing above what unfolded. That is because the collapse of the Wall and its immediate aftermath might have produced a great deal of bloodshed, which would have set back progress in Europe. It was not inevitable that it would be a velvet revolution of the kind that it was.

I traveled to Berlin just a few weeks after the collapse of the Wall, which was still largely intact. I remember having a strange sense that what I was seeing was not quite real. I was in Berlin for a conference that was held in a hotel in West Berlin. After the meeting a number of us decided to drive into East Berlin. The West Germans who were with me were quite nervous. They kept on saying to me, "Do you have your passport with you? Do you have your passport with you?" They all had passports. When we got to the border crossing at the Friedrichstrasse checkpoint, the guards just waived us through! But, the guards were still there. We continued on, and I remember driving to Unter den Linden and the boulevard was deserted. There was the enormous Soviet Embassy on one side of the street there, very close to the Berlin Wall. We went into a small wine bar, and it was as if we were in alien territory. It was very strange. The tavern was largely empty. Perhaps all the East Berliners were in West Berlin having a hell of a good time.

There was something of the miraculous about the rapid fall of the Berlin Wall. As we remember this event, it is important to recall that it took occurred at the place in Europe where the intensity of the armed confrontation between East and West was unrivaled. Still, at the point of the opening of the border, it was here that both sides had historically marshaled such destructive force. And instead of catastrophe—history happened. It has been said, "Statesmen must grab the mantle of history." That is what Helmut Kohl and Mikhail Gorbachev succeeded in doing.

We all recognize that the fall of the Wall in Berlin, whether it was technically the end of the Cold War or not, is a moment in history in which everybody participated. We all remember it. We all know where we were and what we were doing at the time it happened.

A journalist's perspective on the collapse of the Berlin Wall

Hella Pick

I closely followed, from beginning to end, the very tortured negotiations that produced the Helsinki Declaration of 1975. What is forgotten is that the Helsinki Declaration actually set a seal of approval on the postwar division of Europe. It recognized the Soviet Union's domination of the Warsaw Pact countries. At the same time, it gave the West the opening for free exchange of information. At the time, very few on the Soviet side realized that they had, in fact, pulled the genie out of the bottle. Because it was from that time onward that the opening toward the Warsaw Pact countries became possible.[3] Dissidents in Eastern Europe found in the Helsinki Declaration a justification for what they were trying to do and it gave them an underpinning for their activities. Thus, although the Soviets thought they had secured permanent recognition of their control of Eastern Europe, instead they helped open the process that led to the fall of the Wall and the dissolution of the Warsaw Pact.[4]

On the day that the Declaration was finalized the small countries involved in the negotiations held up the conclusion by raising some last-minute objections. This had been characteristic throughout the negotiating process. On that day it was Malta. This led to stopping the clock, a diplomatic device used to pretend that everything is finishing on time. The bureau chief for *Time* magazine was absolutely desperate; because he was on deadline with the magazine due to go to press with the Declaration. But the negotiations continued to drag on. Aiming to bring the negotiations to a near instant end, he went to the press desk and put up a large notice saying a bomb had been planted in the building. Two hours later, when the Maltese delegation finally finished, that piece of paper was still lying there. Nobody had taken the slightest notice. That could not happen in this day and age.

The Poles played a key role in the unraveling of the Warsaw Pact. It began when John Paul II was elected the first Polish Pope in 1979. One of his first official acts was to make a nine-day visit to Poland. He traveled across the country. I followed that trip and it was just the most extraordinary event. I have never seen such crowds. There were millions of people gathered together at one time, and their religious fervour was amazing. Communism had not undermined their faith. After people had turned out all through Poland to see the Polish Pope, the tour ended in Krakow. John Paul II was in the Cardinal's residence and a few of us journalists were in the courtyard where he was bestowing his blessing.

I stood next to Mieczyslaw Rakowski, who at that time was the editor of *Polytika*, one of the few publications in the Warsaw Pact that had a measure of leeway to criticize the regime. Looking at the courtyard scene, Rakowski said: "Poland will never be the same again and the Warsaw Pact will never be the same again." The Pope's visit triggered the drive for greater freedom in Poland and also inspired other parts of the Soviet Empire to dare think that the Soviet stranglehold could be loosened.

During 1981–2, the period of martial law in Poland, I concluded—in sharp contrast to many other observers—that General Jaruzelski deserved to be seen as more of a patriot than as a Soviet puppet. One of the events that confirmed it for me was in 1982 when I came to Warsaw to interview him for the *Guardian*. The interview was scheduled on the day that Brezhnev's death was announced. To my surprise he did not cancel the interview and received me late that evening. Jaruzelski flew off to Moscow for the funeral the next day. The official Communist Party newspaper that morning featured my interview with Jaruzelski as its leading story. Brezhnev's death and funeral was in second place, tucked away at the bottom of the page. It seemed an important signal marking the strained relationship between Poland and the USSR.

During the martial law period, Rakowski came to London on a number of occasions. In London he visited the offices of the *Guardian* and spoke very freely about what was going on in the Warsaw Pact and in Poland itself. He even wrote some Op-Ed articles for the paper. They were not mere propaganda pieces and we interpreted them as a signal of Poland's relative independence and urge to distance itself from the Soviet Union. The Solidarity Trade Union never trusted Rakowski, but as a leading figure in the Polish Communist Party he later played a key role in the negotiations, which led to the establishment of a democratic government in Poland.

Maintaining good relations with Poland was important to West Germany. That is why, after the Wall collapsed, the West German Foreign Minister Hans-Dietrich Genscher immediately set a high priority on winning Poland's trust. He reassured the Polish government that the existing Polish-German border on the Oder-Neisse line, would continue to be recognized as the formal border between the two countries.

I was in Berlin in October 1989, shortly before the collapse of the Wall, when Gorbachev came to East Germany. During that visit, Gorbachev announced that it was the responsibility of the German Democratic Republic (GDR) to manage its affairs. The Soviet Union would no longer guarantee to defend the status quo in the GDR. It was a momentous event.

That evening I went to the Distel Kabarett-Theater, the political cabaret located in East Berlin. The communist authorities permitted the performance of satire sketches at this cabaret throughout the Cold War. The audience, however, was always limited to Communist Party members. The sketches were permitted to make jokes about life in East Germany such as domestic shortages and holidays restricted to travel in the Communist bloc. But, they never strayed into direct political satire; that was out of bounds. On previous occasions when I had been to the Distel, I would take notes to remember the jokes, and those sitting near me in the audience would always stare at me suspiciously. Clearly they were wondering if I was some sort of informer for the East German government. Nobody ever talked to me.

When I went to the Distel Kabarett the night following Gorbachev's declaration of nonintervention, the change in atmosphere was striking. Suddenly, the content of the show changed completely. It became highly dramatic and emotional. The cheap jokes had gone. That night the people sitting around me all wanted to know who I was and why I was there. When they discovered I was a British journalist, I was invited to go to a bar with them. They proceeded to tell me their whole life stories. It was exhilarating. You felt that something had been released in people; it was a happy release. Quite suddenly, the atmosphere no longer bred frustration. People suddenly sensed that life had changed for the better. There was a real sense of liberation.

The division between East and West Germany, which was symbolized by the Berlin Wall, remains something of a real psychological divide between the former citizens of the GDR and the FRG. That is because economic progress in the former GDR has not been as rapid as was hoped. Unemployment is still higher in the East. Nor has investment been as extensive as in the Western part of Germany. Substantial economic differences remain and people are aware of it. This is a gap between the two societies, which has not yet been eclipsed.

In retrospect, it is easy to see how wrong former FRG Chancellor Willy Brandt was when I interviewed him soon after the fall of the Wall. Brandt said: "This is going to be wonderful. Now the GDR are going to get all the new technologies and innovations, and they will jump far ahead of us in the West." Brandt, like so many of us at the time, did not anticipate that, in spite of unification, the former GDR would remain the poor relation for many years to come.

A Russian perspective on the collapse of the Berlin Wall

Alexander Likhotal

I was sitting peacefully at my country house on the evening of 9 November 1989, when I was suddenly summoned to my office at the Staraya Ploshad—the location of the Central Committee of the Communist Party of the Soviet Union (CPSU). Once there, I learned that the GDR had opened the Berlin Wall, and thousands of Germans were moving freely between the East and the West. That was the beginning of the process that eventually produced German unification and an end to the Cold War. We did not, of course, realize all the implications of what was happening in Berlin that November. Only the passage of time allows us to see clearly the implications of the fall of the Wall. Looking back, however, I think that the collapse of the Berlin Wall was inevitable. It was inevitable because much of the twentieth century essentially was built on the religious war between two secular ideologies. One ideology sought to dismantle profit-seeking private enterprise. The other ideology sought to eliminate all public control over free initiative. In reality things were always more complex than that. But most of the century was about this confrontation.

The collapse of the Berlin Wall signified that the communist system finally blinked first. This did not mean that communism definitively lost the ideological argument. I contend that both ideologies were impractical, and had inherent social and economic problems. In this regard, the words of Pope John Paul II are well worth remembering: "The Western countries run the risk of seeing this collapse of communism as a onesided victory of their own economic system and, thereby, failing to make the necessary corrections in that system."[5] In the years since the collapse of communism in Eastern Europe and the Soviet Union, unfortunately, that actually happened and we know it now.

When the Wall fell, I was not yet working directly with Mikhail Gorbachev, so I do not know first-hand his reaction to the collapse. I worked with some of his assistants, however, and I do not think this event was entirely unexpected. It was clear by late 1989 that it could happen any day.[6] I am sure that Gorbachev thought the fall of the Berlin Wall and German reunification would happen. But, as Gorbachev has stated, he did not think it would happen as fast as it did. During Gorbachev's visit to West Germany in August 1989, he held a joint press conference with Helmut Kohl. They both indicated that history would place German reunification on the agenda. And they both agreed that it probably would not happen until the next century.

The question of German reunification produced an intense political struggle within the leadership of the Soviet Union. During this period, I directed a section of the International Department of the Central Committee of the Communist Party. This office provided assessment and analysis for the leadership about strategic events, such as those unfolding situations in East and West Germany in 1989–1990. The papers we produced eventually included the remarks and comments of the Politburo members, who were the highest leaders in the government. In reading these notations, I remember that many of the remarks showed deep concern that events in Germany were reshaping all of the balance of forces in Europe and around the world. The bulk of the comments of senior Soviet leaders, however strange it may seem, added up to: "OK, if we go for reunification, we need to make them pay for it." I remember one notation in particular by Gorbachev, in which he commented, "You imply then that we need to sell our allies."

It was clear that the Soviet communist establishment would not accept German reunification without extreme pressure from the highest leaders. This opposition characterized even the most forward-looking people, such as the head of the International Department, Valentin Falin. Falin was one of our most brilliant intellects, but he was very conservative in the communist sense of the conservatives. He was very much disturbed by Gorbachev's movement toward acceptance of unification, and he tried to pressure Gorbachev on the issue. Gorbachev, however, was adapting to the situation as it unfolded; it is clear that he did not want to place the question of German unification on the agenda. It is also clear, however, that he was responding to the pressures of reality. Obviously, during his many visits to East and West Germany, Gorbachev realized that the people there were taking things into their own hands. He knew that when the people of a nation took control in this way, you could not stop them. For example, in October 1989, Gorbachev visited East Germany for the commemoration of the fortieth anniversary of the creation of the GDR. As part of the celebration, there was a torchlight parade of Communist Party activists in East Berlin. Gorbachev was standing with Erich Honecker on the balcony of a government building watching the parade, when the people in the crowd abandoned the party-approved slogans and began shouting, "Gorby, Gorby, save us once more!" At that point Miecczyslaw Rakowsky, a senior member of the GDR leadership, turned to Gorbachev and translated the chant. Then he asked Gorbachev, "Do you understand? These are party activists. This is the end." Gorbachev responded, "Yes, I do."[7]

The tragic Soviet intervention in Afghanistan, and our eventual withdrawal, played a significant role in Gorbachav's reluctance to use force to maintain communist regimes in Eastern Europe. The decision to invade Afghanistan was taken by only three members of the Politburo. Not all of the members of the Politburo were even informed of the decision before the invasion began. Gorbachev was not a member of the Politburo in 1979, when the invasion occurred. He found out about it from press reports along with the rest of the country and he was appalled at the situation. Gorbachev was dismayed that the decisions, made by so few men, put such a terrible burden on the shoulders of the Soviet people.[8]

The tragedy of the Soviet intervention in Afghanistan accelerated the end of the Cold War. It contributed to Mikhail Gorbachev's thinking about the futility of military force in European and world affairs. When Gorbachev assumed power in 1985, he opposed continuing the war in Afghanistan. He was not alone in this. The people of the Soviet Union, by this time, were more or less aware of the real situation in Afghanistan. People were dismayed by the burden of the so-called "Cargo 200." This was military slang for the coffins shipped home from Afghanistan. It was the people themselves who drove the ultimate decision to withdraw from the Afghan conflict. After the election of the new Soviet parliament in 1989, it was the Academician Andrei Sakharov, in his first speech as a People's Deputy, who demanded that Soviet troops be withdrawn from Afghanistan. This, however, proved to be an uphill battle because many leaders opposed the troop withdrawal. They believed the USSR would lose face if it withdrew from Afghanistan.

The best insight into the relationship between perestroika and the collapse of the Berlin Wall, and what came after in Eastern Europe, did not come from out of the Kremlin. It came from Poland. Adam Michnik was

Solidarity's intellectual leader and contributed a great deal to the success of that political movement. Michnik observed, "Were it not for the Perestroika 'virus,' the Solidarity Movement could never have got where it is today."[9]

Mikhail Gorbachev's new thinking and leadership created the situation in which communist regimes in Germany and Eastern Europe quite suddenly ended, even though that was not his intention. At the same time, he was not unmindful of what such an eventuality might mean for himself and the Soviet Union.[10] In 1991, Gorbachev traveled to Japan. During the voyage, a university student asked this question: "Mr. Gorbachev do you realize this process released by Perestroika can bring you and your government down?" Gorbachev replied, "Yes I know that. But I think that I will win even if that happens—because if that happens constitutionally, and by election, then I think that Perestroika has succeeded."[11] Gorbachev's attitude brings to mind the words of John Kenneth Galbraith, who once said, "Sometimes statesmen need to take the right position and lose."

Although he is regarded as a hero in the West, Gorbachev is less highly regarded in Russia and is a controversial figure there. At the twentieth anniversary of the fall of the Berlin Wall, President Medvedev of Russia noted that Gorbachev's leadership in Russia unleashed the events that produced the collapse of the Berlin Wall. Gorbachev's reputation in Russia suffered after the dissolution of the Soviet Union, but it has substantially improved in recent years.

A British perspective on the collapse of the Berlin Wall

Sir Christopher Mallaby

For years it had been apparent that the regime in East Germany had failed. Its only legitimacy had been the now discredited ideology. It was next door to the most successful German state in history. West Berlin was an island of democracy and prosperity right at the heart of the GDR, a humiliation for the regime. On top of all that democracy then broke out in other Central European countries, so that the GDR became an island of autocracy and failure within a democratic sea. So by early 1989 it was clear that the GDR simply had to be reformed. Gorbachev made clear that he recognized this. At first it appeared that the outcome of this change might be a second democratic state in Germany.

I think one key moment was when the slogans on the streets of Leipzig changed. They had been saying, "We are the People," which was a riposte to the East German authorities who claimed theirs was a people's regime. When the chant in the streets changed from "We are *the* People" to "We are

One People," it was obvious that the status quo could not be maintained. This subtle change in language made it obvious that reunification, till then not a declared policy of the Federal Republic, was now all but inevitable due to public demand. I reported to the Foreign Office that the call for unification from the streets of the GDR was bound to lead the politicians in West Germany to echo that call. From then on I thought reunification would be the result of the process of change in the GDR. The question was how soon. Helmut Kohl, although he was accused of rushing to unity, was actually following the mood on the streets of East Germany.

At the point when the Berlin Wall collapsed, and the regime in East Germany was failing, Prime Minister Thatcher was worried that change was going very fast. In February 1990, when the Two Plus Four forum[12] was established, I think she was relieved that the Four Powers would now have a say concerning the pace of change.[13] In several of her press interviews after that time, however, Thatcher displayed her dislike of reunification and was critical of the Federal government. Why this negative view?

First, it was the very speed of change that concerned the Prime Minister. Then there was the absence of consultation with the allies of the Federal Republic. Thatcher, by late 1989, had invested a great deal with substantial success in developing a constructive relationship with Gorbachev. She thought that the rapid changes in Germany and Central Europe might destabilize Gorbachev's position. That, she feared, could endanger the rise of democracy in Central Europe. In early 1990 FRG Chancellor Helmut Kohl seemed reluctant to recognize the existing Oder-Neisse frontier. Yet that, from the point of view of anyone interested in European stability, was going to be a necessary part of any package of international arrangements surrounding German unification. Finally, Margaret Thatcher was also concerned specifically about the big question of a unified Germany's future status in NATO. Would all of united Germany be in NATO or only the former Federal Republic? Mrs. Thatcher saw, very early, that this issue was going to be difficult.

What was the real underlying reason for Margaret Thatcher's opposition to German unification? I suppose it was residual generational fear from recent history. She was nineteen when World War II ended in 1945. Her memories of that war made her uneasy. She made a logical point that Germany divided could never be a threat to European stability, while a reunited Germany, hypothetically, might one day become such a threat. My criticism was that this attitude ignored the nature of the West German Federal Republic. I was convinced that, if there were unification, it would bring the spread of Rhineland democracy eastward. We were not going to see what happened in 1871, when Prussian militarism spread westward. From my point of view, it was best to help to ensure that unification would make East Germany like West Germany. Above all, I saw unification as a great gain for the West, bringing the end of the Soviet threat to freedom in the West and a peaceful end to the Cold War. German reunification for me was not only about Germany; it was about an immense improvement in security and freedom in Europe.

The Soviet decision not to intervene militarily in Poland, when the Solidarity movement challenged the communist monopoly on power, was an important development, which helped to prepare the way for the rise of democracy in Central Europe and from there to the collapse of the Berlin Wall and the end of the Cold War. The Soviets considered using force to suppress the change in Poland epitomized by Solidarity. The tanks were got ready, but they were not used. Instead, the Soviets thought that the imposition of martial law by General Jaruzelski would be sufficient. They did not want to lose what they called "the gains of détente," which included their purchase of American grain to help feed the Soviet people. The Kremlin was wrong; martial law only delayed the change in Poland, which resumed and then became part of change throughout Central Europe including East Germany.

Poland later played a significant role in the German unification process in 1989–90, especially in the question of German recognition of the Oder-Neisse line as the permanent eastern frontier of Germany. It was important to others involved in the process, especially the Soviet Union, to establish a clear and definite recognition of that demarcation so that the territorial situation east of the existing frontier would not be disturbed. Full recognition of the Oder-Neisse line meant that one-third of Poland's 1937 territory was lost to Germany. Ultimately, the question of the permanent border between unified Germany and Poland came down to a matter of timing. Would the final legal recognition of the reality of the Oder-Neisse line be deferred until after unification, and left to the new German parliament? That was not acceptable to Poland. Or, would this be done by an agreement among the parties before unification took place? That, of course, is what happened with the Polish-German Border Treaty in 1990.

I have two strong memories about the actual fall of the Berlin Wall. The first one is a small source of pride to me. One of the British Army regiments stationed in Berlin, set up what they called a "Tea Point" just to the west of where the Wall had opened. As people streamed through from East Berlin to freedom, they received a scalding, sweet, strong, and free cup of British Army tea. The second memory is symbolic. On the evening of 10 November, some twenty hours after the Wall was opened, I went with my wife through the crossing between East and West known as Checkpoint Charlie. We were going to an evening in the British Embassy in East Berlin with some of the East German church leaders and opponents of the regime. Multitudes of East Germans, who had gone the other way in the morning, were now streaming back into East Berlin in the evening. They passed through the checkpoint without being checked by border guards. As I watched this crowd passing our car, I saw a little boy; he was three or four years old. He was pulling a toy behind him—a large, plastic, red, London doubledecker bus. For me that was one of the moments when I knew the world was changing.

A German perspective on the collapse of the Berlin Wall

Hermann Freiherr von Richthofen

It was the Conference on Security and Cooperation in Europe (CSCE) in 1975, and the implementation of the Final Agreement process, which made the collapse of the Berlin Wall inevitable. Also important in ending the Cold War was the series of successful arms control and disarmament negotiations that significantly reduced military tensions in Europe. The 1987 Intermediate-range Nuclear Forces (INF) Treaty was of particular importance, as it solved the very difficult and dangerous problem of nuclear missile deployments in Europe. At the same time there were the efforts, such as the Single European Act (SEA) of 1986, to bring Europe closer together. By the time of the collapse of the Berlin Wall, Western Europe had built the foundation for the kind of cooperation that was necessary for German unification to occur.[14] And, of course, on the other side, there was Mikhail Gorbachev.

I accompanied the president of the FRG, Richard von Weizsäcker, on his trip to Moscow in 1987. In our meetings with Gorbachev, the Soviet leader spoke in terms of one hundred years before the German question could be solved. By October 1988, Gorbachev's timeline had shrunken to twenty-five years. And, following his visits to the FRG and the GDR in 1989, Gorbachev realized that the time was right for settling the status of the two German states. By then, we had prepared the ground for a settlement with the 1971 Quadripartite Agreement the status of Berlin and full admission of the two German states to the UN in 1973. UN membership was extended with the proviso that the Allied rights and responsibilities with respect to Germany as a whole, and Berlin in particular, remained unaffected. This kept open the question of a comprehensive settlement.

While the division of Germany remained the status quo in 1989, there was tremendous pressure from the people of East Germany to allow them to travel outside of the GDR. Eventually this pressure forced the GDR leader, Erich Honecker, to permit East German citizens to journey to Hungary. After the Hungarians opened their border with Austria in May 1989, a tremendous opportunity for such travel to the West arose. In August, whilst taking their holiday in Hungary, large numbers of East Germans found they could easily slip into Austria and quickly proceed to their real destination—West Germany. Eventually, Honecker permitted the East German citizens who had taken refuge in West German Embassies in Prague and Warsaw to leave the GDR by being transported through the territory of the GDR to the FRG. By then the leadership in East Berlin was so weakened, and Honecker was so incapable of changing things, that the system reached its break point. The East German authorities simply had to open the GDR for the free travel of their citizens. Thus, GDR spokesperson Gunther Schabowski at the famous press conference on November 9, 1989 announced the new interim regulations, which reduced travel barriers between East and West Germany. Following the press conference, rumors spread that all travel restrictions had been removed. Thousands of people suddenly rushed to the Wall. The border guards, who had not received instructions about the new law, eventually opened the barrier and ever growing numbers of people streamed through to West Berlin. The opening of the Berlin Wall and the inability of the GDR to close it again, created the situation in which the Cold War was brought to an end.[15]

There can be no doubt about the attitude of the Federal Republic of Germany concerning the establishment of a united Germany and continued German membership in the NATO alliance. The FRG strongly favored it. Nor, can there be any doubt about the attitude of both the FRG and the GDR concerning what they saw as the irreversible movement toward an economic and monetary union. Where Russia was concerned, Helmut Kohl was very cautious not to put Gorbachev into a delicate position. It was well understood that, if the Soviets withdrew their 400,000 troops from the GDR, then they would have to be resettled in the Soviet Union. This would be expensive and had to be paid for. West Germans were glad to do so. At the same time, we did not want to create the impression that Gorbachev was expected to sell out his allies. Nevertheless, even today, if you talk with former members of the Communist Party of the GDR, they reproach Gorbachev for selling them out to the West. So, indeed, the FRG did provide a fair compensation to the Soviet Union for the cost of its military withdrawal from East Germany. This was the politically correct action and set the foundation for creating a new partnership with Russia.

The collapse of the Berlin Wall put West German Chancellor Kohl in a difficult position concerning unification. Popular forces were building for a rapid end of the division, but Kohl had to be very cautious in proceeding. He resisted pushing hard for unification until it could be sorted out in the FRG. Kohl did not want to risk the entire process by pushing things too fast. In December 1989, however, Kohl visited East Germany to meet with the new GDR leadership to discuss the possibility of creating some form of confederation. During the visit, Kohl stood on a balcony as a very large East German crowd unanimously shouted, "We are one nation!" At that moment it was clear that the East Germans wanted to exercise their right of selfdetermination. They wanted unification. This was perfectly understood by our friends in the United States, who supported us most loyally on the path to unification.

Contrary to how Bismarck unified Germany in the nineteenth century, Helmut Kohl succeeded in unifying East and West Germany through negotiation rather than force. Through skillful negotiation, Helmut Kohl managed to bring a unified Germany, not only into the EU and NATO, but also into Europe at large. It was remarkable that Kohl managed to do all of this as a peaceful process. An important part of this process was permanently settling the Polish-German border.

When the FRG ratified the Warsaw Treaty of 1970, it recognized the fact that the OderNeisse line was the western border of Poland. In an exchange of notes between West Germany and Poland, however, a reservation was made with respect to Germany as a whole. It basically held that the settlement of the western frontier might well be affected by any future change in the status of a new sovereign German state. Thus, from a strictly legal standpoint, there was not a common border with Poland in 1989. Helmut Kohl did not want to deal with the settlement of the border until it was synchronized with the Two Plus Four process, when German unification was also at stake.

Unification and the settlement of permanent borders, in the end, were achieved with the help of the British, the Americans, and the Soviets. I am grateful for the support that Poland and the Solidarity movement gave us in bringing about the peaceful revolution in East Germany. Kohl was on an official visit in Poland to meet with Solidarity leader Tadeusz Mazowiecki, who then was the first Catholic, freely elected prime minister of Poland, the night the Wall fell. He interrupted his visit and rushed back to Berlin the next morning. Then, exemplifying the importance of Poland's contribution to the peaceful revolution in the GDR, Kohl returned to continue his visit.

Mikhail Gorbachev telephoned Helmut Kohl shortly after the Chancellor returned from Poland to Berlin. Gorbachev was very concerned that an outbreak of violence should be avoided. Kohl calmed Gorbachev's concern by assuring the Soviet leader that the flood of people who were streaming by the tens of thousands through the open wall had but one aim; they just wanted to visit with one another and would return peacefully to their homes. Kohl assured Gorbachev that those who were coming into East Germany were very peaceful. They were not terrorist gangs being unleashed to destabilize the GDR. No mobs would assault the Soviet barracks or the homes of the East German state police. Violence was not likely so long as the East German authorities just let people come and go. Kohl pointed out that, after all, both the Hungarians and the Czechs had already opened the borders of the GDR. What difference could it make to open the border in Berlin too? It was time to let go, to move forward. It was no longer enough to keep the old situation as it was. It was time to change.

The Berlin Wall has been physically demolished. But, for some in Germany a "Wall" continues to exist intellectually and emotionally. The majority of former East Germans are very happy in the unified German state. They are part of West German society without any distinction. You have, of course, the old Communist Party members. For them the Wall still exists in their minds. The Left Party, which is largely composed of former GDR officials and their adherents, contends that NATO should be dissolved, and the EU is something they dislike. But, so long as this "Wall" is in their head, they are not considered by most Germans as qualified for any kind of political participation on the federal level.

Finally, in considering the legacy of the GDR, it is important to mention that in the Federal Republic, we tried to face the terrible history of Germany during the Nazi period. This did not take place in the GDR, because it declared itself, as a communist regime, an antiFascist state. It disregarded the fact that living within the GDR were many individuals who were intimately connected with the Nazi period. Bringing those who lived in the former GDR to an understanding of the Nazi past is work that remains to be done. This confrontation with the past, which was deferred during almost fifty years of Cold War, will take time.

Notes

1   Jacques Lévesque, "The East European Revolutions of 1989," in *The Cambridge History of the Cold War, Volume 2: Crises and Détente*, M. Leffler and O. A. Westad (eds) (New York: Cambridge University Press, 2010b), Helga Haftendorn, "The Unification of Germany, 1985–1991," in *The Cambridge History of the Cold War, Volume 3: Endings*, M. Leffler and O. A. Westad (eds) (New York: Cambridge University Press, 2010c) and Mary Elise Sarotte, *1989: The Struggle to Create Post-Cold War Europe* (Princeton: Princeton University Press, 2009).

2   Jeffrey Engel (ed.), *The Fall of the Berlin Wall: The Revolutionary Legacy of 1989* (New York: Oxford University Press, 2009) and Charles S. Maier, *Dissolution: The Crisis of Communism and the End of East Germany* (Princeton: Princeton University Press, 1997).

3   Daniel Thomas, *The Helsinki Effect: International Norms, Human Rights, and the Demise of Communism* (Princeton: Princeton University Press, 2001).

4   Adam Roberts, "An 'Incredibly Swift Transition': Reflections on the End of the Cold War," in *The Cambridge History of the Cold War, Volume 3, Endings*, 527–9.

5   John Paul II, *Cenntesimus Annus: Encyclical Letter on the Hundredth Anniversary of the Rerum Novarum*, May 1, 1991.

6   Jonathan Haslam, *Russia's Cold War: From the October Revolution to the Fall of the Wall* (New Haven: Yale University Press, 2011), 388.

7   Mikhail Gorbachev, *Memoirs* (New York: Doubleday, 1995), 524.

8   See Artemy Kalinovsky, *A Long Goodbye: The Soviet Withdrawal From Afghanistan* (Cambridge: Harvard University Press, 2011).

9   Adam Michnik, *In Search of Lost Meaning: The New Eastern Europe* (Berkeley: University of California Press, 2011), 30.

10   See Archie Brown, "The Gorbachev Revolution and the End of the Cold War," in *The Cambridge History of the Cold War, Volume 3: Endings*, M. Leffler and O. A. Westad (eds) (New York: Cambridge University Press, 2010c) and Andrei Grachev, *Gorbachev's Gamble: Soviet Foreign Policy and the End of the Cold War* (Cambridge: Polity Press, 2008).

11   Vladislav Zubok, "Gorbachev and the End of the Cold War: Different Perspectives on the Historical Personality," in *Cold War Endgame: Oral History, Analysis, Debates*, W. C. Wohlforth (ed.) (University Park: Pennsylvania State University Press, 2003).

12   Two Plus Four was the designation for the talks among the FDR, GDR, Britain, France, US, and USSR culminating in the Treaty on the Final Settlement with Respect to Germany in 1990.

13   See Thatcher, *The Downing Street Years* (New York: Harper Collins, 1993), 792–9.

14   Stephen Szabo, *The Diplomacy of German Unification* (New York: St. Martin's Press, 1992).

15   Philip Zelikow and Condoleezza Rice, *Germany Unified and Europe Transformed: A Study in Statecraft* (Cambridge: Harvard University Press, 1995), 98–101.

CHAPTER EIGHT

The European legacy

The end of the Cold War produced tremendous change in Europe. Within five years of the collapse of the Berlin War, the geopolitical contours of Eastern and Central Europe, as well as that of Eurasia, had been stunningly transformed. In this chapter journalists, diplomats, and scholars reflect upon the legacy of the Cold War in Europe. They focus on the situation in Eastern Europe, especially Poland, Romania, and Russia and the difficulty of escaping the remnants of the totalitarian past.

Bridget Kendall offers a journalist's first-hand perspective on the critical transition period in Eastern Europe from 1989 to the present. Victor Ashe, the former American Ambassador to Poland, reviews the legacy of Polish-Soviet relations as these affect the US role in Europe and Poland today. The lingering effects of Soviet relations with Eastern Europe frame Andei Pippidi's discussion of the Cold War legacy in Romania. The Cold War legacy for Russia and its future in Europe is the focus for Konstantin Khudoley, Alexander Likhotal, Anthony Brenton.

Prelude to the new beginning

Bridget Kendall

Viewing events from Moscow where I was stationed as BBC correspondent in 1989, it did not seem as though the fall of the Berlin Wall made the collapse of the Soviet Union two years later inevitable. Yes, it was obvious that the Communist Party of the Soviet Union (CPSU) would not survive in its old form, and that the liberation of Eastern Europe had many repercussions. But neither seemed sufficient to cause the breakup of an entire country.

Instead it was the events in 1991, which led to the crisis. The trigger was the attempted coup by communist hardliners in August 1991. Overnight it changed everything. The fragile balance of power between the central Soviet authorities and the constituent parts of the Union was shattered. Once the coup had failed and the Soviet President, Mikhail Gorbachev, had returned to Moscow from house arrest in the Crimea, he discovered his already waning political authority had evaporated. The Russian President, Boris Yeltsin, was now in charge and he lost no time in forestalling new efforts to sabotage reforms by banning the Communist Party. Then at the end of 1991 the Soviet flag came down from the spire of the Kremlin and the Russian flag was raised. In Moscow at the time, none of these historic events appeared as having been rendered inevitable by the collapse of the Berlin Wall. Meanwhile the other republics that made up the Soviet Union also took steps to protect themselves. Before long the leaders of Russia, Ukraine, and Belarus had met in secret and agreed to abolish the Soviet Union altogether.

After that it was only a matter of weeks before President Gorbachev resigned and the Soviet flag was lowered from the Kremlin flagpole, replaced by the Russian tricolor. I remember the moment well. It felt as though an irrevocable, historic moment had come about almost by accident.

Today in Russia the answer to the question 'What or who was to blame for the end of the Soviet Union?' is usually personal. Mikhail Gorbachev blames Boris Yeltsin. But many ordinary Russians hold Gorbachev responsible. They will tell you that he was no hero for ending the Cold War and destroying the old Soviet Empire, but a misguided, naive leader who unleashed changes he failed to control, and allowed his own country to disintegrate.

In recent years resentment among the Russian political elite as a result of this difficult transition has fueled an increase in mutual suspicion between Russia and Europe. The Russian war with Georgia in 2008 made some Europeans wonder if the Cold War was really over. It turned out that it was not a trigger for a new East-West conflict. But it was a warning, a symptom of unfinished business and a reminder that tensions at a political level need to be managed carefully.

Nevertheless, Russians today do not see themselves in opposition to Europe. On the contrary, many view countries like France, Germany, and Britain as models for the sort of country they would like to live in. For many, Europe is still their *destination*.

I had an experience recently that gave me an interesting insight into this. I was traveling back to London from Moscow on an Aeroflot flight. Nearly all the other passengers were Russian. At Arrivals, a large sign in the terminal indicated that Europeans were to join one queue, while all other nationalities were to join another. All the Russians headed for the European queue, confident that they were included in the 'European' category. Upon their arrival at the checkpoint, however, they found their assumption was wrong. This was a queue for EU citizens only. To their consternation they were turned back and told to join the queue for "other nationalities."

It was perhaps a trivial incident but it was a telling one. Russians may profess their country's destiny is unique, but they see their identity as European. It would be as well not to rebuff that sentiment, whatever the strains in geopolitics.

Poland and the legacy of the Cold War

Victor Ashe

I absorbed Poland's history during my service as the US Ambassador 2004 to 2009. I came to appreciate how deeply the legacy of the Cold War in Eastern Europe is affected by the tragic and embittered history of Poland in World War II, and its subsequent domination by the Soviet Union during the Cold War. The Cold War is alive and well in Poland, and it influences attitudes and actions even today. It will take the passage of many years before the impact of the Cold War fades in Poland.

World War II in Europe started and ended in Poland. It opened on September 1, 1939 on the Westerplatte Peninsula in Gdansk. The final battle ended in Breslau, Germany in what is now Wroclaw, Poland on May 8, 1945. Poland lost one-fifth of its population during World War II. As a percentage of the population, Poland lost more people than did any other nation in World War II. Ninety percent of the Polish Jewish population was murdered and twelve percent of the nonJewish Polish population died as well. They died predominantly by Nazi hands, but also at Soviet hands, for the first two years of the war.

The ninetieth anniversary of the reestablishment of Poland as an independent nation took place in 2009. Poland, prior to the end of World War I, historically had been partitioned among Russia, Prussia, and the AustroHungarian Empire for over 130 years. It was President Wilson's advocacy at the Treaty of Versailles that brought Poland back together. Poland in 1919–20 fought the Bolshevik Army, which had marched into Poland. It was in a battle in the suburbs of Warsaw that the Bolshevik Army was defeated. This reestablished Poland's legal sovereignty and achieved the practical sovereignty of a foreign army leaving its boundaries.

Poland's geographic location over the centuries has been its curse. It suffered in the twentieth century for being between Germany and Russia, having to endure invasion and occupation. Today, however, Poland's geographic location is its great economic opportunity as it lies between the East and the West. It has managed to sustain economic growth as its eastern neighbors have suffered negative economic growth.

The year 2009 was an auspicious year in recent Polish history. It was the ninetieth anniversary of the recreation of the Polish nation, the seventieth anniversary of the start of World War II, and the sixty-fifth anniversary of the Warsaw Uprising. It was also the thirtieth anniversary of Karol Wojtyla's first pilgrimage home as the Holy Father, Pope John Paul II. It is impossible to overestimate the impact the Pope's visit to his native land had upon the Polish people in 1979. Tremendous crowds welcomed the Pope and he uplifted their spirits. In the wake of the Pope's visit came the August 1980 strike at the Lenin shipyard in Gdansk. From the shipyard strike arose the Solidarity movement that was so critical, eventually, to ending communist rule in Poland. The year 2009 marks the twentieth anniversary of the fall of communism in Poland, which occurred several months prior to the fall of the Berlin Wall. The collapse of communism in Poland was brought through its first free elections, which transpired because of the round-table talks between opposition groups led by Lech Walesa and the governing coalition led by General Jaruzelski. The success of Solidarity in the parliamentary elections demonstrated the further erosion of the Communist Party's effective political power. By the time the Berlin Wall fell, Poland already had its first noncommunist prime minister and was well along the path to ending communist rule.

The tenth anniversary of Poland's membership in NATO is marked in 2009, as is the fifth anniversary of its membership in the EU. Thus, one can easily see the milestones of the end of the Cold War and its aftermath in the events that define the relationship between Poland, Western Europe, and the demise of Soviet hegemony in Eastern Europe.

World War II and the Cold War, however, remain vivid in the minds of the Polish people. This explains in large part the Polish interest in President Bush's Missile Defense Program, as well as President Obama's modification of that program. These presidential initiatives were well were received and supported by the Polish government of the day. It explains why, although deep down the Polish do not really see the see threat from Iran, they are willing to accommodate American requests. They do see a Polish interest in having American troops on Polish soil. The Poles do not believe that NATO membership alone guarantees their security. As a member of the alliance any attack on Poland should automatically bring NATO to its defense. But, the memory of the failure of Britain and France effectively to oppose the Nazi invasion in 1939 remains fresh in the Polish memory. The Poles feel that if the American soldiers were in Poland when an attack occurred, and American soldiers were injured, the United States would respond in kind. In their view the United States is the only power in the world today with the ability to effectively defend Poland, and its willingness to do so is tied to having American soldiers at risk. Additionally, of course, the legacy between Poland and the United States is a long-standing one. Other than the United Kingdom, Poland is the most consistent and reliable ally the United States has in Europe. Out of the deep and lasting friendship it feels for the United States, Poland clearly has shown it will support the United

States, even when it does not necessarily agree with its policies. Witness the "Coalition of the Willing" in Iraq where every public opinion poll in Poland showed opposition to the war. The Polish government, however, supported the war and provided troops for the effort. Close policy engagement between Poland and the United States survived the tension between them over the war in Iraq.

For historical reasons, despite the end of the Cold War, Russia and Poland continue to have misgivings about one another. The current government of Poland is working to reduce tensions with the Russian Federation. The fact that Russian Prime Minister Putin came to Gdansk to participate in the seventieth anniversary ceremonies was, in itself, a great step forward. It would have been hard to imagine that occurring under the prior Polish leadership, when Lech Walesa and Jarosław Kaczyński were the president and the prime minister respectively. Prime Minister Putin's remarks were not greeted with great applause. The mere fact that he came, however, was a step forward in Polish-Russian relations.

The communist ideology that dominated Poland for forty-four years was simply a synonym for the Soviet Union. Without the Soviet Union, the communist rule of Poland would not have occurred. The list of grievances against the Soviet Union is a very long one and remains fresh in the Polish memory. Relations have improved and are headed in a more positive direction. But the legacy of the Cold War influences individual Poles in their attitude and creates restraints under which any contemporary Polish government must be cognizant. It must not go outside those parameters unless it wishes a vote of no confidence. It will take generations before Poland and Russia escape the tragic legacy of World War II and the Cold War.

Romania and the legacy of the Cold War

Andrei Pippidi

Twenty years ago I assumed that the deaths of Elena and Nicolae Ceausescu would catapult Romania toward a world where lies end. I was wrong. I am a historian and realize now that I was embarrassingly naive. As Romania moves through its sixth presidential election since 1990, that illusion cannot be maintained. It is clear that some legacies of the Cold War are slow to disappear even if, as I like to hope, they may eventually become extinct. In 1948 the Romanian People's Republic, territorially diminished and having been imposed with a Stalinist regime, was compelled to join the group of satellite states around the USSR. Economic and political liberties were suppressed.

During the first period of coercion, the costs for Romania amounted to at least 350,000 citizens who died in jails, prisons, and camps. Some place the total figure during the Cold War at two million killed by the regime. This does not take into account the populations of territories now included in Moldova, Ukraine, Bulgaria, and others deported to the USSR after the war. This lasted until 1964, at which time 17,000 political prisoners were released when the leaders of the Romanian Workers Party adopted the so-called Manifesto of Independence and National Sovereignty. This document declared the principle of non-interference in Romanian internal affairs and respect for territorial integrity, and occurred six years after Soviet troops had been withdrawn from Romania. It signaled an important change in relations between Bucharest and Moscow. Therefore, the way was opened for the Ceausescu regime, which came to power in 1965.

Under Ceausescu, the Bulgarian communist path was distinctive from that taken by the Soviet Union. That was because Ceausescu's foreign policy encouraged a Western presumption that Romania acted independently within the Warsaw Pact, and due to the diminution of brutal repression by the regime. In 1968, just five days before the Soviet invasion of Czechoslovakia, Romanian leaders visited Prague to sign a bilateral treaty. The demonstration of Soviet power was also an implicit threat to Romania. Therefore, 1968 marked the end of Ceausescu's attempt to forge a moderate communist line. He began instead to look to the hardline Chinese and North Korean models. As long as Ceausescu remained at the helm of the Romanian government, reform of any kind was impossible. It is still difficult to say how many Romanians were really indoctrinated communists. Many were simply political opportunists or reluctant accomplices of governmental propaganda. The destruction caused by communism ranged from social engineering to false industrialization. As elsewhere in Eastern Europe, the damage was vast since its economic underdevelopment provided the necessary excuse for strong social intervention. In countries such as Romania, Albania, and, until the perestroika years, in Russia the state was all-powerful, reducing society to absolute dependence.

It can be argued that there were no winners in the Cold War. In Romania, however, there are many people—especially many former dissidents—who claim that the West won this war. Many of the people who benefitted from their collaboration with the communist regime understandably prefer to conclude neither side won. It is obvious that a new center of power has emerged on the western side of the Iron Curtain. It consists of the states integrated in the EU. The changes taking place on the eastern side, however, led to the creation of a power vacuum, which produced deep disruption and instability. Here I refer not only to the emergence of the new independent states in Central Asia, but also to the dislocation of the two federations, Czechoslovakia and Yugoslavia; the first situation being a peaceful process but the other one generating violent conflicts and international involvement.

The end of the Cold War did not cause the disappearance of threats to European security, as the war in the former Yugoslavia has already shown, as have the disputes over the borders of Armenia and Georgia. The absence of a consensus on national identity, the clash between historical tradition and present geopolitics can be the origin of dangerous political upsets. Romania's case stands out among other political transitions in southeastern Europe. The combination of a unitary state, proportional representations of minorities, and openness to cooperation across ethnic lines, from every party, kept the ethnic tensions at a much lower level than was expected in the early 1990s.

Romania's relationship with Hungary needed resetting. Bilateral treaties with that neighbor, however, established an agreement based on mutual trust. The normalization of relations between Romania and Hungary was a required as a precondition of membership in the Council of Europe, NATO, and the EU. The accession of Romania to the EU in 2007 was celebrated as a great triumph within Romania. It was only possible because of the assistance of Western diplomacy. It was, indeed, a long delayed rehabilitation of the West. It helped assuage bitter Romanian memories about Churchill's concessions to Stalin following World War II, which allocated to Russia a preponderance of Soviet influence in the postwar Romanian government.

As far as domestic policy is concerned, it is easy to see that democracy, invoked as it is nowadays in ostentatious declarations, is less advanced in the passage of daily life than it is in procedures and formal institutions. Indeed, this situation is unsurprising, as Romanian history has not favored democratic institutions and ideologies. The lack of democratic opportunities can be traced to the remote past. An overview of the transition toward Romanian democracy is marked by residual anti-democratic attitudes that may be identified as coming from the Cold War period. But, we should also keep in mind the previous conditions. For instance, the history of unscrupulous behavior toward the state, which is commonly called "widespread corruption," can be attributed to a tradition of resistance against any authoritarian governance. Particularism and a culture of privilege are also inherited from long experience. Citizens' law abidingness is a measure of their acceptance of the legislative framework of the regime in which they live. The strict laws under communist rule were followed selectively and for the purpose of enhancing one's own interests.

We have seen in the 1990s, and even in the few more recent instances, how the government's intervention influences justice in Romania. For instance, President Iliescu publicly recommended to the Constitutional Court that it should prevent the restitution of private properties that had been confiscated by the communist state in 1950. Further, there is a tendency toward preserving many of the coercive measures that had been taken during the communist period. For example, despite the law on the right to consult one's files compiled by the Securitate (the political police that closely controlled one's private life), such files are selectively accessible. Denying people access to these records is crucial for protecting certain politicians who were guilty of crimes in the past. It also protects those who informed on their fellow citizens. Those in power, however, are quick to use adverse information of even minor significance from Securitate files against members of the opposition party. This is a practice the mass media are always ready to oblige, either through leaks or through silence. They have become tools of corruption.

After decades of living with minimal political communication and lacking the institutional structures of civil society, Southeastern Europe was thrust directly into postmodern political life by the sudden collapse of communism. Without ever having known modernity, with its process of collective action, political parties, and constituency building, Romania confronted monumental problems in building a new political culture. Romania's difficulty in developing an open mass media is informative. In Romania, as in Albania and Macedonia, the old news channels compete for political influence. There are a number of highly publicized instances of blackmail by press.[1] Instead of healing the public's spirits, the Romanian press has gradually lost the purity of the early years after 1989 and is a source of corruption itself. The Cold War legacy of lies and fear blend with the impact of economic fragility in Romania. This has retarded Romania's progress as a civil society.

Russia and the legacy of the Cold War

Konstantin Khudoley

There have been two tendencies in the foreign policy of the Russian Federation since the end of the Cold War.[2] The first tendency prevailed in the early 1990s and during the first presidency of Vladimir Putin—until the 2003 Iraq crisis. It was aimed at integrating Russia into the West as a part of Euro-Atlantic institutions. The culmination of Russia's political journey toward the West came with President Putin's speech to the Deutsche Bundestag on September 25, 2001, following the terrorist attacks in America on 9/11. This is when Putin announced, "The Cold War is over." Russia was following the path to democracy, and declared its willingness to work for better economic and security integration with Europe.

The second post-Cold War tendency in Russia's foreign policy is its recognition of the multipolar world. Since the collapse of the Soviet Union every president and prime minister has emphasized that Russia now exists in a multipolar world. It is necessary, however, to stress that when Russian politicians speak about the multipolar world they often have different conceptions as to its nature. Some of them truly believe that the multipolar world is possible and that Russia will be a major pole in it. The Russian political elite for some time believed that the country possessed sufficient resources to be one of the centers of the world. Others consider the talk about a multipolar world as a form of strategic maneuver in bargaining with the West over Russia's future position in the Euro-Atlantic community. Thus, for some, the discussion of a multipolar world is a strategy for Russia to pursue, while for others it is only a tactical bargaining position.

Today, integration in the Euro-Atlantic community is no longer the goal of Russian foreign policy. For example, in the first years of their presidencies, Yeltsin and Putin both expressed an interest in Russia joining NATO. After Putin, however, when President Medvedev first was asked about the possibility of Russia joining NATO, he replied that this now was out of question. Subsequently, on occasions when the issue of possible Russian membership in NATO was raised, Medvedev continued to say it was not currently possible; but then he would add, "Never say never." Currently a negative attitude toward NATO prevails in Russian ruling circles.

Russia's attempt to be an important center in the multipolar world has really emerged from the Iraq War crisis and the rise in energy prices that coincided with it. Because it is a major energy exporter, Russia has done very well for the past several years. Petro-money came in and the Federation's economy benefitted accordingly. Most Russian leaders now understand that the future development of the Russian economy, and Russia's position in a multipolar world, depends on the modernization of the entire Russian economy. This is a significant shift from the perspective taken just a few years ago in 2005–6, when Russian leaders deemphasized the need for economic reform because of the flow of petro-money. The Russian leadership now understands that the Russian economy is not strong enough for the Federation to be a center pole in the multipolar world. Its main emphasis at present is on the development of superior technology in the military industry.

Beyond the problem of modernizing its economy, Russia has significant political problems in attaining its strategic goal of becoming a major pole in the multipolar world. Most especially, Russia has had tremendous difficulty maintaining the loyalty and support of the surrounding former Soviet Republics. When confronted by situations requiring a choice between the Russian Federation and Washington, Brussels, or Beijing—most of these states have tended consistently to side against the Federation. Russia's difficulty in this respect was made worse by the Caucasus Crisis of 2008, when it engaged Georgia in military conflict over South Ossetia. It is significant that while Nicaragua and Venezuela supported Russia in this conflict, the Federation failed to win the support of Belarus and other post-Soviet countries. Although Russia prevailed over Georgia, the result was not very good for the Russian Federation, as it further alienated its neighbors. Thus, the prospects for Russia becoming the political center of the post-Soviet states are very limited.

Russian efforts to become an economic center in the multipolar world have not been very successful. The provision of significant economic assistance to some post-Soviet states has not produced influence, loyalty, or support from these regimes. Russia so far has practically nothing to show politically for the investment. Further, Russia's attempt to form a customs union among the post-Soviet states did not succeed. There have been some trade agreements between Russia and these countries, but the effort to make the Russian ruble the common currency for these countries has not been successful. After Vladimir Putin returned to the presidency in 2012, the idea of creating a Eurasian union, based on the custom union of three countries, became once more the priority of Russian foreign policy.

An important legacy of the Cold War in Russia is the change in ideology. Communism is gone and no single ideological perspective has replaced it. Although there is talk in some quarters about a cohesive Russian national idea it does not seem to have gone very far. What exists is a mixture of pluralist ideologies among the Russian elite. In practice, the Russian elite does not want to have a single dominant ideology. They prefer to maneuver from one side to another—sometimes liberal, sometimes nationalistic, and sometimes in other directions. Among Russian elites and the general population there is one ideological position that clearly is a legacy of the Cold War, which is nostalgia for the Soviet times. There is an attitude among elites and the ordinary people that in the Soviet days it was good and now it is bad. Nobody really wants to return to the old days. Very few Russians, including old supporters of the Communist Party, really want the return of Soviet power. They are reconciled to the new regime—but nonetheless, people have nostalgia for the good old days and that affects contemporary Russian political attitudes.

It is clear that most of the political and economic elite consider Russia a European country. But, they also feel that the West is often anti-Russian and very unfriendly to their country. This leaves the Russian elite with the attitude that Russia is somehow not a part of the "West," but it is a part of Europe. This is really the position for the most of the Russian elite, and is a matter of controversy among its members, as they confront the need better to integrate the Russian Federation into the European economic and security framework.

Thus, there are many practical problems as the Russian Federation moves through the first stage of its transition away from the Soviet Union. It is a very difficult process and Russia is only at the beginning of a long journey. It must deal with attitudes, suspicions, and hostilities that are part of the legacy of the Cold War. But, new ideas are coming forward for dealing with this legacy—even though Russia is very far from transforming proclamations about its future into practical reality.

There is one legacy of the Cold War that is very clear. One of the most important foreign policies of the Soviet Union was its determination to bring foreign investment to Russia. This remains the policy of the Russian Federation. The government remains determined to bring extensive, long-term foreign investment to Russia. If it can do so, it will fulfill the goals of a foreign policy that transcends the end of the Cold War. But it has yet to happen.

The post-Cold War relationship between China and the Russian Federation is complicated. There are tensions between them that are a legacy of the Cold War, although elites in both countries see the problems as manageable and well within "the rules of the game." Still, Russian officials in the Far East are very worried about the large number of Chinese who are illegal immigrants. The fear is this is the beginning of a Chinese "soft occupation" of the region. The problem is that, with a declining Russian population, the only growing source of labor is coming from China. Finally, it must be acknowledged what when the Russians speak about attracting foreign investment to the Federation, these days they are thinking mostly about China. So the Russian Federation is in the midst of a change in domestic affairs and this influences foreign policy, which as we all know, begins at home. The Cold War is over, but the transformation to a new Russia is ongoing and incomplete.

Russia's future and the illusions of a new world order

Alexander Likhotal

Russia's struggles to deal with the legacy of the Cold War are not the most important problem confronting the future of Europe. I do not mean to minimize or devalue what is going on today in Russia. In Moscow these days people joke that only the mentally retarded bother to criticize the government. That is because the deficiencies are so widespread and well known that it is boring to point them out. There is no freedom of press. There is no free parliament. There are no free courts of the country. So, why bother?

What is more important is to concentrate on what actually happens, and why the situation faced in Russia today is irrelevant beyond its borders. I would say that there is some mystical logic with the figures 11 and 9, 9 and 11. The opening and closing of a century never really coincide with the calendar. In my judgment, the twentieth century ended on the November 9,

1989. But the new century did not really begin until the September 11, 2001. I mean 9/11 or 11/9, however you put it, there is some mysticism to these numbers. And remember, it was on 9/11 of 1990 when President George H.W. Bush addressed the US Congress to declare the coming of the new world order.

Today, twenty years later, what does "the new world order" mean? Well, we somehow missed some very important points along the way. We failed to create this new world order and that is the problem, not only for Russia, but for the rest of the world as well.[3] During the Bush period there were some illusions on both sides. There was a degree of gentlemanly politics practiced by both sides during the period that produced important misunderstandings, which trouble US-Russian relations to this day. For example, in 1990 US Secretary of State James Baker offered Gorbachev assurances that NATO would not expand toward Russia. He said, "We guarantee to the Soviet Union that NATO will not move to the east even one inch."[4] Then the new American administration came into power. Ideologically and politically the Clinton administration wanted to move the dates of the end of the Cold War so as to give the laurels of the event to the Democratic Party. Therefore the dates were moved to coincide with the collapse of the Soviet Union. The political wisdom at that time in Washington was to attribute the end of the Cold War to the collapse of the Soviet Union during the Clinton administration. In my view, however, the Soviet Union would not have collapsed unless the Cold War had already ended—these events did not coincide.

It was within this framework that President Clinton arrived in Moscow in 1994. During the visit Boris Yeltsin told the US president that Russia was, indeed, well along the path to building democracy and a free market economy. And Clinton left fully reassured about the future of democracy in Russia. But, from then until this very day, if you go into any village in Russia and ask the people ""Do you want your president to be elected in open and free elections every four or five years?" They will respond, "Yes, of course we do." And, if you ask them, "Do you want to be able to criticize the corruption of your government and use the free media to do that?" They will say, "Yes, of course." You can continue with this line of questioning until you finally ask the people, "So you have become democrats?" And they will say, "Oh, for God's sake no!" You finally ask, "Why not?" They say, "Because when the democrats came into power they did exactly the opposite of what was promised or expected." Thus, in Russia, democracy is a very tricky word. To understand the legacy of the Cold War in Russia, you must understand the disillusionment about democracy that set in after the Yeltsin years. Also, it is necessary that we understand how Russian attitudes toward the United States have become negative because of America's post-1992 claim of having "won" the Cold War and defeated the Soviet Union, which is symbolized by NATO's expansion into Eastern Europe.

Also notable are Russian perceptions about the Chinese threat. First of all, the Chinese threat might be a reality, but it is a reality not because of China's strength, but because of the weakness of Russia. Whatever happens in terms of the gravitation of certain regions away from Russia and toward China, will not happen due to Chinese military aggression. Gravitation toward China is because of the economic situation and depends on how quickly Russia resolves its modernization agenda. Russia's relationship with China is similar to its relationship with NATO. It remains hostage to its traditional philosophy and Russia thinks it is "us against them." Russia continues to perceive NATO as a threat, and applies this same pattern of thought to its relationship with China. But, the problem is totally different today. The problem now is for Russia and others to comprehend how the efforts of all the nations can be combined to resolve joint vulnerabilities and respond to common threats.

To understand Russia's view of Western efforts to expand NATO, one must appreciate the historical context that frames American assurances that this is not a threat to Russia. It was in the period 1989–90 that discussions about possible NATO expansion took place between the United States and the USSR. The American Secretary of State, James Baker, in his Washington office, told diplomats that NATO would not expand into Eastern Europe. Baker has never denied that this discussion took place. Russia expected NATO would undergo a reorientation and fundamental restructuring at the end of the Cold War. We hoped it would become an organization that engaged all of Europe, including Russia, in a cooperative security system. Unfortunately, that is not what happened. From the Russian viewpoint, instead of moving to a more inclusive Europe-wide security organization, NATO continued as an anti-Russian institution—returning to the mentality upon which it was originally founded. Lord Ismay, NATO's first General Secretary, described the alliance's original mission very clearly when he declared, "We need NATO to keep Americans in, the Germans down, and Russians out." How could the USSR join NATO at the beginning of the Cold War given that mission? How could Russia after the Cold War join NATO, given Western triumphalism and the alliance's expansion toward its territory? Russia sees NATO's expansion into the countries of the former Warsaw Pact as a great breach of faith.[5] Because of it, a tremendous opportunity was missed to build a real architecture for European security in the future.[6]

The post-Cold War years were very difficult for the Russian people. In 1992, the rate of inflation was 2,600 percent per year. In 1993 the entire population witnessed the shelling of the Parliament on television. In 1994 privatization auctions created a few "dollar" billionaires in a country where almost eighty percent of the population lived below the poverty level. In 1995–1996 Boris Yeltsin sought reelection. Thanks to the manipulation of the media, his popularity was raised in three months from three percent to fifty-three percent and he continued in power. That was the end of the free media and a free press in the country.[7] Then in 1998 there was the collapse of the financial pyramid, which sent the rest of the population to the poverty level. After that, everything moved gradually in the same undemocratic direction until 1999, which crowns this story, when the country was introduced to heir to the throne, Mr. Vladimir Putin.[8]

One unfortunate legacy of the Cold War is the tendency for some in the West, in the United States especially, to engage in triumphalism. I cannot believe that anybody in his or her right mind would claim that the Cold War was lost by the Soviet Union. That is because I find it impossible to agree that the opening of the way to freedom for 250 million people can in any way be considered a "lost" war. It is critical that we should not confuse the regime with the nation, which is too often being done in considering the end of the Cold War. This monumental series of events, which culminated in the end of communist rule in Eastern Europe and in Russia, was a tremendous breakthrough for the entire world. We should all be proud, including the Russian people, of what possibilities opened thanks to the end of the Cold War.

We did not, of course, always draw the right conclusions as to the meaning of the end of the Cold War and the collapse of the Soviet Union. The post-Cold War world has moved in unanticipated directions. National and international security, for example, must be understood in completely different terms today. Security now is detached from traditional territorial or national reference points. It has become global in its scope. The threat of terrorism, or as I prefer to call it, the privatization of war, has created a lot of problems for major stakeholders in the world. Worldwide terrorist networks, which exist today due to globalization, are able to take advantage of worldwide vulnerabilities. That is very clear. Threats have become defused and security challenges have acquired an existential dimension. For much of the Cold War, humankind lived under the threat of Mutually Assured Destruction (MAD). It really was a mad situation. Today humankind is moving from a MAD world into a NUTS world; that is to say, we no longer live under the threat of nuclear extermination, but now face the growing threat of Nature Use-up Triggered Suicide (NUTS). Our fear of the finger on the nuclear trigger has been replaced by our fear of the foot on the gas pedal.[9]

Today the former adversaries in the Cold War face tremendous mutual problems. The tremendous challenges stand at our gates and we must respond immediately to them. To do so we must use multilateral approaches that are based, not on the basis of joint interests, but on the basis of mutual exposures and vulnerabilities. This is important due to the multipolar structure of the post-Cold War world. The fate of our children is determined today not only in Washington, London, and Moscow. Our children's future also is being shaped in Beijing, New Delhi, and

Singapore, as well as in many other capitals around the world. Countries around the world are realizing that in the multipolar world they have acquired veto rights over our economic development. That will change everything very soon.

Russia and the end of the Soviet Empire

Sir Anthony Brenton

The end of the Cold War, and the way it ended, is the single most important historical event that has happened in my lifetime. It is essential that we do not lose track of that fact. This volume and its account of the Cold War and its legacy help us assure that important fact is not lost. Earlier, Charles Powell asked, I suspect for rhetorical effect, whether the Cold War had in fact ended. That question nicely places our fingers on the key issue about the heritage of the Cold War, which in a word is Russia. All the rest of the nations of Europe are in one way or another, with various degrees of difficulty, becoming integrated into the EU.[10]

NATO is moving in the sort of democratic and the market economy direction that we all thought it would at the time the Cold War ended. At that time we also had those expectations about Russia. And then it all began to go sour. I served in Russia twice—first 1994–8 and then again in 2004–8. The common thrust during both periods was telling. The first period was dreadful due to the collapsing economy. I was there for the very shoddy presidential election in 1996, the first ever Russian presidential election in all of its history, which produced President Yeltsin. I was in the city of Kazan during the several rounds of the election. I read the instructions from the President of Kazan to the effect that the vote counters needed to do a better job for President Yeltsin this time around.

It was, of course, a time of hyperinflation and of gangsterism. There was a genuine threat to the integrity of the Russian Federation, not only in the form of the war in Chechnya, but in the fact that other bits of Russia, such as Tatarstan, were making themselves increasingly autonomous and threatening to the central authorities. It was a very polarized society; you had the rule of oligarchs and there were more billionaires in Moscow than in New York. The oligarchs were seizing all of the national assets on the one hand, while the very angry Russian population was being impoverished on the other. Externally, the West, in effect, was insouciantly going its own way. NATO was being expanded toward Russia's closest neighbors, despite the assurances the Russians thought they had received to the contrary, and the alliance was conducting a war in Kosovo despite strenuous Russian objections.

It was a very bad time for Russia. It is unsurprising, given those circumstances, that Russia found a strong man, as she has so often before in her history. Vladimir Putin took control and began to put the place together again, in a way that has to be recognized was very satisfactory to most of the Russian citizenry.

Until recently the economy grew fast. It nearly doubled in size over the first decade of this century. This was due not only to oil and gas, but also because the necessary economic benefits from unwinding communism continued to unfold. Putin imposed *poriadok*, "order," which in Russia is considered a wonderful thing.[11] The Russians really feel *poriadok* is necessary for them to control such a big, difficult country.

So, Putin imposed order by throwing out the press oligarchs. He brought the provincial governors firmly under control and made clear they would no longer be allowed to wander off in their own directions. Putin won the war in Chechnya, by brutal means of course, but he won it nonetheless. He tamed the oligarchs, the excessively rich, by locking one of them up for quite a long time. Putin began to reestablish Russia's external national pride. He won war in Georgia; he turned off the gas in Ukraine when they refused to pay their bills. Putin directed a more activist, prouder, richer, more centrally effective Russia. The Russians loved him for it. Along with his protégé Medvedev, his hand-picked successor as president, Putin gets the sorts of popularity numbers in polls that British leaders would die for. But, all of this happened in Russia at the expense of civil liberties and liberal values.

Thus, we have just seen a series of local elections, which even the sort of payroll opposition felt the need to protest. During the last presidential election I was there for, which was the presidential election of Medvedev, there was really very little pretense that this was going to be a fair election. Any threatening candidate was simply excluded from the ballot. There are a few free newspapers in Russia, but not many. The press and the television are very firmly controlled. One of the bright spots is the Internet, which remains uncontrolled, but even this arena of free expression is being threatened. So what we have to live with is a Russia that is diverging quite notably from the way we in the West like to conduct our business. As I see it, that is the current picture in Russia. I will draw five conclusions from that picture, three pessimistic and two optimistic.

First of all our earlier euphoria was visibly misplaced. We are not yet at the end of history, we're in for a pretty bumpy ride. We have a selfassertive Russia still feeling for its place in the world, it's going to remain a challenge for some time to come and we are going to have to adapt our policies accordingly. The original naiveté noticeable in many European countries' foreign policy about Russia feels increasingly naive as time goes on.

Second, I detect tendencies in the West in the direction of liberal guilt, as if we are somehow responsible for what has happened to Russian democracy. That is wrong; we have tried to help them. We have tried to help the Russians in their transition from communism and the Soviet regime. We have tried our best to advise them, but Russia is a big, proud country and it has gone its own way. Where Russia now finds itself is due to Russian factors. It may be, for example, that NATO expansion aroused Russian irritation, but it was marginal. Russia is going to continue to evolve according to its own internal dynamic. That is something to which we must simply adapt. We can try to be helpful, but Russia's transition is not a process we can control. Nor should we feel guilty about the way it has gone so far.

My third pessimistic point is if you contrast how Russia has evolved with the fate of the rest of Central and Eastern Europe, there is a striking difference. The rest of Central and Eastern Europe have, with more or less difficulty, accommodated themselves into Western institutions. One of the best things that the EU has ever done vis-à-vis the post-communist states is to give all of them a goal, on the condition that they maintain democratic values. That has been crucial to the democratic evolution of Europe since the Cold War. Russia, unfortunately, has not followed suit. Now we could not offer that goal; it would have rejected it if we had. This shows that the problem with Russia's post-Cold War transition is fundamentally different from the problem of the transition in Poland, or the other countries in Central Eastern Europe.

I would point to two probable explanations for that difference. First of all, Russia is an ex-empire. We are looking at a tremendous post-imperial transition that has to be made. Russia is not just a country finding a new home in the new international system. Second, there is the question of ideology to which Professor Khudoley alludes in his essay. The Russian elite got used to thinking of themselves as being in the vanguard of the new world; communism, it is worth recalling, was the great Messianic philosophy which was going to solve things for all of us. Russia, if you go down its history, has a certain Messianic history and they have lost that. They are now a big country, but just another country, and that is very difficult to adapt to. These are my three gloomy points about the way things are going to go in Russia.

I have two positive conclusions to offer as to the current state of Russia. First, as Professor Khudoley observes earlier in this chapter, Russia is a European county. It thinks of itself as European country and the values to which Russians aspire are European. The least threatening border that Russia has is the border to its west. It is striking to me that Russia for the moment is adopting the new Chinese model for authoritarian capitalism. But in the long run, this model has no intellectual or socio-logical attraction for the Russian people. The magnet for them remains Europe and European values and that is going to be important as Russia continues to evolve.

The second optimistic conclusion is that Russia is an ex-empire. In considering Russia's relationship with the rest of the world, I am inclined to make the comparison between Russia's post-imperial history and the post-imperial history of my own country, the United Kingdom. Now, you cannot date the end of the British Empire as precisely as you can indicate the end of the Soviet Empire, in effect ending in 1991. But, for us British 1956 is a reasonably good date to pick. Now, if you think about the subsequent 30 odd years of British history following 1956, well they were ghastly. We did not know where we were in the world. We were no longer an empire to be sure. But what were we? We knew we were not a Luxembourg, but we did not know where or how we fitted into the international order. There was a European union with which we were deeply uncomfortable. Our trade orientation was in a completely different direction. Our economy was in very bad shape. It took until the late Margaret Thatcher period before the United Kingdom fully emerged from its post-imperial trauma. It was only then that we finally arrived at our current state of economic and political selfconfidence. So, it took Britain about 35 years to make its post-imperial transition. Now, as I look at the Russians, whenever I address Russian audiences, I say "You guys are nearly half way through the transition from an empire."

As regards the Russians and NATO expansion, I do not know whether assurances were given. All these years later it is not factually important as to whether or not they actually were offered by the Americans. What is important is that the Russians seriously believed those assurances were given. They are feeling betrayed by the subsequent history, and it's worth considering that NATO has now become the cockpit in a way of many of the core disagreements between Russia and the West.

With the Cold War having ended, I cheerfully assumed, along with a great many others, that NATO would fade away. With the passing of the Cold War, its purpose had been served and NATO no longer had a purpose. Actually we found another purpose for NATO, and it is a good purpose. It is needed for dealing with places like Afghanistan. The presumption at the end of the Cold War, held naively in London and elsewhere, was that we would be able to cooperate with the Russians in dealing in bad places with difficult situations. That has happened to some extent. The trouble is that there are very divided motivations among NATO members. People like the Poles and the Estonians are in NATO precisely in order to keep the Russians out and we hit the crunch when the question of Georgian membership of NATO came along. Georgia is a country that the Russians regarded firmly as, to use a nineteenth-century term, in their "sphere of influence." Russia simply was not going to let join Georgia join NATO under any conditions. NATO does have to find a modus vivendi with Russia. The alliance has to accept that there are places where it cannot go, and I would say that Georgia and Ukraine are among those. Still, NATO and Russia do share certain agendas; they have, for example, mutual concerns in Afghanistan, Iran, and so on. This common ground is a good place to look for new sources of cooperation.

Notes

1   Mihai Coman, "Press Freedom and Media Pluralism in Romania," in *Press Freedom and Pluralism in Europe: Concepts and Conditions*, A. Czepek, M. Hellwig, and N. Nowak (eds) (Bristol: Intellect, 2009), 193–94.

2   Konstantin Khudoley, "Modern Russian Policy Toward Europe," in *Russia and Europe in a Changing European Environment*, K. Malfliet and L. Verpoest (eds) (Leuven: Leuven University Press, 2001).

3   See Stephen Cohen, *Soviet Fates and Lost Alternatives: From Stalinism to the New Cold War* (New York: Columbia University Press, 2009), chapters 6 and 7.

4   See Philip Zelikow and Condoleezza Rice, *Germany Unified and Europe Transformed: A Study in Statecraft* (Cambridge: Harvard University Press, 1995), 182 and Ronald D. Asmus, *Opening NATO's Door: How the Alliance Remade Itself for a New Era* (New York: Columbia University Press, 2002), 4–7.

5   See Mary Elise Sarotte, "Not One Inch Eastward? Bush, Baker, Kohl, Genscher, Gorbachev, and the Origin of Russian Resentment Toward NATO Enlargement in February 1990," *Diplomatic History* 34, no. 1 (January 2010), 119–40.

6   See Cohen, *Soviet Fates*, 167–71.

7   See Cohen, *Soviet Fates*, 144–56.

8   See M. Stephen Fish, *Democracy Derailed in Russia: The Failure of Open Politics* (New York: Cambridge University Press, 2005) and Katlijn Malfliet and Ria Laenen (eds), *Elusive Russia: Current Developments in Russian State Identity and Institutional Reform Under President Putin* (Leuven: Leuven University Press, 2007).

9   Alexander Likhotal, "The Road From Copenhagen," speech delivered at the Sustainable World Congress, July 23, 2009. http://www.gcint.org/news/road-copenhagen

10   See Katlijn Malfliet, Lien Verpoest, and Evgeny Vinokurov, *The CIS, the EU, and Russia: Challenges of Integration* (London: Palgrave Macmillan, 2007).

11   See also, Daniel Treisman, *The Return: Russia's Journey From Gorbachev to Medvedev* (New York: The Free Press, 2011). See also Stephen Wegren (ed.), *Return to Putin's Russia: Past Imperfect, Future Uncertain*, 5th edn. (Oxford: Rowman & Littlefield, 2012).

CHAPTER NINE

The Asian legacy

The end of the Cold War and the disintegration of the Soviet Union have had profound implications for Asia. The major communist regimes in this region, China, North Korea, and Vietnam remain as vestiges of the Cold War. The end of the superpower confrontation between the United States and the USSR, however, has affected these regimes in very different ways than their counterparts in Eastern Europe. This is also true for the major noncommunist regimes Japan, South Korea, and India. The rigid relations among nations in this increasingly significant geopolitical region have evolved into patterns of dynamic multilateralism. This transformation and its implications are considered from the perspectives of India, Japan, and China. Amidst a mutual sense of relief over the end of the US-Soviet mobilization of the nations of the Third World, these essays reflect upon the challenges of a multipolar world and the role of Asian nations in it—especially as new relationships emerge with Russia and the United States in the post-Cold War era.

Kishan Rana provides the Asian legacy of the Cold War from the perspective of India. Based on his experience as a career diplomat and as a commentator on diplomatic affairs, Rana holds that the close of the Cold War provided the impetus for a renaissance in India's role in regional and international relations. As an international relations scholar, Yoshihide Soeya provides an assessment of the continuing Cold War divisions, which define and continue to restrict Japan's role as a regional and global player in the post-Cold War era. Ying Rong provides China's perspective on the legacy of the Cold War in Asia. Rong emphasizes the implications of this nation's movement from the periphery of global affairs during the Cold War to its present position as a world economic power at the center of regional and international relations. John Swenson-Wright offers an overall assessment of the Asian legacy of the Cold War. He focuses on how the end of the Cold War has affected regional continuities and discontinuities. Swenson-Wright emphasizes that the different perceptions of government elites and mass populations in Japan and Korea continue to affect the prospects for reconciliation and future cooperation.

The view from India

Kishan Rana

The end of the Cold War coincided with what one can only call a renaissance for India. It was a kind of "second independence" of India, except that this time it was India's liberation from itself. This renaissance freed India from its selfimposed, pseudosocialistic, quasi-statist, and tightly regulated system. The end of the Cold War was an extraordinary turning point for India in several different ways.

In international affairs the logic of non-alignment had run its course. Conditions were right for change. But, more than anything else, it was the collapse of the Soviet Union, which forced the Indian establishment to reconsider its position. India had become rather attached to the Soviet Union for a variety of reasons, which were all very much related to the Cold War. The renaissance was also related to the alliances that the West had brought into our region. In May 1991, Rajiv Gandhi was assassinated in the middle of an election campaign. P. V. Narasimha Rao, a reluctant candidate for the position, then became prime minister. It was at this point that a crisis became an opportunity. India was so broke that it actually sold gold in order to meet its external payment obligations. Thus, the unthinkable became the source of bold action and economic reforms were launched. Narasimha Rao was the prime mover for this historic reform effort. The finance minister, Manmohan Singh was the principal architect of the economic reform, which restructured and liberalized the Indian economy. State control of the economy was quite rapidly demolished. While the economic transition from a state-controlled to a market economy has been uneven, it has consistently moved forward. Every Indian prime minister since Narasimha Rao has advanced reforms in his own way. The collapse of the USSR, and recognition of post-Cold War financial realities, produced significant and ongoing efforts to reform India's economy.

With regard to foreign policy, the collapse of the Soviet Union forced an evaluation of our ties with the West. Pragmatism became the anchor for Indian external policy. Market reform required much greater engagement with the world. In order for India's economy to be competitive there had to be more international trade, increased foreign direct investment, and technological innovation. To accomplish this, India was forced to build new relationships with the West. That, in turn, led to a rapid change in its global posture. In making that change, India has achieved a measure of economic success, but huge problems remain. Approximately a quarter of the population is below the poverty line. Much remains to be done to reduce poverty and produce social services. India has weathered the global recession in a fairly positive fashion. A reasonable rate of economic growth has continued.

Several foreign relations challenges remain. India recently negotiated, with some difficulty, a civilian nuclear cooperation agreement with the United States. The government then found that selling that agreement domestically was a lot harder than negotiating with the Americans. The government almost fell, but it somehow managed to survive. That has led to a qualitative change in the relationship with the United States.

In South Asia, there is the challenge of crafting a new relationship between Delhi and Islamabad. Between them remains a complex series of problems that are again a legacy of the Cold War. Our relations with Pakistan are extremely complicated. We now know that during the last years of General Musharraf's presidency, there was a back channel dialogue that had come within striking distance of a major solution. The Pakistanis insist that this was almost accomplished. The Indian side is a little more cautious. But we know things had moved forward. Then came the huge setback in Indian-Pakistani relationships caused by the Mumbai attacks in November 2008.

On major international issues such as climate change, the World Trade Organization, and disarmament, India is torn between its old positions and new ways of thinking. In the end, India's real challenge is to move from being an outlier nation, stuck on the periphery of global affairs, into a country that is a central actor in shaping solutions to international problems. Indians have never been isolationist vis-à-vis international affairs. Engagement was always India's policy. But sometimes we trapped ourselves in a corner by posturing in ways that were not taken seriously. Now India has to make a transition so that it is perceived as a consensus builder in regional and global affairs. It must, for example, in areas such as climate change, cease its tendency to focus so much on its own sense of righteousness. India will have to recognize how its economic modernization efforts impact global pollution, and find ways to join international efforts to solve this problem without putting a cap on its economic growth.

India continues to have basic identity with the global South as a developing country. It continues to work through this major transition. This will be India's second great transition. To complete it, though, there will have to be consensus at home, which is not easy, and understanding abroad.

India in the post-Cold War era is determined to engage constructively in international affairs. India has, for example, managed to reconstruct its relationship with Russia, which is a positive development. We now are engaged with Russia and China in two groups that have some potential for cooperative relationships. One is the BRIC group, in which Brazil, Russia,

India, and China work together on matters of advanced economic development. The BRIC group has not attracted much international attention, but it has held summit meetings that promote mutual understanding. The other group in which India is involved is a quiet trilateral process with Russia and China. It is not a formal alliance. It is not for the purpose of ganging up against any other group or nation. Rather, it is a quiet process through which the foreign ministers of these countries meet periodically to discuss shared interests. These efforts exemplify the ways in which India seeks engagement on points of commonality with other nations.

At the same time, it is important to note that India's relationship with China is complex. There are elements of competition and there are limits to collaboration, which we will have to work our way through. It makes no sense, however, for India to join anybody else's agenda in order to constrain China.

As seen from Asia, one gets the impression that Europe is not terribly relevant anymore. Europe takes minimal interest, for example, in organizations such as the Council for Security Cooperation in the Asian Pacific. The rather annoying thing is that, all too often, the EU is absent from the meetings of these organizations. We wish for a bigger European presence in Asia because every other major power center meets in Asia.

If one looks at the Cold War in an East-West centric mode, one ends up missing a very large part of what went on during the Cold War: its impact on Africa and Latin America. This matters because the two power blocs mobilized these newly independent nations to serve their regional and global strategic purposes. The United States and the Soviets essentially compelled these nations to choose between them, and that has produced an extraordinary legacy that needs to be examined.

The view from Japan

Yoshihide Soeya

The Cold War produced five enduring divisions among the nations of East Asia, which were exacerbated by post-World War II and indigenous factors. It is important to emphasize that these divisions would not have occurred without the Cold War. Although its end removed the framework, the divisions caused by the Cold War remain. In the post-Cold War era, it is the indigenous factors that must now be understood as perpetuating the divisions in East Asia. The divisions have hardly disappeared at all. This has led some observers to contend that the Cold War has not ended in this region. They point, in particular, to the continued divisions of Korea and China. That is, in my view, very misleading; the end of the Cold War is real. It is over in East Asia, but its legacy continues to affect the region deeply.[1]

The first Cold War division was the division of China. The story of Asia during the Cold War is very different from that of Europe because of China's existence as an independent strategic actor. China never officially sided with one bloc or another during the Cold War. After the defeat of Japan, it was assumed by the Allied Powers that China, under the Nationalist Party led by Chiang Kai-shek, would be a primary actor in the postwar order. This is why China got a seat as one of the five permanent members in the UN Security Council. That, however, is not the role China was destined to play in the critical transition from World War II to the Cold War. The communists led by Mao Zedong prevailed in the Chinese Civil War of 1945–9. Chiang's nationalists were driven to the offshore islands of Taiwan, Penghu, Kinmen, and Matsu. Initially, the United States looked to recognize the People's Republic of China (PRC) and to ignore Chiang's regime on Taiwan. The Truman administration continued to see China as a strategic partner in ordering affairs in Asia. The outbreak of the war in Korea, however, changed the US-PRC relationship. Thus, the division of China between the communist PRC on the mainland, and the noncommunist Republic of China (ROC) on Taiwan, became a permanent feature of the Cold War. It remains a contentious legacy of the Cold War to the present day.

The second important Cold War division affecting Asia is the separation of China and the United States. These close World War II allies were initially separated by the communist victory in the Chinese Civil War, but their division became a permanent fixture of the Cold War by virtue of the breakout of the Korean War. Once the People's Army of the PRC joined the North Korean Army, and directly engaged the UN forces led by the United States, adversarial Sino-American relations were set for the remainder of the Cold War. Eventually, their animosity diminished and their relations normalized. The Sino-American strategic rivalry in Asia, however, endures and deeply affects geopolitical affairs in the region. China's rise as a global power has moved the division with the United States beyond Asia.

The permanent partition of the Korean Peninsula, between the communist Democratic People's Republic of Korea (PRK) and the noncommunist Republic of Korea (ROK) is the third Cold War division. This division was not anticipated when World War II ended. The plan of the Allied Powers was to place Korea within the international trusteeship system following a temporary division of Korea at the 38th parallel. The United States, USSR, United Kingdom, and China in December 1945 agreed to establish a five-year trusteeship for the Korean Peninsula. The plan was to create an independent, stable, and democratic Korea, which would never again become a hot spot for Asian power rivalries. Provisional governments were established in the Soviet and US zones of occupation while the details for a trustee plan were under development. This plan, however, was doomed because of the unfolding conflict between the United States and the Soviet Union that became the Cold War. When the United States and the USSR deadlocked over implementation of the Korean trusteeship, the UN called for free and fair elections to determine Korea's government. The Soviet-backed regime north of the 38th parallel refused to cooperate with the UN election process. Thus, in 1948 the division of the Korean Peninsula became permanent as a direct result of the confrontation between the USSR and the United States.

The fourth Cold War division is the division between Japan and China. Soon after the end of World War II, the establishment of close relations between Japan and China seemed almost a matter of common sense. The economic recovery of Japan, it seemed at the time, would be almost impossible without establishing close relations with China, particularly in terms of its import and export markets. The loss of the Chinese market due to the Korean War and the Cold War, however, led Japan to undertake a new recovery strategy. Japan's future became tied to the United States, especially economically, and this disrupted the prospects for credible, meaningful relations with China.

The fifth division caused by the Cold War occurred in domestic Japanese politics. Had World War II ended later, if only by a matter of weeks, and had the Soviets been able to move directly against the home islands, Japan might well have ended up partitioned into US and Soviet occupation zones. This division could have produced a divided Japan much like Korea. At that time, Japan might have been divided rather than Korea. And rather than a People's Republic in Korea, there might have been a People's Republic in Japan. The fast end to the war prevented this and was a critical turning point. The Korean people today believe that they sacrificed themselves to prevent the division of Japan. I am inclined to believe that is true. It is likely that had Japan been so divided, all of Korea would have fallen within the Soviet orbit. The reality, of course, is that Korea was divided and Japan remained united. Japan was then remade directly under American rule. The Cold War, however, split domestic politics within this united Japan.

In 1946, the Post-War Constitution of Japan was literally written and imposed by the Americans. The majority of the Japanese people nevertheless accepted it as legitimate. In Article 9 of the Constitution, the Japanese people "forever renounced war as a sovereign right of the nation." It further declared: "land, sea, and air forces, as well as other war potential, will never be maintained." The international system for which the Americans wrote Article 9, however, did not come into existence. The Cold War intervened. American strategic thinking shifted dramatically in the presence of the Soviet and Chinese threats in Asia. The United States subsequently realized it needed Japan to contribute to its strategic security posture in Asia. Having taken the logic of Article 9 to heart, much of

Japanese society subsequently refused to accommodate the new Cold War realities, despite US pressure to do so. Instead, the Americans had to settle for the Security Treaty Between the United States and Japan in 1951, which allowed the United States to maintain certain of its armed forces in and about Japan. This made Japan a strategic security ally of the United States in the Cold War. It supported the projection of American power in East Asia and beyond. By agreeing to do this, however, the government created a deep and bitter political divide in Japanese politics that endures to this very day.

There currently is no consensus among policy-makers as to the future orientation of Japanese diplomatic relations. For many years after the end of World War II, in Japanese society and politics there was great support for the constitutional limits on military alliances, which cast great doubt on the legality of the United States-Japan security alliance. This phenomenon was called "Japan's Post-War pacifism." As a result of the end of the Cold War, however, the pacifist groups have diminished in their influence. More conservative groups, which support more Japanese participation in security alliances and the UN's international peacekeeping activities, have grown in influence. This division is a symptom of the inherent contradiction between Article 9 of the Post-War Constitution and the reality of Japan's security alliance with the United States. Japan's task is to somehow resolve that contradiction in view of the realities of the post-Cold War world.

The view from China

Ying Rong

On the day the Soviet Union ended in 1991, when its flag was lowered and the hammer and sickle just disappeared, I received a telephone call from a childhood friend. We had grown up together in the same village and had been classmates until I left for the university in Beijing. He remained in the village, became a member of the Communist Party, and worked for the local government. When he called, I was a junior member of the Institute for International Studies. My friend knew this organization was connected with the Ministry of Foreign Affairs. He assumed I was in a knowledgeable position. So he asked me, "Now that the Soviet Union is gone, what is going to happen to China? What is going to happen to people like us?" These questions were on the minds of many people in China at the time. It was not just a concern for my friend. With my limited knowledge of the situation, I responded to my friend by saying, "Nothing serious is going to happen to China, or its people, as a consequence of the Soviet collapse."

The story of my friend's phone call, indeed, demonstrates the difficult situation China faced at the time of the demise of the Soviet Union and at the end of the Cold War. The economic reforms that began in 1978 were running into difficulties. The domestic political situation was unsettled, as was shown in the Tiananmen Incident.[2] In the wake of the collapse of the Soviet Union and the end of the Cold War, China found itself under sanctions and internationally isolated. The Chinese government was deeply concerned by the overwhelming Western military power demonstrated in the Gulf War. Our relations with the international community in general, and the United States in particular, were very tense due to questions about trade, human rights, and the Nuclear Non-Proliferation Treaty.[3]

Things have changed for China, and again, I think this is exemplified by subsequent conversations between my friend and me. After 1991, he developed an interest in international affairs and became quite expert. He would call me to discuss his questions and concerns about China's global situation. After 1999, however, he stopped calling and we almost completely lost contact. In 2008, I returned to my home town and inquired about my friend. It turned out he had become a successful businessman. He appeared to be quite happy and was doing well. Apparently, he no longer felt the need to consult with me for consolation or advice. Things had changed and he could get along quite well without people like me, and the organization in which I was employed. And in many ways, that is the story of what has happened in China over the past two decades since the end of the Cold War. The economic reforms have proceeded and they have changed things dramatically. What is commonly overlooked, however, is that, to some extent, reform in the political field has occurred as well. There has been an emancipation of minds from the old ways of thinking, which was initiated by the leaders in the Chinese government. This new thinking has restored confidence in China and its place in the world.

A very significant shift has taken place in China. Economic reconstruction and development rather than revolution is now seen as the central task of the regime. This perspective has led China to become more pragmatic in its relations with other major powers. As it has done so, China has grown in experience and confidence as an actor in international affairs. In this, it was fortunate to have the leadership of Deng Xiaoping. Deeply respected within the Communist Party of China, and among the Chinese people, Deng had the vision and sense of pragmatism required to accomplish major economic and political reform despite tremendous challenges.

In the post-Cold War era, China is emerging as a more confident nation, but faces several important challenges. First, China must clarify how it will contribute to development and modernization in Asia. The Chinese government seeks to have China viewed internationally as a harmonious society, which is committed to peace and common development among nations, but substance needs to be added. Second, China must continue to progress in its effort to find a path for economic development which features "socialism with Chinese characteristics." Although China, over the past two decades, has been able to solve much of its ideological problem of balancing socialist and capitalist principles, much more work needs to be done. In particular, if the rising expectations of the people are to be met, then significantly more work needs to done to assure that the benefits of economic reform are better shared with the public as a whole. Finally, China must manage the growing challenge to its environment created by rapid economic development.

China has been able to achieve a great deal in the two decades since the end of Cold War, particularly in terms of contributing to a stable and peaceful region. This it has accomplished first by normalizing, and then by improving, its relationship with its major neighbors. It has made remarkable progress in improving relations with others as well, especially Russia.[4] It is true that China's relationships with India and Japan are very complicated, but as these mature and deepen, cooperation surely will increase. What matters is that these nations look to the future and not to the past. Further progress in China's relationship with its Asian neighbors will have to occur within the context of its interaction with the United States.

As China has become more proactive in engaging multilateral forums, there is a growing realization that the Chinese are moving from the international sidelines to center stage. This means that China must adjust to its expanded global responsibilities. It means, as well, that China must work harder to meet the expectations of the international community regarding its behavior and its engagement.

Understanding the legacy of the Cold War in East Asia

John Swenson-Wright

An assessment of the legacy of the Cold War in East Asia is best organized around five themes. The first is the durability of political and territorial conflict. Second is the enduring strength of alliance relations in the region. The third theme is the growing importance of identity politics in the region. Fourth is the gap between the perceptions of national elites as compared to their domestic populations. Finally, there is how the historiography of the Cold War is changing as a result of the work by Asian scholars. Underpinning these themes we can find evidence of both continuities and discontinuities.

Politically and strategically the most obvious legacy to highlight is the remarkable continuity of the conflicts that matter within the region. The Korean Peninsula remains divided. The Kuril Islands continue to divide Russia from Japan. The unresolved standoff between Taiwan and China persists. The maritime territorial disputes are ongoing. All of these issues persist and act as obstacles for post-Cold War reconciliation. Most of these conflicts originate from the terminal stages of the Pacific War, which acted as a certain curtain raiser for the Cold War. In that sense, the legacy of the Potsdam Declaration and the San Francisco Peace Treaty Process has been to reinforce age-old enmities, despite the disappearance of the Soviet Union as a real and present danger. In other words, the imagery and the strategic landscape of the Cold War, superficially at least, remain little changed.

Of course, what has changed is the significance of such conflicts in a wider global context. If the salience of the security challenges remains pronounced for regional actors such as Korea and Japan, then for other actors, not the least of which is the United States, their importance has changed fundamentally. The Korean War is no longer a proxy war, which the superpowers were content to view as a limited conflict. North Korea's security challenge now is an existential one, given Pyongyang's de facto nuclear status. Pyongyang now threatens not only the survival of neighboring states, but also the global community either directly, through risk of proliferation, or indirectly by an escalating arms race. China's rise remains a concern because of its expanding defense budget. But this image of China as a threat is qualified for the United States, given Beijing's post-Cold War role as a strategic and economic partner. For a state such as Japan, of course, this image of China is not new. Throughout the Cold War we saw many incidences in which Japanese politicians were happy to embrace a form of cognitive dissonance in their relations with China. On the one hand, they sided publicly with the United States in its pre-1971 containment of China. On the other hand, they were happy at the same time to pursue semiofficial trade and cultural diplomacy with the PRC long before Japan's own normalization.

If strategic challenges and territorial disputes have remained persistent and frustratingly intractable, it is no accident that alliances set up to deal with these disputes remain intact. And in their fundamental aspects, the American alliances with Japan and South Korea are largely unchanged. Despite the periodic flareup of tension between the United States and its partners, these two core alliances remain fundamentally secure. Of course, the nature of these partnerships has evolved over time, but what is striking is how incremental the process of change has been.

Twenty years after the fall of the Berlin Wall, there have been no major renegotiations of security agreements between the United States and Japan, or South Korea. Instead, the scope of bilateral security cooperation has shifted to accommodate an increasingly extra-regional and global role for America and its two core Asian allies. In some cases, change is being designed to promote greater local autonomy or to minimize the tensions associated with the high-profile presence of American bases in the region. That such changes have taken place through administrative agreements, road maps, or new defense cooperation guidelines tells us something significant about public discourse surrounding alliance relationships, as well as about the gap between elite and public attitudes toward the United States. There is a discontinuity between the positive rhetoric so often used to characterize these two key American alliances, as compared with public sentiment in Tokyo, Seoul, and Washington.

So why have the alliances survived despite public ambivalence in both Japan and South Korea? In part it is due to the success of professional diplomats in managing the relationship. In the case of Japan, the success story is relatively easy to document. Former US Ambassador to Japan Mike Mansfield, famously characterized Japan as America's most important bilateral relationship, bar none. As a description of diplomatic reality, this is open to challenge, but it is a measure of the rhetorical capital that US officials have routinely invested in Japan. Diplomacy also helps explain the extraordinary success of officials, both in Washington and Tokyo, in transforming a bitter, adversarial relationship into a mutually supportive and durable partnership. Despite current tensions over such issues as American bases in Okinawa, Japanese Self-Defense Forces deployments in the Indian Ocean, and Prime Minister Hatoyama's public tilt toward more Asia-centric diplomacy, there is little to suggest that the relationship is about to fundamentally change. In that sense, the continuing strength of the US-Japan alliance is testament to the effectiveness of the national elite in managing the relationship.

In South Korea, by contrast, the record of US Cold War engagement is much more checkered. In part, this is because of the qualified American support for Korea's past authoritarian governments, as well as the troubled legacy of US indirect involvement in controversial events, such as the Gwangju Incident in 1980.[5]

It is one of the great ironies of America's Cold War involvement in Asia that the United States is much more successful in building secure partnerships with its former opponents, than in developing cooperative partnerships with the countries that were liberated from Japanese colonialism. How should we explain this? One key is perhaps ignorance, or to be more precise, the relatively limited American understanding of local conditions. America's post-World War II councilors in South Korea were extraordinarily ill-informed about the country they had to govern. By contrast, in Japan, there was arguably a more knowledgeable cadre of American specialists, who were better able to manage the post-World War II US-Japanese relationship.

The sharp contrast in the way American officials managed two equally critical alliances in the same part of the world demonstrates the particularity of historical events and the dangers of generalizing alliance relations, despite the best efforts by international relations specialists to squeeze these complicated relationships into neat theories. A legacy of disproportional ignorance is still with us today. Perhaps it helps to explain what critics will argue is the key shortcoming of recent US policy toward North Korea: a failure, in particular, to understand either the local circumstances or mentality of the North Koreans. Compare this with the more imaginative and empathetic, but nonetheless nationally selfinterested approach, which has allowed the United States to reconcile with two other Asian communist states, Vietnam and China. One of the puzzles of the present international relations of East Asia is the inability of successive US administrations to apply the lessons of engagement with Beijing or Hanoi to their relations with Pyongyang.

Another key factor in explaining the mixed record of US involvement in Asia is the emerging tensions associated with identity politics in both Japan and South Korea. In Japan, the clearest example is the debate over the so-called "normal Japan," which involves the gradual process of constitutional revision and the emergence of a newly invigorated Democratic Party. In this sense, the end of the Cold War opened up the arena for public debate in Japan in a manner that had not been seen since 1960, when the bitter struggles against the US-Japan Security Treaty occurred.

In South Korea, a parallel process took place with the decision by the government to declassify diplomatic documents relating to post-1945 relationships with Japan. Part of the self-image of the progressive government was its commitment to a more open style of politics. As a result, the government began to challenge some well-established South Korean political mythologies. Most especially, it questioned the notion of a South Korean nation united in opposition to Japanese colonialism, and committed to national reconstruction during the period of rapid economic growth. The parallel here is the experience of post-Mitterrand France, which has begun to question notions of resistance and collaboration under Vichy. The shock of reenvisioning the past in Korea is all the more pronounced, if only because the period of occupation was much longer. It was thirty-five years in the case of Korea, as compared to four in the case of France.

This new domestic environment of political discourse could not have happened until the aftermath of the ending of the Cold War. The end of the Cold War helps to explain why governments in both Japan and South Korea are prepared to talk about new security partnerships. It helps also to explain the greater prominence of Asia in the strategic objectives of both national governments, and the willingness of the populations of Japan and South Korea to increasingly orient themselves toward the region. Of course, this change in emphasis is not unprecedented. The new direction is a distinct echo of past initiatives. Hatoyama Yukio's Asia-centered diplomacy, for example, parallels the attempt by his grandfather, Prime Minister Hatoyama Ichirō, to moderate the US-centered diplomacy of his predecessor, Yoshida Shigeru, in favor of a partial, albeit ultimately unsuccessful, diplomatic opening to Moscow and Beijing in the mid-1950s.

The good news is that the national elites in Japan and South Korea are trying to contain nationalism. The clearest illustration, in the Japanese context, is the very encouraging commitment by the government to establish a new secular shrine for commemorating Japan's war dead. There is a significant effort to take away the sensitivity of the nationalist issues, as well as to accommodate the concerns of Japan's neighbors. It is also fair to say that your average Japanese is not really animated by nationalistic impulses. To strike a more pessimistic note, however, we have seen the way the Internet is used as a volatile force for fostering nationalism in China. And despite the best efforts of the national elites in Korea and Japan to stress the importance of accommodation, public opinion on the Korean Peninsula, both South and North, remain strongly hostile toward Japan. Thus, in the context of continuing tensions over national identity, I am cautiously optimistic in terms of elite initiatives, but in terms of the fundamentals, rather pessimistic.

Notes

1   See Yoshihide Soeya, *Japan's Economic Diplomacy with China, 1945–1978* (New York: Oxford University Press, 1998), and Yoshihide Soeya, Masayuki Tadokoro, and David Welch (eds), *Japan as a Normal Country? A Nation in Search of its Place in the World* (Toronto: University of Toronto Press, 2011).

2   Tiananmen Square in Beijing was the site in 1989 of mass protests calling for expanded economic and political reforms in China. The protests ended violently when the government deployed military force, including tanks, to clear the square. See Chen Jian, "Tiananmen and the Fall of the Berlin Wall: China's Path Toward 1989 and Beyond," in, Jeffrey A. Engel (ed.), *The Fall of the Berlin Wall: The Revolutionary Legacy of 1989* (New York: Oxford University Press, 2008).

3   The Nuclear Non-Proliferation Treaty (NPT) of 1968 is the international agreement devoted to preventing the spread of nuclear weapons and weapons technology.

4   James Bellacqua, ed., *The Future of China-Russia Relations* (Lexington: University Press of Kentucky, 2010), Stefan Halper, *The Beijing Consensus*: Legitimatizing Authoritarianism in Our Time (New York: Basic Books, 2012), and Ian Storey, *Southeast Asia and the Rise of China: The Search for Security* (London: Routledge, 2011).

5   This incident became a rallying point for the democratization movement throughout South Korea, which was fueled by expanding anti-Americanism. George N. Katsiaficas and Na Kahn-chae, (eds), *South Korean Democracy: The Legacy of the Gwangju Uprising* (New York: Routledge, 2006).

CHAPTER TEN

Reflections on the lessons of the Cold War

The intense confrontation between the Soviet Union and its former Western allies, known as the Cold War, lasted for the better part of fifty years. This vast ideological, economic, and political competition between the two great power blocs led by the United States and the Soviet Union was global in its scope and impact. With an emphasis on endings and beginnings, the essays in the foregoing chapters take the measure of the Cold War. They examine its legacy and set the context for this final chapter, which focuses on the lessons of the Cold War. In this concluding set of essays, prominent scholars and practitioners reflect upon the foregoing essays and the international dialogue on the Cold War they represent. All fundamentally agree that there is much of value to be derived from the systematic study of the Cold War. They also agree that it will take a long time for all of the lessons of this epic period to emerge. Four eminent historians offer the scholarly perspective on the lessons of the Cold War: Andrei Pippidi, Konstantin Khudoley, Jonathan Haslam, and Christopher Andrew. Lord Wright of Richmond, Franklin Miller, and John Warner offer lessons from the perspective of distinguished careers in public service during the Cold War.

The lessons of unintended consequences

Lord Wright of Richmond

First of all, the job of a government is not to win wars; it is to prevent them. I think we should all bear in mind the lessons of unintended consequences, of which the Helsinki Conference was the most striking example. I do not think that the Russians had any idea what a Pandora's box they were opening when they suggested the Helsinki Conference. The end of the Cold War has not prevented serious problems such as the breakup of Yugoslavia. Indeed you could argue that it was the end of the Cold War that caused the breakup of Yugoslavia.

The end of the Cold War has created new opportunities for international collaboration. It is difficult to imagine that the degree of cooperation that has transpired among previous Cold War adversaries, as regards policy toward Iran, Afghanistan, and piracy, could have occurred during the Cold War. Still, there have been disappointments on the path to a new world order, such as the lost opportunity to create a genuine Euro-Atlantic partnership. This is clear from the Russian perspective offered in the essays of Karasin and Likhotal.

Finally, as is readily apparent from the essays in Chapter 6, an important and unanticipated lesson about intelligence during the Cold War is that there are occasional advantages of allowing one's secrets to get to the other side. I do not know to what extent Moscow's extensive knowledge of NATO's secrets actually led to reassurances that we were not about to launch an aggressive attack. But I suspect it may have helped to avert the outbreak of general war in Europe.

The retrospect is much clearer than the prospect

Andrei Pippidi

In approaching the Churchill College Conference, I feared that the time had not yet come for an impartial international dialogue about the Cold War. It turns out that my fear was much exaggerated. The essays demonstrate that it is possible to engage in a constructive and impartial international dialogue about this critical period of recent history. In a sense, the perspectives offered in these essays are an interesting and profitable reunion of old friends and rivals. As a result, I have partially modified my views on this important subject. In all human affairs, the retrospect is much clearer than the prospect. It is much easier to see what has happened than to predict what will happen. The most important lesson of the Cold War is that although the superpowers' rivalry influenced our lives from remote villages to the frontiers of space, this nevertheless was a period when the collision of the past with the future stimulated human consciousness to meditate on freedom, oppression, and responsibility.

The Cold War must never be repeated

Konstantin Khudoley

The Cold War must never be repeated in international relations. World War I created the road to World War II. This must not happen again. I hope that the Cold War will be the only Cold War in the history of international relations. We can learn, for example, from the negotiation and effect of the Helsinki Final Act. When Brezhnev brought this agreement to the Politburo of the Communist Party, nearly all of the members predicted that it would adversely affect Soviet control of Eastern and Central Europe. They told him, "This will be the end." Brezhnev, however, insisted on its approval. He held that it was better to sign the Helsinki Act than to continue to endure the risks of another world war without such an agreement. In any crisis this is the best way to deal with problems—through negotiations rather than war.

Although we have not returned to a state of cold war in international relations, significant problems remain. There remains, for example, the issue of the continued militarization of international affairs. While there currently is no arms race comparable to that during the Cold War, the proliferation of arms sales around the globe continues. Despite the passing of the generation that waged the Cold War, the legacy of their decisions and rivalries remain. It will take generations to remove the legacy of the Cold War.

Avoiding future delusions and ignorance

Jonathan Haslam

As an historian, I am very skeptical that politicians learn anything from history at all. In this sense, any discussion of the lessons of the Cold War, or any other war for that matter, is entirely futile. The Cold War was absolutely necessary. It was necessary in the same way that other wars have been necessary—to sustain a balance of power. Without a balance of power, you get hegemony and despotism. That is a basic, realist view.

Having said that, if one looks back on the mistakes and achievements of the Cold War, and compare them to the mistakes and achievements that you find in international relations today and yesterday, I am struck to find that one of the greatest mistakes made was the failure of the antagonists to take the other side seriously. That does not sound quite how it felt in the 1970s or in the 1980s, but it was certainly the case in the 1940s. The

Foreign Office in London, for example, found during World War II when one of its members came back from the Moscow Embassy that no one in the department spoke any Russian whatsoever. The United States found itself in the same situation. That is why, to get ready for the post-war world, it started language programs through the Rockefeller Foundation in 1944–5. But in Moscow during the war, Roosevelt's Ambassador Averell Harriman, soon discovered he usually had only one man who spoke really good Russian serving as a political officer. The man he wanted was George Kennan. But Kennan was taken to work on other European matters. Then when Kennan arrived, Harriman wished Kennan had never arrived. Kennan preached gloom and doom incessantly. But there was a real problem because the State Department did not take expertise on Russia seriously. President Roosevelt clearly did not take Russia seriously; otherwise he would have filled the embassy with people who actually spoke the language and had Russian expertise. So you had London and Washington utterly unprepared for what then hit them at the end of World War II.

Now, on the Russian side, of course, Stalin wiped out most of the diplomatic corps in purges. This left Russia in a rather sticky situation as it recreated its foreign office with young men from factories and outer Siberia and trained them up in foreign languages. This produced people like Gromyko, who was a joke in the United States when he was ambassador because his English was utterly incomprehensible. He learned English from books as an agronomist for goodness sake. This is not an ideal situation for diplomacy. This set of countries did not take each other seriously enough to handle the challenges before them. The paucity of language skills in the respective diplomatic corps of both sides reflected a more general failure really to take diplomatic relations with one another seriously. This repeated itself throughout the Cold War and produced very inaccurate assessments of what was going on with the other side. In the late 1960s, there was a wonderful CIA memo saying the Soviet Union is getting much, much less ideological, the KGB is sort of fading out, and we can look forward to a pleasant future. Unfortunately, the British Ambassador to Moscow shared this erroneous assessment. The delusion that the other side had suddenly been transformed and had become more like us proved horribly untrue. It led to miscalculations that virtually guaranteed the collapse of détente in the 1970s. So I think what was striking about the Cold War was the delusions that were held on both sides and the preponderance of ignorance. But I have absolutely no faith that present governments in the world will avoid either of these mistakes in the future.

A fairly rough road ahead

Franklin C. Miller

Three lessons emerge from the essays in this volume and the international dialogue they reflect. The first is the enormous role played by leaders and personalities in shaping events. The stories told about Churchill, Gorbachev, Reagan, Roosevelt, Stalin, Thatcher, and Truman remind us of the role of human beings in shaping history and how incredibly important that is. There is one important subject the dialogue really did not get into: the role of implementation when the leader sets the policy course. Sometimes the bureaucracy does as the leaders want and sometimes it does not, but that is a subject for future consideration. It is, nevertheless another important element of the Cold War.

The second lesson is the role of intelligence in international affairs. More accurately, it was the mischaracterization of intelligence and the misinterpretation of data that often got both sides into bad spots. This is a reminder that simply because you gather all sorts of materials does not mean that you actually know what is going on.

The third lesson, which I think is terribly important, comes to something that Susan Eisenhower said in her essay. She pointed to the importance of understanding and misunderstanding in human affairs. Time and again this set of essays points to the enormous role played by misconceptions, misperceptions, and misunderstandings among the governments of the United States, the United Kingdom, and the Soviet Union. It underscores the need to correct those misunderstandings whenever possible, especially when one is dealing with a partner who sometimes displays extreme paranoia. Reducing mutual misconceptions does not eliminate the genuine clash of interests between antagonists in global affairs, but it is an essential feature of effective international relations.

These essays reflect with great certitude a consensus that the Cold War is over. I agree the Cold War has ended. It nevertheless is important to understand that we still have a fairly rough road ahead of us, especially in our relations with the Russian Federation. Problems with mutual misconceptions and misunderstandings remain. There is the critical issue, for example, of how the West deals with the fact that it wants a Europe that is whole and free, yet the Russian leadership views the emergence of democracy in Ukraine and Georgia as a threat to their existence. Further, Russia is a major energy exporter but this raises the issue of a dangerous Western dependence on oil and gas from the East. Finally, we have the President of the United States and the Prime Minister of the United Kingdom talking about a world in which there are no more nuclear weapons, while at the same time Russia continues to manifest an aggressive military posture.

For example, in the past several years Russia has flown strategic bombers into US-UK air space, has held a military exercise that simulated hitting Poland with nuclear weapons, and recently announced a doctrine aimed at its principal enemies, the United States and NATO. To be sure, there are bumps ahead that we all need to work out.

Taking the long view

Christopher Andrew

When seeking to understand Soviet policy during the Cold War, few Western policy-makers or their advisors took the long view. The West suffered, and arguably still suffers, from what I have called Historical Attention Span Deficit Disorder (HASDD). A long-term view of Soviet policy-making would have emphasized the problems of "telling truth to power" in a one-party state, which the history of all previous highly authoritarian regimes showed to be inevitable. In one-party states, political intelligence analysis is necessarily distorted by the insistent demands of political correctness. It thus acts as a mechanism for reinforcing, rather than correcting, the regimes' misconceptions of the outside world. Autocrats, by and large, are told what they want to hear. One British SIS Chief defined his main role as, on the contrary, to "tell the Prime Minister what the Prime Minister does not want to know." Western intelligence agencies, of course, have sometimes fallen far short of this exalted calling. Though the politicization of intelligence sometimes degrades assessment even within democratic systems, however, it is built into the structure of all authoritarian regimes.

Cold War Soviet intelligence analysis remained seriously undeveloped by Western standards. Nikolai Leonov, who was dismayed to be appointed Deputy Head of the KGB Foreign Intelligence Assessment Department in 1971, estimates that it had only ten percent of the importance of the CIA's Directorate of Intelligence [Analysis]. Its prestige was correspondingly low. But, in the absence of a long-term view of the limitations of one-party states, the achievements of Soviet intelligence collection led many Western analysts to exaggerate the likely success of Soviet intelligence analysis. Only in retrospect was it realized that, in the words of Sir Percy Cradock, former Chairman of the British Joint Intelligence Committee and Margaret Thatcher's Foreign Policy Advisor, that "the main source of weakness" in the Soviet intelligence system was "the attempt to force an excellent supply of information from the multifaceted West into an oversimplified framework of hostility and conspiracy theory."

Among the most impressive evidence that Gorbachev's "new thinking" began to break down this oversimplified view of the West during his first year as general secretary, came when he denounced the distorted political reporting by KGB foreign intelligence. The fact that KGB headquarters had then to issue stern instructions to foreign residencies in December 1985 entitled, "On the impermissibility of distortions of the factual state of affairs in messages and informational reports sent to the central committee of the Communist Party of the Soviet Union and other ruling bodies," is a damning indictment of KGB subservience to the standards of political correctness expected by Soviet leaders over the previous two-thirds of a century.

Perhaps the biggest gap in the official written record of the Cold War is a sense of how frightening it sometimes was. Officials were unlikely to put on file their own feelings of personal anxiety (or worse). Nor do US presidents commonly reveal in their memoirs what it was like to have their fingers on the nuclear button and how they faced the nightmarish possibility that, if deterrence failed, they would be US commanders-in-chief during the world's first thermonuclear war. Since the later stages of Dwight D. Eisenhower's first term at the White House, presidents have been followed everywhere they go by a military aide carrying the "nuclear football," an attaché case containing the launch codes for nuclear weapons. From Khrushchev onward, Soviet leaders were accompanied by a similar "small suitcase" (*chemodanchik*). General Andrew Goodpaster, Eisenhower's Staff Secretary and Defense Liaison Officer, who briefed Eisenhower on the introduction of the nuclear football, had no doubt when I interviewed him half a century later that it had marked a turning point in the history of the US presidency. That turning point, however, is rarely mentioned in histories of the Cold War.

We now know that in Britain, if thermonuclear war had appeared imminent during the 1960s and 1970s, about two thousand people, headed by the War Cabinet with their chief advisors and intelligence staff, would have retreated to a huge Ministry of Defence bunker (successively codenamed BURLINGTON and TURNSTILE) near Corsham in the West Country. If war had followed, they would have spent what remained of British history desperately hoping against hope that some of the Britain above them might somehow survive. But we do not know how many of the two thousand would actually have gone to the bunker. Had they done so, they would have had to leave their families behind, knowing that if war began they were unlikely to survive. Such unanswered questions about the human response to preparations for thermonuclear war require much further research.

I usually suggest to Cambridge undergraduates at some point when I'm teaching contemporary history that they ask their grandparents (and parents, if they are old enough) what memories they have about the Cuban Missile Crisis. I have been struck by the impact of the crisis even on many quite young children that such memories reveal. Most Americans now aged

33.

From Stettin in the Baltic
   to Trieste in the Adriatic,

   an iron curtain has descended
   across the Continent.

Behind that line
   lie all the capitals of the ancient states
   of Central and Eastern Europe.

Warsaw, Berlin, Prague, Vienna, Budapest,
   Belgrade, Bucharest and Sofia,

   all these famous cities and the populations
                              around them

   lie in the Soviet sphere

   and all are subject
      in one form or another,

   not only to Soviet influence
      but to a very high and increasing
         measure of control fr Moscow.

PHOTO 10.1 *Page from Churchill's speaking notes for his historic Iron Curtain Speech in March 1946 (Courtesy of Churchill Archives Centre)* between their late fifties and late sixties remember the "duck and cover" drills during the crisis, which taught them to hide under school desks and adopt the brace position in case of nuclear attack. Because there were no organized drills in British schools, recollections on this side of the Atlantic are more various. Some children, particularly at primary schools, were kept in ignorance by parents and teachers and now have no memory of the crisis. But others do remember. The mother of a former student of mine who was six at the time recalls hearing her father, a naval officer who was on leave during the crisis, discussing the threat of nuclear attack with her mother. Though the child's parents spoke in a way their daughter was not supposed to understand, their peculiar conversation only succeeded in attracting the little girl's horrified attention. She stood up in class next day and announced to the other children: "You are all going to die." The school was sympathetic but telephoned the little girl's mother (who still remembers the telephone call) to take her home for the rest of the day.

No attempt to learn the lessons of the Cold War can be complete without a serious attempt, while there is still time, to compile an oral history of the fears that it generated among children as well as adults.

There will be no second chance

John Warner

My generation has struggled with the issues of war and peace that permeated the Cold War our entire lives. In 1917 a young doctor left his beloved state of Virginia, donned the uniform of a captain in the US Army Medical Corps, and quickly shipped off to France. He served in the trenches, was wounded in combat, and received many decorations—including the *Croix de Guerre*. That captain was my father, and he often told me that he treated the wounds of as many British "Tommies" as he did American "Yanks." After the war ended, he returned to the United States and civilian life to raise a family and enjoy the blessings of a hard-won peace. In our home there was a shelf above the fireplace. My father put two things on it: his old cap from World War I and the three-volume book titled *The War to End All Wars*. As a boy, with my father working through the book with me, I read every page of that history of World War I. Together we tried to understand the causes, costs, and consequences of that terrible conflict. During the last year of World War II, my father drove me to the station where I boarded a train with hundreds of other seventeen and eighteen year-old kids to enter military service.

In my lifetime, I have witnessed the tail end of World War II, Korea, Vietnam, and now Afghanistan and Iraq. Since World War II, there have been some twenty-five significant engagements where presidents of the United States, in the role of commander in chief, have packed off our troops in the cause of freedom. So at some point, we have got to learn what to do because with the advent of the nuclear weapon, there will be no second chance if this terrible device falls into the wrong hands.

As I look back on my long years of life, I have not seen a more complex framework of challenges than those facing the free world today as regards state and non-state threats to global security. First, we face terrorist threats from a relatively small number of persons and groups who, because they are driven by ideology, are willing to take any risk in the pursuit of their cause—including surrendering their own lives. Second, we also face a framework of state-sponsored terrorism in the form of North Korea and, of course, Iran. When the threat is state-based, diplomacy is possible. Hopefully diplomacy will work to deter these nations from acquiring their own nuclear capability, which is not in the interest of the free world. I am hopeful that the prevention of nuclear weapons proliferation can be achieved without the use of force of any type. Still, in the wake of the Cold War, we collectively face a state-sponsored and non-state terrorist threat made the more lethal due to their pursuit of weapons of mass destruction.

It took decades to resolve the Cold War. It is likely that it will take decades to fend off the international terrorism threat that we are suffering today. It took the strategic and inspirational communication of leaders such as Winston Churchill and Ronald Reagan to provide the vision that allowed us to endure, and ultimately to end, the Cold War. One lesson from the Cold War is that strategic and inspirational leadership will be required for us to endure and prevail in the global war on terror. It is a prerequisite to building public support for missions such as NATO's in Afghanistan that are essential to this effort.

A second lesson from the Cold War is the critical importance of diplomatic engagement with our adversaries. Throughout the Cold War we negotiated with the Soviets. The lines of communication remained open. We will need to summon the courage to reach out and try, in the most impossible of situations, to persuade terrorists to forego bringing harm to innocent people in the pursuit of their cause.

The Cold War now lies behind us. The reality of international terrorism lies before us. In rising to the challenges of the post-Cold War world, I think we should draw upon the wisdom of Winston Churchill. In his famous "Iron Curtain" speech, delivered in the United States at Westminster College in 1946, Churchill argued that the newly created United Nations offered tremendous hope for world peace, but warned:

> We must make sure that its work is fruitful, that it is a reality and not a sham, that it is a force for action, and not merely a frothing of words,

that it is a true temple of peace in which the shields of many nations can some day be hung up, and not merely a cockpit in a Tower of Babel.

If there is going to be a "true temple of peace," it will have to be built by the workmen of many nations. Churchill understood that the path to peace would be difficult and long, but he knew that "if we persevere together ... we shall achieve our common purpose in the end." That is the challenge before us. We must work together and persevere until our common purpose is achieved—as was done in the great Cold War.

BIBLIOGRAPHY

Andrew, Christopher (2009), *Defend the Realm: The Authorized History of MI5*. New York: Alfred A. Knopf.

—(2010), "Intelligence in the Cold War." In *The Cambridge History of The Cold War, Volume 2: Crises and Détente*, M. Leffler and O. A. Westad (eds), 417–37. New York: Cambridge University Press.

Andrew, Christopher and David N. Dilks (eds) (1984), *The Missing Dimension: Governments and Intelligence Communities in the Twentieth Century*. London: Macmillan.

Andrew, Christopher and Oleg Gordievsky (1990), *KGB: The Inside Story of its Operations from Lenin to Gorbachev*. New York: Harper Collins.

—(eds) (1991), *Instructions from the Centre: Top Secret Files on KGB Foreign Operations, 1975–1985*. London: Hodder & Stoughton.

—(eds) (1992), *More Instructions from the Centre: Top Secret Files on KGB Global Operations, 1975–1985*. London: Frank Cass.

Andrew, Christopher and Vasili Mitrokhin (1999), *The Mitrokhin Archive*. London: Allen Lane-Penguin Press.

—(2005), *The World Was Going Our Way: The KGB and the Battle for the Third World*. New York: Basic Books.

Asmus, Ronald D. (2002), *Opening NATO's Door: How the Alliance Remade Itself for a New Era*. New York: Columbia University Press.

Barrass, Gordon (2009), *The Great Cold War: A Journey Through the Hall of Mirrors*. Stanford: Stanford Security Studies.

Bellacqua, James (ed.) (2010), *The Future of China-Russia Relations*. Lexington: University Press of Kentucky.

Beschloss, Michael R. (1991), *The Crisis Years: Kennedy and Khrushchev, 1960–1963*. New York: Edward Burlingame.

Bowie, Robert R. and Richard H. Immerman (2000), *Waging Peace: How Eisenhower Shaped an Enduring Cold War Strategy*. New York: Oxford University Press.

Brodie, Bernard (ed.) (1946), *The Absolute Weapon: Atomic Power and World Order*. New York: Harcourt, Brace and Company.

Brown, Archie (2010), "The Gorbachev Revolution and the End of the Cold War." In *The Cambridge History of the Cold War, Volume 3: Endings*, M. Leffler and O. A. Westad (eds), 244–66. New York: Cambridge University Press.

Brown, Harold (1983), *Thinking About National Security: Defense and Foreign Policy in a Dangerous World*. Boulder: Westview Press.

Brzezinski, Zbigniew. "An Agenda for NATO: Building a Global Security Web," *Foreign Affairs* 88, no. 5 (October/September 2009): 2–20.

Bush, Vannevar (1945), *Science, the Endless Frontier: A Report to the President on a Program for Postwar Scientific Research*. Washington, DC: US Government Printing Office.

—(1949), *Modern Arms and Free Men: A Discussion of the Role of Science in Preserving Democracy*. New York: Simon & Schuster.

Clancy, Tom (1985), *The Hunt for Red October*. New York: Berkley Books.

Cohen, Stephen F. (2009), *Soviet Fates and Lost Alternatives: From Stalinism to the New Cold War*. New York: Columbia University Press.

Coman, Mihai (2009), "Press Freedom and Media Pluralism in Romania." In *Press Freedom and Pluralism in Europe: Concepts and Conditions*, A. Czepek, M. Hellwig, and N. Nowak (eds), 177–96. Bristol: Intellect.

Dallek, Robert (2004), *An Unfinished Life: John F. Kennedy, 1917–1963*. New York: Back Bay Books.

Eisenhower, John S. D. (1974), *Strictly Personal: A Memoir*. New York: Doubleday.

Eisenhower, Susan (1995), *Breaking Free: A Memoir of Love and Revolution*. New York: Farrar, Straus and Giroux.

Engel, Jeffrey A. (ed.) (2009), *The Fall of the Berlin Wall: The Revolutionary Legacy of 1989*. New York: Oxford University Press.

Engerman, David (2010), "Ideology and the Origin of the Cold War, 1917–1962." In *The Cambridge History of The Cold War, Volume 1: Origins*, edited by M. Leffler and O. A. Westad, 20–43. New York: Cambridge University Press.

Farmelo, Graham (2009), *The Strangest Man: The Hidden Life of Paul Dirac, Mystic of the Atom*. New York: Basic Books.

Fish, M. Stephen (2005), *Democracy Derailed in Russia: The Failure of Open Politics*. New York: Cambridge University Press.

Fox, William T. R. (1944), *Superpowers: The United States, Britain, and the Soviet Union—Their Responsibility for Peace*. New York: Harcourt, Brace and Company.

Fursenko, Alexandr A. and Timothy Naftali (1997), *One Hell of a Gamble: Khrushchev, Castro, and Kennedy, 1958–1964*. New York: Norton.

—(2006), *Khrushchev's Cold War: The Inside Story of an American Adversary*. New York: Norton.

Gaddis, John Lewis (1987), *The Long Peace: Inquiries into the History of the Cold War*. New York: Oxford University Press.

—(1997), *We Now Know: Rethinking Cold War History*. Oxford: Oxford University Press.

—(2005a), *Strategies of Containment: A Critical Appraisal of American National Security Policy During the Cold War*, revised and expanded edition. New York: Oxford University Press.

—(2005b), *The Cold War: A New History*. New York: Penguin Press.

Gorbachev, Mikhail (1995), *Memoirs*. New York: Doubleday.

Gorbachev, Mikhail and Zdeněk Mlynář (2002), *Conversations with Gorbachev: On Perestroika, the Prague Spring, and the Crossroads of Socialism*, trans. George Shriver. New York: Columbia University Press.

Gordievsky, Oleg (1995), *Next Stop Execution: The Autobiography of Oleg Gordievsky*. New York: Macmillan.

Grachev, Andrei (2008), *Gorbachev's Gamble: Soviet Foreign Policy and the End of the Cold War*. Cambridge: Polity Press.

Haftendorn, Helga (2010), "The Unification of Germany, 1985–1991." In *The Cambridge History of the Cold War, Volume 3: Endings*, M. Leffler and O. A. Westad (eds), 333–55. New York: Cambridge University Press.

Halper, Stefan (2012), *The Beijing Consensus: Legitimatizing Authoritarianism in Our Time*. New York: Basic Books.

Hanhimäki, Jussi M. (2012), *The Rise and Fall of Détente: American Foreign Policy and the Transformation of the Cold War*. Herndon: Potomac Books.

Hanhimäki, Jussi M. and Odd Arne Westad (eds) (2003), *The Cold War: A History in Documents and Eyewitness Accounts*. Oxford: Oxford University Press.

Harper, John Lamberton (2011), *The Cold War*. New York: Oxford University Press.

Haslam, Jonathan (2002), *No Virtue Like Necessity: Realist Thought in International Relations Since Machiavelli*. New Haven: Yale University Press.

—(2011), *Russia's Cold War: From the October Revolution to the Fall of the Wall*. New Haven: Yale University Press.

Henrikson, Alan (2008), "FDR and the World Wide Arena." In *FDR's World: War, Peace, and Legacies*, David B. Woolner, David Reynolds, and Warren Kimball (eds), 35–62. New York: Palgrave Macmillan.

Herken, Gregg (2002), *Brotherhood of the Bomb: The Tangled Lives and Loyalties of Robert Oppenheimer, Ernest Lawrence, and Edward Teller*. New York: Henry Holt.

Hershberg, James G. (2010), "The Cuban Missile Crisis." In *The Cambridge History of the Cold War, Volume 2: Crises and Détente*, M. Leffler and O. A. Westad (eds), 65–87. New York: Cambridge University Press.

Hines, John G., Ellis M. Mishulovich, and John Shull (1995), *Soviet Intentions 1965–1985: An Analytical Comparison of US-Soviet Assessments During the Cold War*. Vol. 1 (September). McLean: BMD Federal.

Howard, Michael (1967), *The Mediterranean Strategy in the Second World War*. New York: Praeger.

Hull, Cordell (1948), *The Memoirs of Cordell Hull*. Vol. 1. New York: The Macmillan Company.

Jian, Chen (2001), *Mao's China and the Cold War*. Chapel Hill: University of North Carolina Press.

—(2008), "Tiananmen and the Fall of the Berlin Wall: China's Path Toward 1989 and Beyond." In *The Fall of the Berlin Wall: The Revolutionary Legacy of 1989*, Jeffrey A. Engel (ed.), 96–131. New York: Oxford University Press.

Kalinovsky, Artemy M. (2011), *A Long Goodbye: The Soviet Withdrawal From Afghanistan*. Cambridge: Harvard University Press.

Kalinovsky, Artemy M. and Sergey Radchenko (eds) (2011), *The End of the Cold War and the Third World: New Perspectives on Regional Conflict*. London: Routledge.

Katsiaficas, George N. and Na Kahn-chae (eds) (2006), *South Korean Democracy: The Legacy of the Gwangju Uprising*. New York: Routledge.

Kemp-Welch, Anthony (2010), "Eastern Europe: Stalinism to Solidarity." In *The*

Cambridge History of the Cold War, Volume 2: Crises and Détente, M. Leffler and O. A. Westad (eds), 219–37. New York: Cambridge University Press.

Kennan, George F. "The Sources of Soviet Conduct." *Foreign Affairs* 25, no. 4 (July 1947): 566–82.

—"A Fateful Error." *New York Times*, February 5, 1997: A23.

Khudoley, Konstantin (2001), "Modern Russian Policy Toward Europe." In *Russia and Europe in a Changing European Environment*, K. Malfliet and L. Verpoest (eds), 25–38. Leuven: Leuven University Press.

Kramer, Mark, "Colonel Kuklinski and the Polish Crisis, 1980–81." *Cold War International History Project Bulletin* no. 11 (Winter 1998): 48–60.

—(2009), *The Kukliński Files and the Polish Crisis of 1980–1981: An Analysis of the Newly Released CIA Documents*. CWIHP Working Paper No. 59 (March). Washington, DC: Cold War International History Project.

Latham, Michael (2010), "The Cold War in the Third World, 1963–1975." In *The Cambridge History of the Cold War, Volume 2: Crises and Détente*, M. Leffler and O. A. Westad (eds), 258–80. New York: Cambridge University Press.

Leffler, Melvyn (2007), *For the Soul of Mankind: The United States, the Soviet Union, and the Cold War*. New York: Hill and Wang.

—(2010), "The Emergence of an American Grand Strategy, 1945–1952." In *The Cambridge History of the Cold War, Volume 1: Origins*, M. Leffler and O. A. Westad (eds), 67–89. New York: Cambridge University Press.

Leffler, Melvyn and Odd Arne Westad (eds) (2010a), *The Cambridge History of the Cold War, Volume 1: Origins*. New York: Cambridge University Press.

—(2010b), *The Cambridge History of the Cold War, Volume 2: Crises and Détente*. New York: Cambridge University Press.

—(2010c), *The Cambridge History of the Cold War, Volume 3: Endings*. New York: Cambridge University Press.

Levering, Ralph B., Vladimir O. Pechatnov, Verena Botzenhart-Viehe, and C. Earl Edmondson (2002), *Debating the Cold War: American and Russian Perspectives*. Lanham: Rowman & Littlefield.

Lévesque, Jacques (2010), "The East European Revolutions of 1989." In *The Cambridge History of the Cold War, Volume 2: Crises and Détente*, edited by M. Leffler and O. A. Westad, 311–32. New York: Cambridge University Press.

Likhotal, Alexander, "The Road From Copenhagen." Speech delivered at the Sustainable World Congress, July 23, 2009. http://www.gcint.org/ news/ road-copenhagen

Lüthi, Lorenz (2011), "Chinese Foreign Policy, 1960–1979." In *The Cold War in East Asia, 1945–1991*, T. Hasegawa (ed.), 152–79. Stanford: Stanford University Press.

Mahnken, Thomas G. (2008), *Technology and the American Way of War*. New York: Columbia University Press.

Maier, Charles S. (1997), *Dissolution: The Crisis of Communism and the End of East Germany*. Princeton: Princeton University Press.

Malfliet, Katlijn and Ria Laenen (eds) (2007), *Elusive Russia: Current Developments in Russian State Identity and Institutional Reform Under President Putin*. Leuven: Leuven University Press.

Malfliet, Katlijn, Lien Verpoest, and Evgeny Vinokurov (eds) (2007), *The CIS, the EU, and Russia: Challenges of Integration*. London: Palgrave Macmillan.

Mason, T. E., T. J. Gawne, S. E. Nagler, M. B. Nestor, and J. M. Carpenter. "The Early Development of Neutron Diffraction: Science in the Wings of the Manhattan Project." *Acta Crystallographica* Section A: Foundations of Crystallography. 2013 January 1; 69 (Pt. 1): 37-44. Published online 2012 December 5. Doi: 10.1107/S0108767312036021.

Mastny, Vojtech (2010), "Soviet Foreign Policy, 1954–1962." In *The Cambridge History of the Cold War, Volume 1: Origins*, M. Leffler and O. A. Westad (eds), 312–33. New York: Cambridge University Press.

Michnik, Adam (2011), *In Search of Lost Meaning: The New Eastern Europe*. Berkeley: University of California Press.

Mikoyan, Sergo (2012), *The Soviet Cuban Missile Crisis: Castro, Mikoyan, Kennedy, Khrushchev, and the Missiles of November*, edited by Svetlana Savranskaya. Stanford: Stanford University Press.

Miscamble, Wilson D. (1992), *George F. Kennan and the Making of American Foreign Policy, 1947–1959*. Princeton: Princeton University Press.

Molotov, V. M. (1993), *Molotov Remember: Inside Kremlin Politics— Conversations With Felix Chuev*. Chicago: Ivan R. Dee.

Naimark, Norman (2010), "The Sovietization of Eastern Europe, 1944–1954." In *The Cambridge History of the Cold War, Volume 1: Origins*, M. Leffler and O. A. Westad (eds), 175–97. New York: Cambridge University Press.

Nau, Henry R. and Deepa M. Ollapally (eds) (2012), *Worldviews of Aspiring Powers: Domestic Foreign Policy Debates in China, India, Iran, Japan, and Russia*. New York: Oxford University Press.

Njolstad, Olav (2010), "The Collapse of Superpower Détente, 1975–1980." In *The Cambridge History of the Cold War, Volume 3: Endings*, M. Leffler and O. A. Westad (eds), 135–55. New York: Cambridge University Press.

Paul, John II. *Cenntesimus Annus: Encyclical Letter on the Hundredth Anniversary of the Rerum Novarum*, May 1, 1991.

Pechatnov, Vladimir. "The Big Three After World War II: New Documents on Soviet Thinking about Post War Relations with the United States and Great Britain." *Cold War International History Project*, Working Paper 13, July 1995.

—"Fulton Revisited." *Russia in Global Affairs*, no. 2 (April/June 2006). http://eng.globalaffairs.ru/number/n_6572

—(2010), "The Soviet Union and the World, 1944–1953." In *The Cambridge History of the Cold War, Volume 1: Origins*, M. Leffler and O. A. Westad (eds), 90–111. New York: Cambridge University Press.

Pechatnov, Vladimir and C. Earl Edmondson (2002), "The Russian Perspective." In *Debating The Origins of the Cold War: American and Russian Perspectives*, edited by R. Levering, V. Pechatnov, V. Botzenhart-Viehe, and C. Edmondson, 85–151. Lanham: Rowman & Littlefield.

Perry, William. "Testimony to the US Senate Armed Services Committee." Hearing on Department of Defense Appropriations for FY 1977, Part 8: Research and Development. February 28, March 7, 9, 14, and 21, 1978.

Radchenko, Sergey (2009), *Two Suns in the Heavens: The Sino-Soviet Struggle for Supremacy, 1962–1967*. Washington, DC: Woodrow Wilson Center Press.

—(2010), "The Sino-Soviet Split." In *The Cambridge History of the Cold War,*

Volume 2: Crises and Détente, edited by M. Leffler and O. A. Westad, 349–72. New York: Cambridge University Press.

Reynolds, David (1994), *Origins of the Cold War in Europe: International Perspectives*. New Haven: Yale University Press.

—(2005), *In Command of History: Churchill Fighting and Writing the Second World War*. New York: Random House.

—(2006), *From World War to Cold War: Churchill, Roosevelt, and the International Histories of the 1940s*. New York: Oxford University Press.

—(2007), *Summits: Six Conferences That Changed History*. London: Allen Lane.

—(2010), "Science, Technology, and the Cold War." In *The Cambridge History of the Cold War, Volume 3: Endings*, M. Leffler and O. A. Westad (eds), 378–99. New York: Cambridge University Press.

Roberts, Adam (2010), "An 'Incredibly Swift Transition': Reflections on the End of the Cold War." In *The Cambridge History of the Cold War, Volume 2: Crises and Détente*, M. Leffler and O. A. Westad (eds), 513–34. New York: Cambridge University Press.

Sarotte, Mary Elise (2009), *1989: The Struggle to Create Post-Cold War Europe*. Princeton: Princeton University Press.

—(2010), "Not One Inch Eastward? Bush, Baker, Kohl, Genscher, Gorbachev, and the Origin of Russian Resentment Toward NATO Enlargement in February 1990." *Diplomatic History* 34, no. 1 (January), 119–40.

Savranskaya, Svetlana and William Taubman (2010), "Soviet Foreign Policy, 1962–1975." In *The Cambridge History of the Cold War, Volume 2: Crises and Détente*, edited by M. Leffler and O. A. Westad, 134–57. New York: Cambridge University Press.

Soeya, Yoshihide (1998), *Japan's Economic Diplomacy with China, 1945–1978*. New York: Oxford University Press.

Soeya, Yoshihide, Masayuki Tadokoro, and David A. Welch (eds) (2011), *Japan as a Normal Country? A Nation in Search of its Place in the World*. Toronto: University of Toronto Press.

Stern, Sheldon M. (2012), *The Cuban Missile Crisis in American Memory: Myths Versus Reality*. Stanford: Stanford University Press.

Stokes, Gale (2012), *The Walls Came Tumbling Down: Collapse and Rebirth in Eastern Europe*, 2nd edn. New York: Oxford University Press.

Storey, Ian (2011), *Southeast Asia and the Rise of China: The Search for Security*. London: Routledge.

Szabo, Stephen F. (1992), *The Diplomacy of German Unification*. New York: St. Martin's Press.

Thatcher, Margaret (1993), *The Downing Street Years*. New York: Harper Collins.

Thomas, Daniel C. (2001), *The Helsinki Effect: International Norms, Human Rights, and the Demise of Communism*. Princeton: Princeton University Press.

Treisman, Daniel (2011), *The Return: Russia's Journey From Gorbachev to Medvedev*. New York: The Free Press.

Wegren, Stephen K. (ed.) (2012), *Return to Putin's Russia: Past Imperfect, Future Uncertain*, 5th edn. Oxford: Rowman & Littlefield.

Westad, Odd Arne (ed.) (1998), *Brothers in Arms: The Rise and Fall of the Sino-Soviet Alliance, 1945–1963*. Stanford: Stanford University Press.

—(2005), *The Global Cold War: Third World Interventions and the Making of Our Times.* Cambridge: Cambridge University Press.

Wohlforth, William C. (ed.) (2003), *Cold War Endgame: Oral History, Analysis, Debates.* University Park: Pennsylvania State University Press.

Woolner, David B. (1998a), "Coming to Grips with the German Problem: Roosevelt, Churchill and the Morgenthau Plan at the Second Quebec Conference." In *The Second Quebec Conference Revisited: Waging War, Formulating Peace, Canada, Great Britain and the United States in 1944–1945,* David B. Woolner (ed.), 65–104. New York: St. Martin's Press.

—(ed.) (1998b), *The Second Quebec Conference Revisited: Waging War, Formulating Peace: Canada, Great Britain, and the United States in 1944–1945.* New York: St. Martin's Press.

—(2008), "Epilogue: Reflections on Legacy and Leadership—the View from 2008." In *FDR's World: War, Peace, and Legacies,* David B. Woolner, Warren Kimball, and David Reynolds (eds), 227–42. New York: Palgrave Macmillan.

Woolner, David B., Warren Kimball, and David Reynolds (eds) (2008), *FDR's World: War, Peace, and Legacies.* New York: Palgrave Macmillan.

Xia, Yafeng (2006), *Negotiating With the Enemy: US-China Talks During the Cold War, 1949–1972.* Bloomington: Indiana University Press.

Zelikow, Philip and Condoleezza Rice (1995), *Germany Unified and Europe Transformed: A Study in Statecraft.* Cambridge: Harvard University Press.

Zubok, Vladislav (2003), "Gorbachev and the End of the Cold War: Different Perspectives on the Historical Personality." In *Cold War Endgame: Oral History, Analysis, Debates,* W. C. Wohlforth (eds), 207–42. University Park: Pennsylvania State University Press.

—(2007), *A Failed Empire: The Soviet Union in the Cold War From Stalin to Gorbachev.* Chapel Hill: University of North Carolina Press.

Zubok, Vladislav and Constantine Pleshakov (1996), *Inside the Kremlin's Cold War: From Khrushchev.* Cambridge: Harvard University Press.

INDEX